Wakefield Press

I AM THE DAUGHTER THEY STOLE

Eileen Cummings, an Elder of the Rembarrnga and Ngalakan people of Central Arnhem Land, Northern Territory, Australia, holds an honorary doctorate from Charles Darwin University. Stolen from her family when she was four years old, she grew up to advise four chief ministers in the Northern Territory government, and was lead plaintiff in the Northern Territory Stolen Generation Class Action. This is her story.

Jana Anvari holds a PhD in archaeology from Flinders University, South Australia. Her primary research topic is the interactions between people and the built environment at early farming sites in the Eastern Mediterranean. She is passionate about facilitating the telling of women's experiences under challenging conditions.

Claire Smith AO is a professor of archaeology at Flinders University, South Australia. Since 1990, she has worked in relationships of trust with members of Eileen's family at the Aboriginal communities of Barunga, Beswick, Bulman, Manyallaluk, Weemol and Werenbun, Northern Territory. This book emerges from Claire and Eileen's conversations and friendship over some 30 years.

By Claire Smith

Country, Kin and Culture: Survival of an Australian Aboriginal Community

Prospect Hill: Memories of a burned village
(with Heather Burke, Jordan Ralph,
George Merryman and Jo Smith)

I AM THE DAUGHTER THEY STOLE

Eileen Cummings

with Jana Anvari and Claire Smith

Wakefield Press

Wakefield Press
16 Rose Street
Mile End
South Australia 5031
www.wakefieldpress.com.au

First published 2026

This material is based upon work supported by the Australian Research Council under Award No. IN220100079 and the National Science Foundation under Award No. 2243258. This publication is supported by the Healing Foundation.

Edited by Julia Beaven, Wakefield Press
Designed and typeset by Clinton Ellicott, Wakefield Press

ISBN 978 1 923388 18 5

A catalogue record for this book is available from the National Library of Australia

CORIOLE
McLAREN VALE

Wakefield Press thanks Coriole Vineyards for continued support

Dedicated to my mother and father,
Florrie Murray Lindsay and Jugaduk Lindsay

In loving memory of my daughter,
Sheena Marie May (nee Cummings),
who passed away 6 October 2025

Contents

List of Figures

Foreword

Aunty Eileen's book, *I am the Daughter they Stole*, documents the remarkable life of a remarkable woman. It begins from the time Eileen was tricked as a four-year-old into getting into the Chevrolet truck that separated her from her mother for 15 years, to her becoming the first Aboriginal teacher in the Northern Territory and providing policy advice to four Chief Ministers over 26 years. This intimate memoir takes readers on the journey of her extraordinary life.

I first met Aunty Eileen Cummings during the 1980s when I was a journalist with the ABC in Darwin, Northern Territory. From that moment I saw a woman, who despite all she'd experienced, show great kindness and incredible strength.

Aunty Eileen was taken away from her family and community when she was just four years old. She was taken from Mainoru Station, in the heart of Arnhem Land, to the Croker Island Mission. It was the heartbreak of her mother that drove Aunty Eileen to be a tireless advocate for survivors of the Stolen Generations.

I had seen firsthand the sad legacy left for the Yanyuwa and Garrawa families in my own community of Borroloola, the trauma and deep loss felt as a result of children removed from our families.

During the late 1990s, when Aunty Eileen was developing the Aboriginal Family Violence Strategy for the Office of Women's Policy, we would meet regularly. I was impressed that Aunty Eileen was visiting all Aboriginal communities in remote areas of the Northern Territory, so that their views and voices could be woven into the policy. Her aim was that the policy be 'with, by and for Aboriginal people'.

In the early 2000s, Aunty Eileen approached me to support the NT Stolen Generations Group as they sought acknowledgement and redress for being taken away from their mothers as babies. I admired their commitment, integrity and passion. Over the next two decades I met regularly with the Stolen Generations survivors, and with Aunty Eileen to discuss critical issues. I was honoured to support them.

Aunty Eileen later led the Northern Territory Stolen Generations Corporation. She was the lead claimant for a class action that saw a landmark redress scheme set up by the federal government to recognise the pain and suffering of Stolen Generations survivors.

I am delighted to recommend *I am the Daughter they Stole* to readers of all ages. This first-person biography provides insights into the impact of government policies that shaped, and continue to shape, the lives of Aunty Eileen and other Aboriginal people in the Northern Territory and across Australia.

It also provides an opportunity for readers to reflect and acknowledge the strength, courage and resilience of Stolen Generations survivors like Aunty Eileen.

Senator Malarndirri McCarthy
Minister for Indigenous Australians

'Brown Skin Baby'

My brown skin baby, they take him away

As a young preacher, I used to ride
My quiet pony 'round the countryside
In a native camp, I'll never forget
A young black mother, her cheeks all wet
My brown skin baby, they take him away

Between her sobs, I heard her say
Police's been taken my baby away
From white man, boss, the baby I have
Why he let them take baby away
My brown skin baby, they take him away

To a children's home a baby came
With new clothes on and a new name
Day and night, he would always say
Oh mummy, mummy, why they take me away?
My brown skin baby, they take him away

The child grew up and had to go
From a mission home that he loved so
To find his mother, he tried in vain
Upon this earth they never met again

My brown skin baby, they take him away
My brown skin baby, they take him away
My brown skin baby, they take him away

Song written by Bob Randall, 1963

The title of this book is based on something my mother said to me when I saw her again, as an adult, after I had been taken as a child: 'You are my daughter, Eileen, that they stole from me.' So many of our Stolen Generations people have never really had the reconnection that I've had. That's why I'd like to tell my story to show people that even though we were disconnected from our family, there is a way of reconnecting.

1

Childhood at Mainoru Station

I was born in 1943 on the Mainoru cattle station, Central Arnhem Land. I was delivered by my grandmothers in the Aboriginal traditional method of birthing on the cool sands of the Mainoru Riverbank – no hospital for this birth. I was told that my delivery was quick and safe and that the grandmothers and other women were excited to see this child. I was very pink, as all babies are at birth; the women saw that I looked a little different from other babies born in the camp. I was then brought up from the river to meet the family and station manager. I was the first child born to my mother, Liguwanga, of the Ngalakan/Rembarrnga tribes of Central Arnhem Land. They named me Wykundu, 'flowing waters', and my skin name is Gaman. As I grew up, it was decided that I should also have an English name, Eileen. My mother's English name was Florrie.[1]

Before I was born, my mum's family had moved to Mainoru station to work.[2] When mum's sister, Aunty Ivy, married the wrong way, grandpa got upset. She was older than Florrie – Mum was the eldest from her mother, but my grandfather had two wives and Ivy belonged to that other wife. But she went and married wrong way, the wrong skin group and not her promised husband. In those days, they would have punished people who married the wrong way. But because Granddad was head of the Ngalakan tribe, they weren't going to kill his daughter. But Grandpa got annoyed, that's why he left her behind and took the rest of the family up to Mainoru to work – Mum, her mother, and her two brothers, Dick and Larry. Grandfather took them from Urapunga to Mainoru, up through all that bush country. The Wilton is our Country; our Country is all of the Wilton River from Urapunga, so he could go anywhere. He moved them up the Wilton and they ended up at Mainoru. Mum showed me later where they walked. She said, 'We never went on any truck. We put them things in carts and them big billy goats pull everything.' They're pulling the cart up with all their baggage in there, but they walked it all, long distances. Mummy Lucy was actually born out there at Lucy Creek where Baghetti is now sitting. Baghetti is an outstation there at Bulman and Lucy Creek is named after her. When I was an adult, I asked my brother Ronnie, 'Why is that creek named after Mummy Lucy?' And Ronnie told me, he said, 'Because that's where Mummy Lucy was born.' So my grandmother must have been pregnant when she was coming down to Mainoru. Mummy Lucy was born at Lucy Creek off the Bulman River, whereas Florrie and her brothers were born at Urapunga, I think. The stationmaster at Mainoru, old Jack McKay, was looking for workers, and some of the people used to come from Ngukurr – Roper River station – to Mainoru to work. And Grandpa then thought, Oh, well, we'll just go up the river and go to Mainoru. And his children could work for Mainoru station. Old Jack built them little huts around the station, they all had little tin huts around Mainoru that they lived in and put a little fire out the front and cooked.

So, I'm Rembarrnga/Ngalakan. Ngalakan from my grandfather, and Rembarrnga from my mum and her mum. Mum's father, Yilparrara, was a great leader, medicine man, warrior and ceremonial man, not only big in statue but in his role as head of my family and clan. He was the Ngalakan leader, the main ceremonial man of all the Arnhem Land region, right down to Ngukurr. And he had five brothers; they're the Ngalakan mob from Ngukurr. My grandmother, Wuylya, was

Rembarrnga, so my mum identifies as Rembarrnga/ Ngalakan, and I do too. She's Rembarrnga from her mum and Ngalakan from her father. My mother's Aboriginal name was Gudgud. She had two Aboriginal names – Liguwanga, I think, is her skin name, and Gudgud was her Aboriginal name.

My family were the Murrays and the Martins. Uncle Larry Murray and Uncle Dick Murray were my mum's brothers. Mummy Lucy was her sister. Lucy married Uncle Willy Martin, and so she became a Martin. Mum met her husband at the station and married him, Jugaduk, because that's his Country. Bulman's on his Country. Before she married, Mum was a Murray, and then she became a Lindsay when she married my dad. I believe they married in the mid-1930s. My mum's husband raised me from a baby, he's been a father to me all my life and I called him 'Dad', old Jugaduk. After me, they had my brother Ronnie. We are their only children. My brother Ronnie was born in 1946 when I was about three. My mother was very young when she had me. She must've been about 17, 18. But of course she wouldn't have known because all she said was, 'I was a young woman'. That's all she said. And she was a beautiful young woman. She was tall and sort of regal and powerful looking. She walked with her head high and she had great posture. I remember her like that. But Mum was humble and so beautiful.

I never found out who my white father was. My mum and dad worked in a cattle plant. All the stockmen would go to another cattle station, pick up cattle and move them – that's what you call a cattle plant. And a lot of them in the wartime had to do that. They had to get cattle from Victoria River and take them all the way to Mataranka where the army services were, both American and Australian army were there. Mum and the other workers worked in the cattle plant. When mum got back to Mainoru, she was pregnant.

Later in life, when I travelled throughout the Territory for work and talked to those women, they told me some of the horrible things that happened to them on those cattle stations. I heard so many stories from the women about the abuse and suffering they endured from pastoralist or miners who came to the Territory to seek their wealth and fortune. Old Jack McKay at Mainoru, he never abused the women there. Yet I was told by our women that in other cattle stations, they abused the women. Some of the stories were horrific. But that's part of the history of some of our women. When they told me, they said, 'They used us for their good time and sport, Eileen.' I just couldn't believe that. Not many have been able to have that dialogue with our women on the remote communities. But because I was working there, that's what I learnt. It still hurts me to this day. That's why it's taken me so long to talk about what happened to our women. I wanted to highlight the issues our women went through when they worked on cattle stations for white men in remote parts of the Territory; to talk about our mothers and our women because a lot of our women had no say in becoming pregnant. They had no say in the removal of their children. Our mothers were never given choices in what they did. That's why we got all this breed of half-caste kids. Some of those liaisons weren't like rape, they were good relationships, but for most of the women I've spoken to it wasn't a choice. Always I could see the hurt and they lived with shame. I think about it quite a bit, and I get quite emotional.

Dad never talked about it because he was my father as far as I was concerned, old Jugaduk. But you wonder how those men felt, hey? Our people, our men, our fathers. When you listen to some of the stories the women told, they said, 'They'd say to our men that the women had to do it.' They'd threaten them. There was a threat behind it all too, so that if they didn't allow their wives to do it, they wouldn't get rations. Or may get killed.[3] Some of the men told me that when I was travelling around.

They'd say, 'Some of us tried to fight. I picked up a shovel spear once.'

I said, 'And what happened?'

'They told me they'd shoot me.' And you know what a shovel spear is? It hasn't just got one sharp point. It's jaded – that's a shovel spear. And they used that to kill, our people did, when they're fighting against the other tribes. That was to kill, not to maim. That was the killing spear.

The other day, one of my grandsons and I were talking about it and he said, 'Nana, you know what those men did? They raped our grandmothers.' That's what he said the other day. 'My great-grandmother was raped. All the women were raped.' I've never heard my boys talk that way before. He just gave me a big hug. I looked at him and I was so proud of what I'd been able to raise in my children, that one of my grandsons could see it. The boys often said, 'We were raised by strong Aboriginal women,' and I was so proud to think that one of my grandsons understood the work I'd been doing with family violence for such a long time. I felt that I have helped my people to understand what had actually happened to them. Our mothers were the silent sufferers. Nobody worried about them, did they.

I can understand why Mum never talked about it. I tried to ask her, because all of us Stolen Generations[4] kids, we want to know where we came from. I asked her once when I was an adult, I said, 'Mum, where is my father?' 'Him finish.' And I thought she meant, you know, when you say 'him finished', he must be dead. So I thought he was dead. 'Oh. All right. And so you're not gonna tell me his name?' And she reckoned, 'Na, him munanga,[5] anyway. Him big fella munanga,' she reckoned. But as far as she was concerned, he was finished in her life and she didn't want to discuss him at all, so to her he was dead. And I didn't talk about it with her again. I thought, maybe we better just leave it. I don't want any man like that as my father anyway. A lot of other Stolen Generations children have never found out who their fathers were. A lot of us haven't, because it was never recorded. And when you asked the mothers, they didn't want to talk about it. They didn't want to relive and they didn't want to remember. But this is the history I come from. This is what happened to our women and my mother and my aunties and whoever else was there.

My childhood at Mainoru was wonderful. Old Jack McKay, the pastoralist, looked after all my mob. To us, the McKays were our people. They cared for us. He never married, old Jack, neither did old Sandy, his brother. The McKays lived at the station for a long time, but Sandy was out at Milikapiti on Tiwi Islands, teaching, so I didn't meet him until later in life. My mother told me they thought very highly of Jack MacKay and loved and respected him. She said he was a hard man but a kind man, provided you worked. When they had ceremonies or a funeral to go to, he let them go and would provide for their meat and everything. Jack felt all those who worked for him were his people and he took good care of them. He mightn't have paid them money, but they always had food and they always had tobacco. And nobody got paid money at that time. The Aboriginal men and women worked long and hard and only received rations, a hut, and no pay. I felt safe with Jack. I felt he really cared for me and my family. See, that's why I loved being at Mainoru, Mum and all our people were there working, and they were part of the community. They were part of the station, and I was part of the station. And my grandparents were there, my parents were there, my uncles and aunties. I was very close to my uncles and aunties, my mother's brothers and sister; and to all the people, there were other families there too.

As a child, I was really happy. I remember having such a wonderful childhood. I never wanted for anything. We went hunting, fishing and camping on the river. It was always an exciting and enjoyable time because I had my whole family around me, not only my grandparents, but my uncles and aunties and their families, all my little cousins. Most of the Aboriginal families lived in tin shanties on the edge of the cattle station and woke every day to work on the station and in the gardens that supplied the vegetables and fruit, in particular paw-paws, bananas and pineapples. Mum had her own goat herd for milk and meat and she tended these with great care. I loved the goat milk, we used to boil it up, and the cream used to be so thick. You know, we heat it up and then the cream would just sit on the top like that and we used to eat it with syrup and damper. That's how we ate it.

Mum worked on the cattle station, in the station house, cooking, cleaning and doing the laundry. On most days, I was there at the station house with Mum while she worked, or I was running between the camp and the station house and cattle yards. One day, I thought I would just cut up some meat for myself. Mum was cooking in the kitchen and they used to hang the meat in a larder. I went into that and got the big butcher knife and began to carve the meat. I think Dad Jugaduk was down at the stockyards, but then he came up to see Mum and he found me helping myself to meat, and almost had a heart attack! He gave me a bit of a smack, but then he just took the knife away from me, allowed me to eat the meat that I'd sliced. He also cut some more pieces for me because I told him I was hungry, but he said, 'Yes, but you don't cut the meat. We will do that, Mum or me or old Jack will do it for you, not you.' Well, I thought I was really smart and would do it myself!

Sometimes when Mum was working, my grandparents, my mum's mother and father, were looking after me. On other occasions, Mum went off with my dad and the other guys, and they went mustering the cattle and bringing it back, and they'd be gone for about a week. Mum would be gone for a week at a time sometimes, to the mustering camps with her husband and her brothers. And I'd be there with my nana and pop. They were my carers.

My grandfather was a big ceremonial man, and he'd take me to ceremonial places. I remember sitting on his shoulders, he was about seven foot tall, and he used to carry me on his shoulders and take me for walks out bush and everywhere and to places that a lot of other kids weren't allowed to go. But because I went with him, I could go anywhere. I remember that really clearly. A thing that made me wonder, was why I was frightened of heights later in life. I think it was because I used to sit on my grandfather's shoulders and he'd carry me everywhere on his shoulders. Nana was only a tiny little lady, and she'd be walking along next to us.

We often used to go swimming in the river at Mainoru. We weren't allowed to go down to the river unless an adult was with us. We went fishing and turtle hunting because I used to eat a lot of turtle then. We also collected mussels from the rivers, and yabbies. We'd bring it back to the house where we were living. We were in little huts around the cattle station. I had a really happy life at Mainoru station.

We had ceremonies at Mainoru, but also often we'd go to Elsey station for ceremonies when I was a little girl. Our whole family and then the people from Elsey and from Ngukurr would be there. We used to attend these things and I remember going back to Elsey station where the waterfall[6] was when I was older, with my grandchildren, and I said to Aunty Nelly, 'I remember this place. I remember the fish being in the river and everything and playing in the sand here.' Aunty Nelly[7] was Uncle Willy Martin's sister. And she said, 'Yeah, that's where we used to come to the ceremonies.' So we normally took all the family, the Murrays and the Martins, back to that place and some of the other families too that lived at Mainoru. And we met up with the families from Elsey station and some even came from Ngukurr. So it was a group of about a hundred of us, I suppose. But I was only a child at that time, so maybe my figures are wrong – because it seemed like a big group, but when you're little, anything's big.

We used to have to travel all the way from Mainoru, which is a fair distance.[8] And I asked Mum later, 'How did we always travel when we went to these things?' – because we didn't have any cars. Mummy Nelly said, 'Most times we walked or we got people to pick us up.' I know there were a few ceremonies at Elsey station; the other place was Beswick Falls. When I was an adult, we'd go down for the festival at Barunga community; that happens every June. Some of us would go and camp at Beswick Falls. When I went back to Beswick Falls, I remembered having been there as a child and, again, Mummy Nelly said, 'Yeah, that's where we used to go for ceremonies.' So it's amazing that I remembered.

Sometimes we went out to Ngukurr, and also to Urapunga station, where my mother and uncles had been born. That's quite a long way, but we travelled like that because that was part of our life, the Aboriginal system. If we went to Ngukurr, the Ngukurr people ran the ceremony. If they came out to Beswick, then my people from Mainoru ran that one and the Beswick people. When we went to Elsey, the Esley people ran them. So each area was run by the different groups because they've got the ceremonial responsibility for each area. We'd go to those and meet up with all different groups at these ceremonies. And that's why Mum knew all those languages. Mum's English wasn't very good when I was a child, but she spoke nine different languages in the Arnhem Land region. Because my grandfather was the ceremonial man for Arnhem Land, they often travelled to those ceremonies together, because Grandpa had to run them. And so Mum understood and spoke all those languages. Yeah, she was amazing, that old girl. Sometimes they even used to go down the centre, down to Yuendemu and Lajamanu, to ceremonies because of Grandpa's status. So she must have picked up those languages as well, because she went down to all those different Countries. Later, everybody started speaking Kriol and my mother spoke pretty clear Kriol. So my family took me to ceremonies when I was little. And when I left, I lost all of that, they took it all. I had to go back when I was an adult, to go back through ceremony.

2

Stolen

This all came to a big halt because at that time I was called a half-caste since I had a white father and a black mother. They wanted to take us away from our mothers and our people to educate us and assimilate us. The government thought by removing the children they would grow up in the white system and leave their Aboriginal life behind.[9] My people knew about this because Jack McKay, the pastoralist, had told them. 'They'll come and try to take Eileen,' he told Mum, and she's saying, 'But why?' That was always her question, 'But why?' Because she couldn't understand government rules and government policies, I suppose. Jack said that the Native Affairs used to go out there. There was a settlement they called Tandangal, near Beswick station. You know how they are, the stations are thousands and thousands of kilometres big, really big stations. Well, Mainoru was quite a big station, and even though they just lived in one little area, the whole station was his. There was a community set up called Tandangal and a lot of people were living there. The Native Affairs used to come out there, looking for children. Jack was always aware they were coming to look for us. And they knew about me, because there happened to be a policeman there when I was born and he registered my birth. So I think our people were aware that it was going to happen, especially if the pastoralist told them. If you had a good pastoralist, they'd tell you. We were lucky we had old Jack McKay. He was a good man.

So Mum kept me close. When she worked at the station

house, I was with her all the time. Jack McKay let me run that place like it was my home. He only sent me down the camp if I was naughty. Most of the time I was there at the station house with Mum. They didn't tell me about the danger, but when they knew somebody official would come to the station, Mum used to just say, 'Oh, you're going to go bush with your grandparents.' So my grandparents used to run away with me and hide me. A lot of our people did that. And Grandpa knew the ceremonial grounds, so he'd take me bush where nobody was allowed to come. Because we've got sacred sites and areas where white men weren't allowed to come, and that's where he'd take me. Native Affairs came out there quite often and Jack would just say, 'None of the kids are here. No, we've got no kids here.' And by that time I was probably down the scrub with my grandparents somewhere. But on this particular day it was only me running around on the veranda at the station house. Mum was in the kitchen cooking and old Jack and the other men were down the stockyards. Everyone was down the stockyards doing stock work.

I remember the patrol officer in khaki uniform coming to Mainoru in a red truck. I was four and a half, this was in 1948. I ran out and was looking at him on the truck. The truck came to the house and one of the men working in the garden said, 'Old Jack, that old man's down the stockyards.' The patrol officer asked me, 'You wanna come for a ride?' And I said yeah, because I was a curious child. I thought it was only for a ride around the community, not to take me right away from Mum. So I ran down the steps and got on the truck. I think they put me in the front, you know how those old Chevrolet trucks had a seat there. So they had me in there. And I was sitting there and waving, thinking I was special like a princess, waving to Mum. Mum came out to look for me, and she was standing on the veranda of the station house watching me go. And I was waving, I thought it was really good, I was just going for a ride in the truck. Then all of a sudden, the truck didn't swing around to where I could see Mum again. And I thought, Well then, when I get back there, I can jump off and go back to Mum. That's what I was thinking in my little head. Anyway, next minute the truck took off out of Mainoru. And I thought, Might be we're just going for a longer ride? But then when the truck started to go further out, I realised I wasn't coming back. As you go from Mainoru station back out onto the main highway to Katherine, I started bawling because I was thinking, Where's Mum? Where are we? Where's Mum? I started crying and the patrol officer was trying to keep me quiet. He patted me on my head and said, 'It's all right,' and he gave me a drink of water to shut me up, I think. He didn't stop or anything, he just kept going. And I think we went through the rivers and everything. We never even stopped there, we went straight through the rivers. As I was going past all those familiar places, the rivers we used to swim in, I knew that I was going away from my mother.

At first old Jack didn't realise I'd gone either. The patrol officer didn't go and talk to Mum and say they were going to take me. It's like robbery. He just picked me up and took me away. Jack was down in the stockyards and he came up because Mum got upset, I think she might've ran down there to tell Dad that they'd taken me. And when they took me, there was another little boy playing there, he was Mummy Lucy's son, my cousin Leslie, but his mother grabbed him and took him. Later on I found out he was brought in and put into Retta Dixon home.

So I went on the big long road from Mainoru to Katherine without anybody, just myself and the patrol officer. After a day of travelling they took me to the Maranboy police station to await other children from Beswick, Bamyili[10] and Nutwood Downs. So the officer left me at Maranboy police station – on my own, mind you. Nobody was there with me. But in their report[11] they're saying that I was there with all the other kids. I wasn't. I was there on my own. I stayed there for about three days before they brought the other kids. And I was really scared because I was thinking, I'm here by myself. I don't even know anybody. They put me in a big shed of some kind at the police station. I had a bed, but nobody was with me. I never saw anybody. The policeman was there, but he never talked to me. I think I blocked out the details, because I was so young. And then Uncle Willy Martin came down to check on me because Mum must have said, 'If you go past Maranboy, go look for Eileen.' So he came looking for me and he found me. And he just said to that policeman: 'What you leaving this little piccaninny in here by herself for?' That's what he said. He went and got one of my aunties from Bamyili to come, Aunty Rosie. She was married to Tiny Swanson, a white miner working at the George Fisher mine. Little tiny lady, she was. Rosie came up because they said she was related to me somehow, and so Uncle Willy made sure somebody came up to see me. 'Will you go back and sit up with that piccaninny, she's there on her own.' So she came up and sat with me, sat every day. But she wasn't allowed to stay with me at nighttime, she'd have to walk back. I don't remember anybody being with me at night. And that's who they said was my mother, Rosie. They put it on my record that my mother was Rosie, but Rosie wasn't my mother, she was a relation of my mother's. In Aboriginal custom, your aunts are also your mothers. Rosie was a cousin-sister to my mother and she was there with me at that police station. And we were waiting for three days.

When the other children came, that was three days later. Lorky[12] was coming from Tandangal, up near Beswick, and Rita[13] was just there at Maranboy at the mine.[14] Her mother was married to that old white man, George Fisher. Well, not married, but living with him. She didn't have a bad marriage.

But her mum, Daisy, used to take Rita all the time back to Barunga, and that's where they picked her up, from Barunga. But even when the white father and Aboriginal mother were in a relationship, they took the kids. Some men tried to argue and fight with the government, white men, and they never won because they said, 'We are still taking the children. That child is under Native Affairs.' So they just took you. Lorky was the oldest of us, she was seven or eight. Lorraine, but we call her Lorky, that's her nickname from us. Her mother was trying to hide her all that time, and they did hide her for a long time. They used to run to Beswick Falls and all that bush country and hide her there. Then one day, she was walking around somewhere and they came and just picked her up. And when she got picked up, our people said, 'You have to go with the little ones. You're the oldest, you gotta go and look after all them kids. Don't let the little kids forget who they are.' She had to come with us, whether her mother liked it or not. The mothers, all our relations said, 'Well, she has to go with them. We still got all them little piccaninnies.' Rita was not quite two years old. That's what my mum told me later, that's why Lorky had to come with us. 'You know that big girl you always talk about?' I said. 'Lorky, Lorraine.' And she said, 'Yeah, her. We gone make sure she come to look after you kids.' And Lorky, because she was eight years old by the time she was picked up, she knew us all from the ceremonies.

We all spent another day and night at the police station, then the patrol officer took us by truck to Darwin. We stopped at Pine Creek. There was a home there next to the water tower, a home for children. It used to be a holding place because we know that a lot of the Croker Island people went there before they went to Croker in the 1930s. They've got a plaque there where the home used to be. And that's where we went, to that home and the hospital. We thought we were gonna pick up other kids, but the only kid we picked up from Pine Creek was Tommy Olsen. He'd been down the pit with his father, an old white man. Tommy was about five or six and that old man must have known that they were going to come and get him at some stage because he had taken him away from his mother and he was raising him. The patrol officer went down to the mine and picked Tommy up and brought him back to the truck. Tommy was just full of soot, you know, he come out of the mine full of soot and they put him on the truck. I don't even remember them bathing him.

At Pine Creek, we also picked up four men prisoners going to Fannie Bay goal. And that's what I always say about duty of care. They had no duty of care for us. They left me alone at the police station for three days, and when the others came, they put us all on the truck and we went to Pine Creek and the patrol officer picked up those prisoners and the Aboriginal lady with some sort of disease to bring her to Darwin hospital. They were all on the truck with us. So there was no duty of care for the children. As we were driving to Darwin, we were in the back of the truck, crying for our mothers. None of us spoke much English, but anyway, nobody was explaining anything to us. And we were so afraid of being on the back of this big truck, too frightened to move in case we fell off. So we're sitting in the middle of the truck, holding on. And then Rita spewed all over Tommy's head because I think she was getting car sick. Poor thing, Tommy, he was in worse condition than ever. And I think Lorky, she found a bucket or some bottle with water so she just poured it on his head to clean him. Poor thing, he was screaming and crying, but she was trying to clean him, I think. So can you imagine when we got to Darwin, we must have looked like nothing on Earth, you know. There was no time to bathe or really stop for toilet time; so you can imagine the sight of us when we arrived in Darwin, we must have looked like we had never had proper care in all our lives.

We got to Retta Dixon[15] in Darwin, and were there for nearly a week before going to Croker. At Retta Dixon, we met two other kids from our area, Tarni and Shirley,[16] they're sisters. But for a long time, as a child, I believed that they was with us all the way from Maranboy, and they weren't. Even when I grew up, I think I still believed that. But Lorky said to me one day when we were at Croker Island, she said, 'No, Tarni and Shirley didn't come with us from Maranboy. We met them in Darwin at Retta Dixon.' She reckoned, 'You remember their mother bringing them to Retta Dixon? Well, that's when they came to us.' I still don't know to this day why their mother was with them, because nobody ever explained that to us. Because our mothers weren't allowed to even come and see us, but Lorraine said somehow their mother was in Darwin with them and she brought them to Retta Dixon. And then I don't know what happened to her, she must have gone back. They were from Nutwood Downs down near Elsey and that's a long way.

When Shirley and Tarni came to Retta Dixon, Lorky recognised them from ceremonies. She'd say, in language, 'You remember when we went to Elsey or Ngukurr?' And I'd say, 'Yeah.' 'Well, these two are from them.' And I started to remember them because they all had come to ceremonies with me. Because we used to have whole ceremonies at Elsey station, and they used to come there with their mother, but they were actually from Nutwood Downs. In the end, it was six of us: Lorraine, myself, Tarni and Shirley, Rita and Tommy Olsen. We didn't know Tommy before, his family's from Pine Creek. But he was with us and he wouldn't leave us, so we somehow thought he was part of our family. Wherever we went, Tommy went. Even in Retta Dixon and Croker, he became attached to me and Lorky, Rita and Shirley. He was like our family, a brother. Rita was only around two years old, and Tarni was even younger, about 18 months. Shirley was the same age as me. Rita and Tarni were still suckling off their mothers when they took them, those two.

We tried to run away, but went in the wrong direction and ended up near the back of Bagot and down near that creek, Racecourse Creek. You go through Bagot, through that back road there, past the little community there. We went down the back way through the scrub. Lorky, me, Rita, Shirley and Tarni and Tommy Olson. We were going towards the sea and we ended up at Racecourse Creek, which is near Fannie Bay. The patrol officers found out that we were missing and went looking for us. One of them came up in a car and he looked at us. 'Where do you kids think you're going?' he said. Lorky looked at him and said, 'Home.' And he said, 'Well, you're going the wrong way.' He brought us back to Retta Dixon and we were crying, and they were still trying to separate us, but we just clung to Lorky, so they couldn't do anything. They just let us be. Rita and I were on each side of Lorky, we weren't going anywhere, and Shirley was carrying Tarni because she was a baby.

When I was an adult, I looked up the report that the patrol officer wrote about us when we were picked up. Claire[17] had seen it, so she said, 'You want to go?' So I went to the archives, we got one here in Darwin and it holds all the government records. Of course, a lot of it is blacked out. You see the reports and they've got a black line through them because they don't want us to read what they wrote about us. They've written some horrible things about us. But I saw my report, I got a copy of it, but it's very short.

It was the policy of the Commonwealth Government from the early 1900s to 1967 to remove all 'half-caste' children with black mothers and white fathers to missions and institutions.[18] With the Stolen Generations from the Territory, there were about 2000 children removed, in the Territory alone.[19] We had seven institutions in the Northern Territory and in those seven institutions there were 2000 children who had been removed. The government thought by removing the children they would grow up in the white system and leave their Aboriginal life behind.[20] They were mistaken. How can a child that had been reared in that way, to be part of those ceremonies and everything, just forget it? We couldn't forget it because we'd gone through ceremonies and practised the Aboriginal way of life; we would not forget where we came from or who our mothers were. They couldn't take away our Aboriginality. That was part of us and part of our life.

I suppose they thought education would compensate but it didn't. Education doesn't replace the hurt of not having a mother and not having a family. I'm not better off because I missed out on the most important things. We missed out on our culture and our family. Nothing can replace that. When I left, it was like I had nowhere. I had nothing. They took us completely, isolated us, changed our names, took us as far as they could from our Country and our people.

I understood all of this later, through my work. But when I was taken, nobody explained it to us. Even when they moved me from my mother, they didn't tell me where they were taking me. They didn't tell my mother where they were taking me, or why, and whether I was ever going to come back. They just took me. And so it must have been sad for her to think, They've taken her and I'm not gonna ever see her again. And my family and the people at the station, they couldn't understand why I was taken. I had a really happy life, I felt, and that's why Mum could never understand why they took me away. She always said that she was a hard worker all her life. When I saw her again as an adult, I kept telling her that that was a policy, and she couldn't understand policy because she was almost illiterate. And I kept saying to her, 'But Mum, look at my skin. That's why they removed us as children and put us into missions and institutions.' And she said, 'But why? I didn't do anything wrong.' But it had nothing to do with that. And because she thought they took me because she was a bad mother, she had to live with that guilt all that time I was away.

What Jack McKay did, was he built his own school there so that they couldn't say the kids weren't being educated. After they took me, he was quite angry about it. He didn't like the government's removal policy, he thought children should remain with their mothers, families and clans. That's why Jack took it on himself then to build that school, so none of us kids would be taken again. He knew the hurt it was. He wrote to Native Affairs, he used to often write letters to them, and he said, 'If that's the reason you're taking children, well, I'll build my own school on the station.' And he brought his sister and her husband, both qualified teachers, from Queensland to Mainoru to run the school. Mr and Mrs Dodd. He was the first pastoralist to build a school on the station. And it worked in that area, it stopped the kids from being taken.

Then, when I was on Croker, Jack McKay used to write every Christmas to Native Affairs and say, 'Can Eileen come home for the holidays? Can we come and get her? I'll come into Darwin and pick her up and take her home so she can see her mother and her people.' But they wouldn't let me go. He used to ask every Christmas, his niece Heather told me later. She said, 'Eileen, he used to always ask if you could come back for Christmas and they wouldn't let you.' She said, 'He came in there that many times, Eileen, every Christmas to pick you up.' What a kind and generous man he was, old Jack McKay. And that road used to be terrible at Christmas time. But nothing, they wouldn't let me go home. I never went home. I didn't see my mum again until I was 19, and I never saw my grandparents again.

Left: 0.1 Eileen Cummings, Claire Smith and Michelle Cummings, June 2019

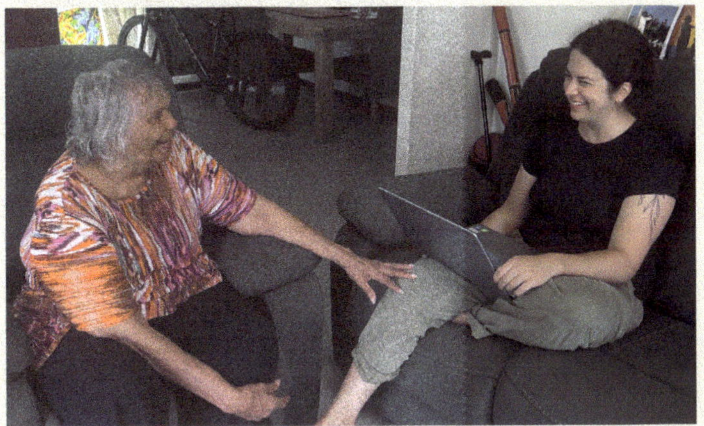

Above: 0.2 Eileen Cummings and Jana Anvari, January 2025

Right: 1.1 Eileen Cummings' mother and father, Florrie and Jugaduk Lindsay, c. 1965

Above: 1.2 Florrie Lindsay and Lucy Martin, 1975

Right: 1.3 Jugaduk Lindsay (MAGNT, Pict 047, Dodd Collection)

Below: 1.4 Women at Mainoru, Northern Territory

Top: 1.5 Branding at Mainoru Station, 1960s (Lawley-Brown, P., LANT, Lawley-Brown Collection, PH0694-0013)

Above: 2.1 Maranboy Police Station, 1920s (LANT, Bruce Sutherland Collection, PH0619-0009)

Below: 2.2 Mrs Dodd teaching children at Mainoru school. Jeanette McDonald and Glen Stuart (afterwards Wesan) in front row, Jill Curtis in middle row centre (MAGNT PH047, Dodd Collection)

Left: 3.1 Map of Croker Island (NTSGAC collection, 36270006)

Below: 3.2 Croker Island Mission from the air, c. 1958, with the new government school in the foreground (NTSGAC Collection, 002_Croker from Air)

Bottom: 3.3 Looking down on the mission from the tank, 1950s (NTSGAC Miss Clarke's Collection, 36350006)

Above: 3.4 Croker Island Mission girls, early 1950s. Eileen is in the front row, third from left

Left: 3.5 Seaview Cottage at Croker Island Mission

Right: 3.6 Eileen Cummings in her Girl Guide's uniform, early to mid-1950s

Below: 3.7 Christmas party on the Croker Island Mission, 1952 or 1953

Top: 3.8 Lillies collected by the children for a church service, Croker Island Mission

Left: 3.9 Lorraine Rouster on the day she left Croker Island for Adelaide, 1958

Below: 3.10 Pavalina Nickloff, Eileen Cummings and Florrie Cousins on the beach, late 1950s

Bottom: 3.11 School sports day, 1957. Eileen Cummings holding the blue flag as team captain (NTSGAC Miss Clarke's Collection, Sports Day 1957)

Left: 3.12 Eileen Cummings on Arbor Day, c. 1958 (NTSGAC Collection, 157)

Below: 3.13 Domestic science class, Croker Island school, presenting a meal, c. 1959. Eileen is 5th from left (NTSGAC Collection, 150)

Bottom: 3.14 The old Croker Island school, early 1950s (NTSGAC Miss Clarke's Collection, 3637000)

Above: 3.15 The new Croker Island school

Left: 3.16 Bob and Amy Randall's wedding, 1958 (NTSGAC Collection, 36310003)

Below: 3.17 Amy and Alan Randall, late 1950s (NTSGAC Collection, family24_3_09_0014)

Bottom: 3.18 Aunty Dolly Crocker, Eileen Cummings and Mum Amy Randall at award ceremony, Parliament House, Darwin

3

Growing Up on Croker Island

After a week at Retta Dixon home Native Affairs sent us to Croker Island Mission by boat. This was to be our home until we turned 18. We are asking Lorky to explain what a boat was, and why we were going on a boat, and she was trying to work it out in her head. We had all them paperbark boats on our land. Our people used to go across the billabongs and that in paperbark boats. And then to tell us we were going out on that big sea – we didn't even know what that was. We'd never seen an ocean before. And poor thing, she was trying to explain it to us in our language so we could understand, and we were crying, 'We don't want to go. We don't want to go.' When we got to the wharf: 'That! That thing is the boat,' she said. It was a frightening experience. We were on the boat sitting there like little lost sheep, didn't know what to do. Poor old Jack Scrymgour was trying to console us. He was the older boy from Croker Island on the boat, working as a deck hand. Uncle Willie was the captain and he was a Malay man. The boat, named *Larrapan*, used to take children and supplies to the mission. They had a crew there, they were all trying to look after us. Jack tried to give us Vegemite sandwiches, which we threw into the water. We didn't know what the black stuff was on our bread. We came to the point where we passed the Tiwi Islands and were going towards Cobourg and we could see the trees and everything on the land. I'm saying to Lorky, 'That's Mummy?' And she's saying, 'No, that's not Mummy. Mummy long way.' And I would say,

'When we going to see Mummy?' And she'd say, 'No mummy, dear. Mummy home.' She just kept saying, 'Mummy home.'

We arrived on Croker at night and could see lanterns. There were white cottage sisters, the superintendent and older girls and boys to meet us with dinghies. They tried to put us into a dingy to take us to shore from the big boat. Some older girls had white turbans over their heads. As we later discovered, they had had their heads shaved for punishment and they were bald. But to us, they looked scary and we screamed as we did not want any of them to touch us. We were kicking and screaming as they put us in the dinghies and then on a truck to take us to the mission. At first they tried to split us up and get us away from Lorraine. But they couldn't, the first night, because we wouldn't let her go. We kept on clinging onto her. So we all stayed with Ms Somerville.

The next day they sent Lorraine and Shirley to Reynella, which was sort of the teenagers' cottage. Rita and Tanya had to stay with Ms Somerville in the little people's cottage at Somerset. I was sent by myself to Malila. That's where I became best friends with Laura, she and I were in that cottage together with her younger sister, Eva. So we had a couple of older girls living there and they were in one big room. Then we had a couple of teenagers, and then us little ones in the middle room; that's where I was with Laura. And we grew up in Malila, not far from the school. Once they'd built that big new school, we just walked across the road to school every day.

There were eight cottages with nearly a hundred children. They had older girls in Alkoomi cottage at one end of the mission, the next lot of girls in the middle at Reynella cottage, and then the little ones down the bottom in Somerset. So the girls were all at one end, except Malila, where I was growing up, that was up near the other end. And we were surrounded by boys, the little boys' cottage, Seaview, and teenage boys in Illawarra and Delaraine. And then the big boys' cottage, Victory, was right in the middle of the community. We had eight cottages, and you'd have a minimum of eight children in each cottage. There were five children in the bedroom in my cottage, five in one of the other bedrooms and four in the other bedroom. We just had those skinny little cyclone beds. Each cottage had three bedrooms, and then another little room where the cottage sister lived, so the house was almost a four-bedroom house. We had a change of cottage sisters. If they were there for two to three years or something like that, then they'd leave and you get another one. So we didn't have continuity in care, except some sisters stayed longer. Ms Somerville who took care of the toddlers, she was there all that time and I think she took really good care of the little ones. And some of the older children were sort of attached to her because she was the one who took them away and cared for them in wartime.[21]

The bathroom, it was a big room attached to the house with concrete floor and no roof on it. And there'd be a bathtub if we wanted to be in the bathtub, but we never used to, we used to go straight under the shower. Next to that was the kitchen, and that was quite big. And down the back were those pit toilets. So we used to have to walk up to that at nighttime if we wanted to go to the toilet, and that was really frightening. We'd have a torch walking there to the toilet, but I hated pit toilets because I was frightened something was going to jump up and bite me. But it wasn't really going to happen, the pit was so deep nothing could jump up, probably.

We had three boats, the *Larrapan*, the *Warrawi*, and one other, that used to bring all our stores out. We had cauliflower in tins and it stank and smelled horrible because a lot of our food was in tins, like tomatoes. Why tomatoes, when we grew our own tomatoes on the mission? But we hardly had any apples and oranges. Sometimes we'd have them, but most of our fruit came from our vegetable garden. The only times we had oranges and apples, probably once a year when they probably were in season and the boat would bring it out for us. But we never went hungry, the mission had plenty of food, milk, meat, fruit and vegetables. We had vegetable gardens and, some Saturday mornings, we had to go and weed those vegetable gardens because we had carrots and tomatoes and all those sorts of things. In our fruit gardens, we had lemons, limes, mandarins. We had a fruit I've never seen again since, we called it African quince. It had a big hard shell, like a coconut shell, really hard. And when it was on the tree, it was green. When it was ripe, we used to crack it open and eat the food that was inside that shell. And you know where I thought I saw it? You know *Lion King*, that fruit in *Lion King* that the monkey cracked open? That's what it looked like. It had the biggest tree, and the trees are still at Croker Island. And we had five corners there, you know, that fruit with the five corners. We had a lot of cashew nut trees. And we used to have to pick the watermelons. We also had a peanut farm, and we had to harvest the peanuts. We'd have to pull them out and shake them and let them dry. We had every fruit: we had bananas, custard apples, pineapples, every sort of fruit you could think of. And we had a big piggery. Uncle Mick Yarmia and Uncle Timothy Yarmia looked after that, and they would chase us away from that piggery, because we used to tease the old boar. We were real mad children, we seemed to have quite a freedom to do a lot of things. Laura and I got up to a lot of mischief.

Then on Saturdays, the superintendent would often take us to another part of the island for the day. So we'd go fishing and hunting at another part, like Second Bay or Cape Don down the bottom of the island, or Cape Croker. We'd go to different places in the truck, all sit in the back of the big truck and go for these picnics and spend the whole day somewhere.

At Second Bay, they used to have fresh water running out of the cliffs where we played and there'd be billabongs and things we could play in. And the sea, of course, we always had the sea there. The missionaries also took us camping each school break, in different parts of the Island. So it wasn't a bad place to grow up. And yet, underneath all of that, there was all these other things happening.

When we got to the mission, the government gave us all English names and from then on I was known as Eileen Smith. I was Eileen Murray when they picked me up, but they changed my name to Smith. They changed our names. They changed our birth dates and everything. And they told us we weren't allowed to speak the language. That's why we used to run around corners and talk to Lorky. And if they caught us speaking the language, they'd punish us in some shape or form. But most times it was just a smacking. So we used to sneak around and still do it but, in the end, we forgot about it. We were all separated and so it was harder for us to get together to speak our language. So slowly we forgot about it. But Lorky never did, because she was seven or eight when she left. She still could talk language. And Lorky would talk language to us on Croker so that we could sort of remember little bits and pieces. Because I remember when I first went back to Mum, I could sort of understand what she was saying in language.

The missionaries were telling us that our mothers were gone. And we were thinking, must be our mummy's dead, if they're telling us, 'Your mummy's gone, so don't look for your mummy. Your mummy's not here, she's gone.' And 'gone' to us in the Aboriginal context means that they passed. They were dead. I think they wanted us to believe that, that she was dead. But she wasn't. She was still alive. So those things hurt me quite deeply. The only reason I survived I think was because I had Lorraine; she always reminded me about where we came from, who our mothers were, who our people were. Lorky would say, 'No, Mummy not gone. She home.' So we were always reassured and she'd say where we came from, who our mothers were, she remembered all our mothers' names, the Aboriginal as well as the English name. And she'd tell us, 'One day we go home.'

The worst part of it all was I always missed my mother. It was something that never went away. I used to cry at nighttime because I was missing my mother and my family and my grandparents, and the missionaries would say to me, 'Your mum's gone. So stop crying, Eileen, and go to bed.' But I'd see things at nighttime, I'd always think that I could see somebody there in my room, and maybe it was my people protecting me in some way; I could feel and see them. In the back of my mind, I always knew I had my mother and my people, I knew I had them somewhere there, and someday I was going to go and find them. Because Lorraine never let us forget. If she'd let us forget, we would've forgotten about it like other kids. She always maintained who they were, where they were, what their names were, what their Aboriginal names were.

Lorraine was like our mother, our surrogate mother. She came along with us when we were taken because our people said, 'You're the oldest, you gotta go and look after all them kids.' She made sure we knew our language, who our mothers were, which Country we came from. Lorky did all of that and she was only seven or eight. All our lives, she was like that, she watched over us like she was still our mother. When we were going to Croker, we only spoke our native tongue, none of us spoke much English, but Lorky spoke some, and she'd be rattling off language to us and talking to us, trying to console us, trying to explain things to us. But, of course, she didn't really know the white system that well herself. And Rita and I, I think we were part of her dress. Sometimes she'd pick up Rita when she was younger and Lorky could pick her up and carry her, and then I would be still clinging on to her dress on the other side, holding onto her skirt to make sure she wasn't going to let me go. And Shirley would be struggling along with Tarni, carrying Tarni who was only two years old.

It was good having her. As we were growing up, we always had her there, even though she was in a different cottage. But I think to myself, what if we didn't have her? What would have happened to us? She was there to protect us and look after us. But she also kept reminding us where our mothers were, who our mothers were, who our people were. She never let us forget that. I think that's why we found it easier to go back home and find our people. A lot of other people didn't have that, but we had it because of her. Lorky also connected us with other kids on Croker that had been taken from our area. We wouldn't have remembered, we were still little kids, but Lorky was seven and she remembered everything. We used to get really jealous, too, if anybody tried to take our Lorky anywhere. Those older girls bonded with her and wanted to be friends with her. But we'd be running after her, holding on to her, we didn't want anybody else to take our Lorky. She was our security. And Rita and I used to be chasing her all the time, holding on to her. She was wonderful.

Croker Island wasn't a bad place to live. We were allowed to roam and do things after schools and on the weekends. We had to go to church every Sunday, and every week day we had to go to school. But Saturdays were pretty clear, on Saturdays we'd go out, roaming around to the plains and to fishing places, swimming places. There was a season just before wet season, called goose season, and we'd go out to the plains to get those goose eggs. And at the same time, we'd pick up bunches of water lilies for the church for Sunday. We'd do things like that together. So our life was full of fun and activities – fishing, swimming in freshwater springs and the clear blue sea, and we also learnt to ride Timor ponies.

Nobody was really there to supervise us, we never had missionaries with us, we had the older girls and boys to make sure that we were okay. But it would be just us kids, walking. We'd walk miles, and it was all barefoot. The missionaries made us wear shoes for school and stuff, but we were running around barefoot all the time. When you look at Croker Island now and think how far we walked as children, you'd wonder how we did it. But we'd be running along the road laughing and playing and talking to each other, and the boys would be on their ponies chasing us, and we'd be running and jumping into trees and everything. It was all fun, you know. The boys used to be off on their ponies all the time, riding. But most of us girls, we'd walk everywhere and we'd walk miles. We'd go fishing to Second Bay, we'd go everywhere. We'd swim across the Japanese Creek. We called it Japanese Creek because the older kids told us Japanese people had come down in the wartime. At Japanese Creek, there was nice, fresh, clean water coming out of the cliffs and we used to stand under it. We'd get a billy of spring water and boil it up to make tea and things like that. And we'd swim across the creek to gather wild apples, with beautiful pink and white flesh. Not the apples that you get in the shops, but wild apples. And the seed was really big inside of them, but the flesh was quite thick around it. We used to swim the creek to get these apples and then swim back across the creek again, with our apples tied up in our shirts. And then if somebody got hurt, we would take them back to the mission and say, 'Oh, so-and-so got cut,' or something happened. And the nurse would say, 'How did that happen?' 'Well, so-and-so was cutting something and cut their hand.' Nobody was there to supervise us, we were kids and we thought we were bulletproof, we could go anywhere.

One day when I was nine years old, several of the girls and I decided to take old Mick's canoe – he was the gardener – out into Mission Bay so we could dive for cockles. It was a big log canoe, really narrow, you just sit in there single file. There were about four of us sitting in it, and we took it out in the middle of the bay to go diving for cockles. We had forgotten to get permission and old man Mick saw us and told the superintendent that we didn't ask him to take the canoe. I don't think he was mad that we'd taken his canoe, it was more the fear that something would happen to us and that he'd get blamed for it, I suppose. It was dangerous because we were right out in the middle of the bay and we were children. So he had to report us to the superintendent, and they had to come and get us. They sang out to us from the beach, 'Get your little tails back in here right now.' So we paddled back into shore, but we had the biggest mob of cockles, so we weren't worried about that. But we got into trouble about taking the canoe; did we get a flogging! Afterwards, we just boiled them cockles up over the coals and ate them all. And we gave some to old Mick, and he said, 'What's this for?' 'Because we took your canoe,' we told him, but he just looked at us. One thing we did learn was to never take Mick's canoe again without his permission.

My best friend Laura and I used to get up to a lot of mischief. One day we decided to go picking plums in a place named Lover's Valley and little be known to us the boys were shooting birds on the foreshore off the point of Mission Bay. We were happily gathering wild plums when a shot rang out. Laura says she was shot in the back as we were running, so she jumped on my back and I carried her over the hill. We fell in a heap and we searched for a bullet mark on her back, but instead we found a twig from the plum tree. We rolled around laughing until we heard the boys coming towards us so we hid in the bushes. Another time Laura and I were near Back Jungle spring where our water supply came from and we found a billy can full of wild cherries and we thought our luck was in. We climbed into a gum tree and proceeded to eat the cherries and then we heard yelling from one of the boys that someone had stolen his cherries! We were giggling and eating when he started to shoot up into the tree and we both fell in a heap at the bottom, picked ourselves up and ran for our lives. Another time Laura and I decided to tease one of the older boys by whistling at him while hiding in the bushes. He thought this was one of the older girls so he began to stride with pride down the road and then found us laughing and realised it was only us young girls and not one of the older ones. He became angry and started throwing stones at us so we ran away again. She and I were always teasing someone, especially the boys. We often ran between the cottages and one day as we were running, I ducked under the clothesline and told Laura to duck but she didn't and she got hooked up and dumped on her back. We laughed and laughed about this.

On Fridays we'd go to the store because the Iwaidja people, who lived at the other parts of the island, would come in every Friday to go to the stores for their rations and they'd trade shells, their pandanus weaving mats, bags and things like that. And I remember one of the old people brought a turtle shell, and they polished the shell, it was so beautiful because all the colours came up. So we used to walk around there every morning when they came in on Fridays, on our way to school to see what they were trading. Whatever they traded, they got flour, tea, sugar, milk, tobacco and even some beef from the store. As children were very interested in what they were trading.

When we went out to the toilets some nights we'd hear the didgeridoos and the clap sticks going down on the beach, from the Iwaidja people, because Malila was probably the closest cottage to the beach. It was still a fair way to walk down to the beach and to where they were, but you could hear the sound floating across. The missionaries were trying to stop us from having anything to do with it. They told us we weren't allowed to have anything to do with that anymore. But how can you not, when you could hear it every second or third night, the clap sticks going and the didgeridoos going and them singing. And we really wanted to be part of it all because we remembered what we participated in as little children. Aboriginal children are part of ceremonies from the time they can walk. How can a child that had been reared in that sense, to be part of those ceremonies and everything, just forget it? I'd want to run down there, but we weren't allowed to. And it was in middle of the night. Laura said to me one night, 'Eileen, you only go out there because you want to listen, ey?'

And I said, 'Probably.' I used to go out there and then sit and just listen to them.

The next day I'd say to her, 'I want to go down there.' She said, 'And how are we going to go down there? We've got to go to school.'

'Yeah, but I'd like to just go down there and sit with them,' I said, because I missed being with my mum and my people.

The next day I'd see Daisy, she didn't live with us in the cottage but she was Iwaidja and lived with her parents at the beach. I saw Daisy and I'd say, 'I wanted to come down last night because I could hear the singing and the clap sticks and the didgeridoo.'

'Well, why didn't you?' she'd say and I would reply, 'I would've got into trouble, from the missionaries.'

She would say, 'Oh, okay. Well you can come down on the weekend.' So we'd go down on the weekend to where old Mick and Timothy lived. They were the old Iwaidja people and they worked for the mission. They looked after our gardens, they looked after our pigs and our goats. Mick was a kind man, but very stern when he had to be, especially when we were to weed the gardens and tend the goats. We often gave him a headache because we teased the big old boar in the pig pens and he would chase us away as he was very protective of the gardens and the stockyards, always yelling in Iwaidja, his native tongue. His brother Timothy was just as stern and very mindful of his job in the gardens and stockyards.

So we used to run away to the Iwaidja people on the beach, because we wanted to be part of their activities. Never at nighttime, though, we weren't allowed out of the cottages at night. And that's how we ended up learning how to eat stingrays, dugong, turtles – sea turtles, not freshwater turtles, because I was brought up on freshwater turtles in the bush, but these were big sea turtles. The old ladies taught us how to eat turtles and stingrays and crabs and fish and all those wonderful seafood. They taught us how to gather them and how to eat them. Medic and Hazel were Mick and Timothy's wives, and Medic and Mick were Daisy's parents. They even took us to show us how to get oysters off the mangrove roots, to cut the mangrove roots because oysters used to grow on the roots. We would take them back and cook them. We did a lot of stuff with them, with the old Iwaidja people at Croker Island. And some of the older girls and boys from Croker Island taught us, too. Aunty Medic and Aunty Hazel used to make us johnny cakes and damper and we'd sit there and eat with them. Then we learnt how to eat the wild tomatoes. There was a special way to eat them. You have to peel the skin off and eat the flesh without it touching your lips. Otherwise you ended up with big, swollen lips. So we used to eat all these bush foods and everything because they taught us how.

But that was all happy times for me because even though they weren't really my people, they were like my people. Then later on in life, Daisy said to me, 'You know, we were linked through kinship. My mother is linked to your mother.'

'And when I was growing up on Croker?'

'We weren't allowed to talk about it.' But Lorraine sort of

had an inkling, she knew about it and she'd say, 'They'll look after us.' She used to say that all the time, but I didn't know why, because I didn't know about any connection. But we're in the same kinship group. I said to Daisy, 'Well, why didn't you tell us?' and she said, 'Mum and Dad said we weren't allowed to talk about it when you were kids.' They knew they'd get into trouble from the mission, I guess. So even though we'd moved from Mainoru all the way to Croker Island, which to me seemed miles and miles away from Country, when you look at it and you look on the map now you can go from Mainoru to Cobourg and straight across to Croker. So the Aboriginal songlines are there. But as a child, I didn't know that.

On the mission, we all did jobs. We had to do jobs from when we were about nine or 10 or something, all the way through till we were in our teens. But we thought it was part of the mission. We used to have to look after the goats, but we loved it because we missed school for the day. Like, I might've done it one week, but we had to go through all the kids, so we probably wouldn't have had another chance for about another six weeks. We'd take them for the day somewhere so they could feed and roam. Then we'd take them back to the stockyards, close the paddocks and leave them there. And then the boys would go there after lunch and take them out again. It was something that we loved because we missed school for that period of time. There were about a hundred goats, I suppose. And we'd boil up milk while we were out looking after the goats. We'd get one of the goats and milk it. I loved that goat milk, and the cream used to be so thick and lovely. You know, heat it up and then the cream would just sit on the top and we used to eat it with syrup and damper.

One day Laura and I, we were looking after the goats. We had the herd next to the airstrip up near the hills because we'd taken them a long way from the stockyards, and next minute the boys appeared, they were mustering cattle and they brought the cattle from the plains towards us. The goats bolted, we ran and climbed up a tree, Laura and I. The smallest little tree, I think the cows could have knocked us over, and we're screaming at the boys, 'Don't bring the cows here. The goats are going to run away!' We're screaming at the boys to take the cattle further away, but they didn't. The cattle just ran straight through where we were looking after the goats. The goats took off up to the hills. So we had to go and chase them and bring them back to the stockyards. And the boys were just laughing their heads off. They thought it was the biggest joke, but we didn't.

Every second Saturday the missionaries would wake me up and tell me I had to go and cook for the boys, make the breakfast in one of the boys' cottages, some of the girls had these duties. Sometimes we'd cook porridge, other times we made eggs, bacon and toast. We used to have big teapots to make the tea. The boys used to pour their own tea, but we used to have to make it all. Then also, after we'd put the breakfast and cleaned up the dishes and everything, then we'd pull out the meat, cut up all the meat and get the vegetables ready for the cottage sister to cook the next meal. And then I'd be off and they let us go play then. One day I was cutting the meat up in the kitchen and Tommy Olson, the boy that we picked up from Pine Creek, came running into the kitchen and he shouted really loudly, 'Harrrrrr, Eileen,' like that. Silly Tommy gave me such a fright. I had a big butcher's knife in my hand and spun around with that butcher's knife still in my hand. He reckon, 'You nearly stabbed me!', and he's screaming his head off. But then we both cracked up laughing. And I said, 'Don't sing that to Miss Proctor, she'll start screaming at me.'

We also did gardening in our vegetable patches and fruit patches. Making breakfast for the boys at the boys' cottage, that didn't faze me, working in the gardens didn't faze me. I was quite happy to do that, I thought that was just part of growing up on Croker Island. The only scary part about all the work I did was having to do the sheets and towels in a big copper boiler and then pulling it out with a big stick, putting it into cold water to rinse and then hanging it on the clothes line. And it was hot, as hot as hell. Only sometimes the big girls were there to help us. But we had to do it ourselves and I was really scared of doing the washing. I was frightened because I thought I might get burnt because those sticks used to be really long and we'd dig it in under the sheets that were boiling in that copper, dig that stick in and then lift the sheets and towels out, with all the hot water pouring out and then chuck it into a trough of cold water. That is the scary part of it. I used to hate it when I was little.

One other thing that wasn't so fun, as children we were given all sorts of medication. One we all hated was the medicine to treat hookworm. The taste was awful. They'd line us all up, give us a big tablespoon of that medicine – 'Open your mouth' – straight down your throat. The medicine made many of us quite sick. Many hallucinated and vomited. Me, I used to get sleepy and go to sleep. So it affected us all in different ways. I reckon they were experimenting on us, to be quite honest. Because that medicine, none of us had hookworm. You can see hookworm in your faeces, you can see it if you had it. We used to go toilet anywhere out in the bush and we never saw any. But that's what they treated us for, hookworm. And there was also cod liver oil. We used to have that all the time because they said it was good for our health. A lot of people took it in the old days, from all accounts, but why? It was horrible, disgusting. We'd be nearly spewing when the nurse used to chuck it down our throat and she'd just say, 'Hold your nose.' They'd open your mouth and pour it down your throat. So we had cod liver oil and that hookworm medicine, they were the worst ones I experienced, I think.

The doctors would come out there every six months or

something to check on us, to make sure we were all healthy. We had doctors coming there all the time, and dentists. But I had beautiful teeth then when I was young; not anymore, though! On the missions, we had all that medical attention all the time. So you can't say that we didn't have that. But we must have been quite healthy. Many of us had coughs and colds, measles and chicken pox at some time of our lives. But I don't ever remember having my heart checked. Over the years I have seen many children in the Territory suffer with heart disease, but we on Croker must have all been quite healthy. They checked us for leprosy. None of us had leprosy, but they still checked us. They used to take blood, I think. Then they checked our limbs to see if we were all functioning. But we were all running like mad kids anyway. So there was nothing wrong with us that I could see.

So, it wasn't a bad place to grow up. And yet, underneath all of that, there was all these other things happening. And a lot of us would never talk about it. The abuse, beatings and punishments. Even when we grew up, we wouldn't talk about what had happened to us. We had this happy part of our life there, but underneath it all, there was this other sad part, too. And when we got beatings and that, we just thought that was part of the mission. So we felt that maybe it was our fault and not the missionaries. One form of punishment was that we couldn't go out on the picnic outings they provided every weekend. Sometimes too, if I'd done something, like I went eating bush foods and eating fruit that I picked off the trees instead of waiting for dinner, they'd send me to bed without supper because, they said, 'You've already eaten now.' And on many occasions I did, because, being a child, and finding fruit trees and finding bush tucker – I'd eat them! The other thing was the missionaries used to bald the women's heads if they'd done anything wrong. The older girls, not the kids. And that's why we had seen all them women with turbans on their head when we first arrived on Croker, and started screaming because we didn't know who they were. It was a form of punishment that if they did anything wrong, the older girls, like smoking or they ran away from the mission – when they got back, they'd have their head shaved. The other punishment was smacking us, or the superintendent actually used to use his strap or belt. But why beat us, when they also had these other forms of punishments, like not going on outings? Why beat the kids? Because we were all kids. I went there when I was four and a half, and some of the kids were two, three years old. But I don't remember getting beaten until I was about 10 or 11, I suppose.

I remember getting a beating a couple of times from the superintendent. One time was because of the canoe, when we took old Mick's canoe, and another time was because a boy and I were fighting on the cricket pitch. I got him out, so he got mad at me and threw the bat at me. And we never had real cricket bats, we had sticks made from Cyprus pine, and they were all splintered, and one got me on the foot here. I still got the scar to this day. It cut me quite deep, and my foot was bleeding. So I turned around and I got the ball that I had in my hand and donged him in the forehead. The superintendent was watching us playing on the field, and he told us, 'Colin and Eileen, get up here. I want to talk to you.' So we went up. He took us down to the store where he held his belt and gave us a hiding. He strapped me on my hands and legs for fighting with Colin. With a strap, you know, them belts. And sometimes the buckle will cut you. Colin got the same. And then he told us to go, but said, 'You better not fight again.' That was the only two strappings I ever got that I can recall. But other children got really bad treatment, and they got hidings and strappings and things like that. I didn't, that was the only one I've got for fighting with a boy. I fought the boys because the boys always said, 'Girls can't do anything,' and I said, 'Oh, yeah?' because I was always pretty good at sports. So I'd show them up, the boys, and they'd say, 'Yeah, but you can't do anything, Eileen.' I'd say, 'Yes, I can.' So there were fights.

There was one really bad thing I recall as a child on Croker. There was this young fella, he was older than us, and he was actually locked up. He would've been about 11 or 12 or maybe older. And the missionaries said that they couldn't control him, so they put him in this facility, because every time they let him out, he just went silly, and became quite violent and aggressive towards the missionaries. It was a room as part of a house where the boys lived, at the end of the house. But it was partly open, with mesh over it. We used to climb up above him and look down at him, and we'd say, 'Malcolm, you hungry?' So we'd pass him bread and fruit or whatever we had. I think they fed him meals, but we felt sorry for him and we thought that was bad of them, having him locked up like that. But we also thought it was fun and games that we could go to this caged child and feed him and talk to him. He never ranted and raved, so we had no fear of him, we just felt pity.

Later on in life, I wanted to really look at some of the records they had on Croker Island. But I never got the chance to, you have to go to Sydney to see the Methodist Overseas Mission's archives. I never had time to go and have a look, and I felt that the missionaries didn't want you to look at what was written about us. So I don't know what they really wrote about me, because I never looked. This is my recollection of what happened to me.

Even though there was lots of fun times as children at Croker, I became a loner there, I became withdrawn. I used to get up in the tree and sit in the tree by myself and they'd be singing out for me, looking for me. This must've been when I was about seven or eight. So even though I had all those fun times as I was getting older and enjoying being with other kids and Laura, there was a time when I felt I was quite alone. I used to get up in the tree, it was a poinciana tree just outside the cottage, and I'd sit up there for hours and hours. Sometimes I'd eat the beans off the tree and sit there and look around at the mission. And the cottage sister would be singing out, 'Eileen, where are you? Where are you? You got to get in here, you got to come for tea,' or something like that. And I wouldn't come down. I remember that part of my life as lonely because I didn't want to relate with the children. I was sitting in the tree one day when Eva was swinging on one of the branches and the branch cracked, and she fell and broke her arm. When she got up off the ground, I thought she had a snake on her arm because her arm was the shape of a snake because it had broken that badly. I started screaming from the top of the tree. That's when they found I was up there. I came down the tree to try and help her, but then the older girls came and picked her up and carried her into the cottage. I remember that quite clearly. I know we had lots of fun there with all the other kids. I was quite sport minded. I was quite bright in my studies, everything. But I still felt very lonely. But I didn't really talk about it, instead of talking about it, I used to run away and hide in the tree, often just before suppertime. There was about three years of it, I think from seven to nine or 10, I was doing that.

Also, that's when Rita left. She was only a little kid when she left Croker. I would've been eight or nine, and she would've been about six or seven, and she was sent to Dalmar Children's Home in Sydney with another girl. That's why I felt really lost, because she'd gone. We were crying, and I was really broken hearted, because even my best friend, Laura, was sent to Adelaide to a foster home. I would've been about 10 or 11, I think, when Laura left. Laura was a year younger than me, and she would've gone with the Tragers down to Adelaide to live with them as their foster child. See, Mr and

Mrs Trager were the teachers on Croker Island, and when they'd been there for two years they left and took Laura with them. But she had a brother and sister there at Croker. Roger was her twin, and Eva was her baby sister. So Laura didn't have her siblings with her. They sent Rita first, and she was still young, and then Laura. I call it the chain: one link was broken all the time.

So when I think about Croker, that still is there for me. Even though I had all those fun things happening on Croker Island, I still think about that period of my life that wasn't happy. I don't know what you call it, whether it's withdrawal or loneliness or something. And there was nobody there to help me deal with it, because the missionaries never really dealt with any of our issues. If you cut yourself, you'd go to them and they'd put a band aid on it and tell you to go play. There was no hugs or no consoling you to say 'Are you all right? You'll be all right'. There was no warmth or kindness in the interaction between us and the missionaries. And so where was I supposed to go if I needed that as a child? All the other girls were there. Laura was with me all the time and the older girls, Amy and Dolly, were really good for me. They'd take me with them wherever they went, fishing and swimming, I'd go with them. But I remember that period of my life, about three years of it, where I think I really longed for my mother, I longed for someone, I think. I felt I had nobody. That's why I can't believe that I got over it, because who was there to help me? Who was there to give me the directions to get out of it?

When I got to 10 or something, I started to really show interest in school because that's when that new school was built and new teachers came, and I was able to develop. Before that, I went to school every day, but I still had these lonely times. But I got older and I started to find more interest in school and there were more things to do because the government teachers they sent were more qualified, they were able to give us more as teachers. The missionaries, I didn't feel they did that. It was only when I started to enjoy school that I got out of my loneliness. That dark part of my life on Croker, I never really talked about it to anybody. I sort of shut it away. And then when I started to change and develop at school, I wasn't lonely anymore. I had all of this other stuff to do, and I had the boys there, Peter and Billy, who had the same ambitions as me in wanting to learn. But how many of our kids would've gone through that and never got out of it? Maybe that's why a lot of them drank later in life. Because I reckon that's part of Stolen Generations, because we were removed from our mothers and our people.

When I was older, I started to go to the Randall's, I think I was about 12 then. The Randalls were my foster parents, Bob and Amy Randall. They were Stolen Generations people on Croker Island. Mum Randall was from Ti-Tree, and Dad was from Mutitjulu, Uluru. They picked him up there, took him to the Bungalow[22] and then sent him to Croker Island. Mum and Dad Randall met and got married on Croker. Mum was one of the older girls in the cottage where I was living, Malila cottage, with her sister Dolly. They used to look after us in the cottage, they were always supporting us and looking after us. When she married Bob, they had a little house of their own at the back of Malila cottage. I used to go down a lot and help her and clean and do things, like washing. And when Alan came along, their first son, I bathed him and played with him. I loved Alan. I was in their household quite a bit and the Randalls became a foster family for Max and myself. Max wasn't behaving himself, so the missionaries asked Bob to take Max in care. Dad Randall had Max back on track and he did chores around the yard, helping Dad with the pigs and chooks and everything else. He was the foster son and I was the foster girl. We were just like a normal family but each night I had to return to the cottage whereas Max was under the full care of the Randalls. These were happy days and for the first time since I had been taken, I experienced a real family home. It was a great time having people who loved and cared for us. The Randalls had experienced the removal policy and were wonderful role models for Max and me.

I had started school at five. We all attended school as soon as we turned five years old. We went to school Monday to Friday. On Sundays, we had church and Sunday school. When I started school, I was doing everything with my left hand, and they hit me on the knuckles with a ruler so that I would change to my right hand. And I had to learn to write it with my right hand, not with my left. In those days, they wanted you to do everything with your right hand. And yet, even when I played sports later on in life, I could still do things with my left hand. When I first started school, we had those little slate boards to write on with chalk. And it was only a little tiny building and all us little kids were in there. I don't know where the big kids went, I can't remember. But then when I got to about 10, they built a big school and sent out government teachers to teach us. Before, we had missionary teachers. But soon as they built a big government school, they sent government teachers to teach us. That's when I started to really get into school. I loved it, because we had this beautiful big school, we had everything there. And I loved sports. School sports days were fun and so enjoyable, as I was good at sports and the school captain at all sports days. Sport was always the thing that held me together. I played a lot of sport, as I grew up and later on in life I played every woman sport you could think of.

So when they built that new school, that was good. I loved old Mr Cormack and the other teacher, I can't remember his name now. I loved the way they taught us and I really got a lot out of their teaching. I always wanted to learn, I was one of those really inquisitive children, I always wanted to know things. I loved school, I really loved school. And there were two boys, Peter and Billy, who were like me too, always wanted to learn. The three of us, we'd be sitting around a map or something when Mr Cormack was writing up his next lesson and we'd be questioning him as he's doing it. So when I look at my life and look at some of the other kids' lives, I seemed to grab the opportunities differently. Whereas the other kids just wanted to, maybe, to survive, I suppose – for me, I wanted everything, not only survival. I wanted to learn, I wanted to know about other things, I wanted to know about other people.

Often, Peter, Billy and I, we'd say to Mr Cormack, 'We want to look at the globe.' And we used to study all the different countries of the world on it. I was really curious because coming from the bush, I didn't even know Australia, you know what I mean? I had to learn about Australia. And then we started to learn about other countries, and had Fijians and Tongans coming out as missionaries to Croker Island. To me, it was interesting that there were other brown people in the world, not only us. It really made me think about the world as a whole. And we'd sit there and we'd spin that globe around and point to different countries and the teacher would tell us about the different countries. I thought it was great, I loved hearing about other people. And then as I grew older, of course, we started to hear about apartheid and all the stuff in America and Africa. The missionaries sometimes let us watch a movie on Friday nights. And you know what? One of them was *A Tale of Two Cities*. It was about Paris in that really bad time when people were starving, and they let us watch that when we were kids! It was interesting because it was another part of the world. The world was something I wanted to really explore. And I did, later on in life.

As we got older, kids started being sent away. Until we

were 18, we were being ruled by Native Affairs. They were the ones controlling everything, not the missionaries so much. I think sometimes they consulted with the missionaries and teachers, but it wasn't the missionaries that made the decision, it was Native Affairs. The government said, 'Well, we got to get some of these kids out of here,' because too many kids were coming to Croker and they didn't want to go over a hundred. We only had eight cottages there, so they wouldn't have been able to cater for more. A lot of kids were sent to Adelaide. At one stage, the government was going to send us down to Quorn, out in the country in South Australia somewhere. The government came and told that to the missionaries and the missionaries said, 'No, we are not taking the children to Quorn.' Most of the missionaries were from Adelaide or Queensland, so when they were told we were going to Quorn, they were against it. Instead, kids were sent to different places, but most to Adelaide.

Rita had already been sent away and Laura was in Adelaide as a foster kid with the Tragers. And then they took Lorky away and sent her to Adelaide, that was in '57 when she left. She was sent down to Adelaide to look after other children; about five children went with Lorky. Tarni and Eva went with her, Eva was Laura's younger sister, she flew down with them from Croker to Darwin and then to Adelaide. Lorraine was with them at the home, but then they split the children up. They put the boys into a boys' home and the girls in a girls' home. These were Methodist church homes in Adelaide. And Lorky was sent to work at Minda Home. She was around 16, 17 and she never even had the opportunity to finish her education. How old would I have been then – 13, 14? But I missed her. I felt really alone. I felt that nobody was with me anymore.

Shirley and two other girls, Betty Graham and Annette White, were sent to work at the Methodist women's lodge in Brisbane as domestics. Shirley would've been about 17. Tommy, when he got older, he went to work on Elizabeth Downs cattle station down near Daly River. A lot of the boys went to the cattle stations to work. Maxi Cummings went there as well, the Randalls' foster son. Once he turned 18 years, he went to a cattle station to work.

I stayed behind on Croker, but then the superintendent said, 'Eileen, you're going to Darwin High School to finish your education.'

'And why?'

'Well, you can't do it here', he said, because even though we had secondary school at Croker Island, to actually go to the next stage after Year 9 and to third year high, you'd have to do this in Darwin. So they sent Roger Knowles and me to Darwin to do the third year of high school. We were top of our class all the time at school, myself and a group of boys: Richie Reynolds, Leslie Jones, Harry Allard, Peter Hansen and Billy Patterson. They were the boys closest to me, I had a good relationship with them. Billy and I excelled in school. Peter did okay. He jumped out of it at the age of 16 because he wanted to go work, but he was still a bright boy. Other boys also came into Darwin to train in the workforce. Billy ended up being fostered by some family in Adelaide, him and his brother Joe. And Roger and I came into Darwin High School for our third year high. It was bit frightening for me at first, but I had Roger with me, Laura's brother. It was hard to leave Croker because I'd got used to being there. But I knew if I wanted to achieve more in school, I had to do further studies. I was happy to come to Darwin because the Randalls were there. They had moved to Darwin by this point and I used to come visit all the time for holidays. So it was quite easy. I came at Christmas in 1959, staying with the Randalls, and then the missionaries took me to the United Church Hostel in January 1960.

During this time, I lived in the hostel across from the school. We crossed the road to the high school every day. The school used to be on Cavenagh Street, so was the Uniting church, and behind the church was the church hostel. They took all us kids from remote communities, not only black kids, white kids too. Any children that didn't belong to Darwin, they came and stayed at the hostel with us. We had kids from Batchelor, Katherine and Pine Creek. Veronica Young was from Pine Creek, her parents ran the pub there. She became one of my best friends; we kept in touch after school, her and I. We had a big mob of kids there, and only Roger and I were from Croker. At the hostel, Matron took us for picnics on Saturdays. Not Sundays, because Sunday we had to go to church because we were living at a church hostel. Sometimes the Randalls would come with us because Matron liked Dad Randall coming along just in case something happened to us because the staff were all women. We had a matron and two sisters at the hostel to look after us kids. And I still had contact with the Croker Island mob, not only through the Randalls and Roger, but also Leslie and Harry and some other boys from Croker. They used to come see Roger and me at the hostel, because they lived up in the church hostel at Myilly Point. After they left Croker, they lived there and went to work. The boys visited us and rode motorbikes all the time. I loved them motorbikes. I wanted to go on the motorbikes with the boys whenever they visited.

Even before I went to Darwin High School, I had come in to Darwin every Christmas to be with the Randalls. When Mum Randall was having Johnny, the second son, they moved to Darwin, but were still working for the Methodist Overseas Mission in the stores there. First they had a house at East Point and then the missionaries helped them get the house at Stuart Park, and that's where we went all the time. Max and I would come in and stay with them for the Christmas holidays when

I was still on Croker Island, I would've been about 13, 14. We flew in a plane from Croker to Darwin, in DC3s, quite big planes, carrying about 40 people. One year, when Max and I was in Darwin for holidays and were going back to Croker Island, we landed at Bathurst Island. In those days, they didn't have a proper strip, it was all dirt, you know, and the plane got bogged. The nuns and them came over to the airstrip and said to Max and me, 'You have to stay here for the night until we can get the plane out of the bog.' I was crying a bit because there were so many children running around us. I just started to be in my teens – 13, 14, I think, and this woman came to me and held my hand – to this day, I've never forgotten her, Gabriela, she was one of the Garden Point[23] people. She grew up on Garden Point Mission, her mother was a Tiwi woman. But by this time she was working at the mission at Bathurst Island. She said, 'Well, I know the Randalls. I'm going to take Eileen.' She was one of the older girls there, she took me back to the dormitory, and she looked after me till the next day, till the plane was taken out of the bog. She wouldn't let me out of her sight, I was with her the whole time. And one of the older boys was looking after Max. The next day they got the tractors to pull the plane out of the bog and we travelled on to Croker Island. Years later, I found Gabriela, and whenever I went to the Tiwi Islands for work I'd visit her, and I got to know her children and husband.

When I was going to Darwin High School, I stayed with the Randalls at Stuart Park. The family grew over the years with two more children, Dorothea and Anita. I grew up with all the Randall kids, I spent many happy days with them going on Sunday picnics and swimming. And I stayed in contact with the Croker Island mob through Mum and Dad. Dad took us to gatherings every Friday night at the AIM[24] church in Stuart Park with many Stolen Generations members. We had sing alongs and eats brought by each family. The women would cook scones and cakes, and there were cordials, tea and coffee and all of that. Dad had started this gathering because he wanted us to have somewhere we felt happy and secure after leaving the missions. Dad brought everybody together, and he'd play his guitar and everybody would be singing along. It was really good fun.

He was wonderful, Dad Randall. On Saturdays sometimes, we'd go to the shopping centres and buy big bags of groceries and drop them off at the homes of families that were struggling. See, some families had about six to seven, or eight to nine children, and he'd take them food. And all us kids would be in the car with him. Alan and Johnny, Dori and Anita and I would be jumping around in the car and saying, 'Where are we going?' 'Oh, we're going to aunty so-and-so's place.' 'What for?' 'We're going to drop off food.' So we went to a lot of the homes of the old Croker Island mob because he was supporting them. He worked for the Methodist Overseas Missions, but he did this in his own time, because they were Croker Island brothers and sisters in hardship. Nobody asked him to do it, and the people didn't talk to him about their hardship, he just did it.

The Randalls' house became a refuge for a lot of our people, Mum and Dad looked after them. Even though he could have shunned all the people that used to come drunk and disorderly, he never shunned them, there was always a bed for them, there was always food for them if they were hungry, or a shower. So in a way, he practised that missionary spirit he grew up with. And he never drank in all his life and Mum never drank. And yet, they helped all these people. I remember the house was always full of people, and sometimes the beds were taken. Alan would go and sleep in the room where the girls were, and Johnny would come and sleep in my room. He always said, 'Sister Eileen, I'm coming into your room. Somebody's got my bed,' he'd say, and he'd come into my room and sleep at one end of my bed, and I'd be sleeping at the other.

The Randalls never had alcohol in their home. They grew up on Croker Island, yet they never went down that path. So I had really good role models around me to keep me off the alcohol, because all the people who came to the Randalls' home, us kids were there watching them, doing things for them, getting them what they needed. Having to look after the old Croker Island mob that were drunk and coming to the Randalls' all the time – looking at them might've put me off. Mum and Dad Randall didn't drink, and Aunty Dolly, Mum's sister, didn't drink. But her husband did, and sometimes I'd go to Auntie and Uncle's place and help with Uncle Alfie. And I thought, Oh, I don't want to go through this when I get married. I'd help them wherever he was drunk, help Aunty Dolly put him in the car and take him home, things like that. I think that's what put me off drinking. Also, I had a lot of religion in my life, and it seemed to stop me from doing the things that other people would do.

When I got to 21, I started to go out with some of the Darwin kids that I knew from high school. And they'd all get drunk and I'd be the sober one driving. 'Well, but this is no fun,' I said. One thing I tried was gin and tonic, but then I'd just stop and I'd be back on soft drinks. For most of my life, I didn't drink alcohol, I just didn't like drinking. And so, who got lumbered with driving? Eileen! I did try and smoke when I was 19, but I chucked that away. I hated the smell, I just couldn't stand it.

Dad was the support to many other Stolen Generations groups. He had his own little pony club. He did things so the children could have something, because he's always felt that our people were downtrodden, that they couldn't have the same things as other people. He was one of the people who founded Aboriginal organisations in Darwin, like the legal aid service, like the health services. He helped to establish and develop all of those. He also founded a boxing troupe. Our boys used to box on Croker, we had a boxing troupe there and they trained them. There was a boxing troupe in Darwin, but a lot of the Aboriginal boys didn't want to go to it. So Dad decided to run his own. He had an area in the back of his yard where the boys trained. And then he got a training ring up at the basketball courts and he was allowed to use that as a boxing ring. Dad's troupe wasn't only the Croker Island boys, there were other boys from Darwin. They had training during the week and sometimes they had championships. Dad would run tournaments against the other boxing troupes. He set that up to provide something for the Aboriginal boys.

That's the life I had with the Randalls. That was the man and woman who helped to raise me and look after me. He was always saying, 'Eileen, if you can't respect yourself, nobody else will,' and I said, 'What do you mean, Dad?'

'Well, you have to be proud of your achievements. You have to be proud of who you are. Nobody else will do that, but you yourself. And if you want to get ahead in life, you have to be able to do that. We're here to support you, but you've got to do it.' He always said that, and I used to think, well, no wonder he's the man he is.

So, in a way, a lot of support systems were in place for me. And probably that's why I ended up doing what I did, because I had that support system in place. That, I think, grounded me so I didn't go out and drink like a lot of other people. Dad still had that missionary way. We went to church every Sunday. We had activities for everybody, not just for the family. And he wanted to keep the Croker Island people together. The children who were removed and placed on Croker Island Mission had a close bond; I call them my Croker Island family. And the Randalls were my family, they loved and cared for me.

Dad Randall also started that movement to travel back

to Country. His first trip was back down to Mum Randall's Country, to Ti-Tree. He took her back there to see her mother and took his children so they could see their grandmother. We didn't know Nana then. He started that movement where people go back to Country if they could, if they knew enough about it. Well, he knew about it because he worked for a long time for the Methodist Overseas Mission. And he took Mum and the children up to Ti-Tree to see her mother. He also took Aunty Florrie back, one of Mum's cousins, because she was from Ti-Tree as well, and Aunty Dolly, Mum Randall's sister. They all went back to meet their family for the first time. He started all of that before he then moved back to Mutitjulu, to Uluru.

Dad wrote the song 'Brown Skin Baby'. He wrote that because when he started to go back to Country he could see how our mothers who were black had to give up their brown-skinned children because they called us half-caste children. So he wrote a beautiful song about it, talking about children who were removed from their mothers. He wanted to help us Croker people go back to Country to see our people, to meet our mothers again, and all of that.

4

First Aboriginal Teacher in the Northern Territory

When I was finishing high school, they said, 'Eileen, what do you want to do?' I said, 'I want to be a teacher.' I loved school. On Croker Island, from time to time, the teacher would call us up to the front of the room to help with the lessons when I got to Year 8 or 9. I found that really rewarding and exciting. And so from that time onward, I thought about becoming a teacher because I'd experienced that wonderful teaching from those teachers there. I loved working with children, so pre-school was the one I went for. Then they said, 'Eileen, if you want to be a teacher, we've got to send you Brisbane.'

'Where am I going to go in Brisbane?'

They said, 'We got our own Methodist training college there. You'll live there with a lot of other students from the Territory.' So I was happy to go there, but I was a little apprehensive because I was going on my own. Darwin was small, but Brisbane was huge.

I didn't even go back to Croker after finishing high school. I stayed with the Randalls and then old Jack McKay came to take me shopping. Native Affairs told him I was going to Brisbane because he always wrote to them to know what was happening to me. So he knew I was going and he came from Mainoru into town and told the missionaries, 'I'm coming in to take Eileen shopping. I want to get her some clothes and whatever she needs for Brisbane.' Jack felt I should go away to school with the right clothes. So he and Sandy arranged this in Darwin. Sandy came in from the Tiwi Islands because he was teaching at Milikapiti, and I'd never met him until that day. I knew about Jack because he'd often, even when I was at school, even if he didn't see me, get in contact with the Randalls to see how I was, so he could tell Mum. When I was about 17, ready to go to Brisbane, old Jack came to pick me up to go shopping. He had his brother Sandy with him. Jack had said to old Sandy, 'Come and meet me in town. We're going to take Eileen shopping,' but then he reckoned, 'I don't know how to take girls shopping.' Sandy said, 'And how am I supposed to?' because they were both bachelors then. Old Jack reckoned, 'But you teach all them young women at Milikapiti. So you must know something about girls.' I thought, Oh, well, if Sandy's his brother, he must be all right. So Sandy took me shopping and bought me the most beautiful dress; I actually wore it on the plane to Brisbane. But he reckoned, 'Eileen, we can't get you any underclothes.' I said, 'Why not? I'll pick them out.' 'No, I'll get one of the missionary ladies to take you.' So I had to go with one of the women from the Overseas Missions. He was so funny, old Sandy, such a lovely man. They both were so beautiful.

I was down in Brisbane probably end of January or early February when the school year started. I was 17. I lived at the Methodist Training College and Bible School because it was a boarding place for all of us from the missions. It was also a theological college where young men were training as ministers, both Australians and people from the Pacific. A couple of the girls were training as nurses. The college was at Kangaroo Point and we crossed on the ferry to go to the city.

Then I found out Shirley, Betty and Annette from my Croker Island mob were working at the church hostel – they called it the Lodge – and it wasn't far from our college. Shirley had come to Croker with me, remember? That made me really happy, because they'd come and pick me up weekends and take me out with them. So I had the girls there, I had Croker Island people with me. And then some weekends, Mr and Mrs Reverend Moore and his family would pick me up because they were running a church in Brisbane. He was the superintendent when I was still on the mission. When they finished their two years, they went back to Brisbane. They'd pick me up some weekends to go to their place and I'd go to their church with them on a Sunday, spend the day with them and go back to the training college on Sunday afternoon. So, again, the influence of the church was quite big for me. I remember when I was at the Training College, the boys played rugby. I didn't play any sports at that time, except on sports day I ran and did all the sports activities with the college. The boys were playing rugby and we'd go and watch the games, all us young people from the college, every Saturday. On Sundays we had church. So, once again, my life was surrounded by church and sport. And probably that's why I didn't get into drinking and doing the things the other children were doing.

At the college, Jocelyn became one of my good friends. And I saw Rita again during this time. She was sent to a home in Sydney as a young child, but by this time she was 18. She said, 'I want to be with you. I'm coming to Brisbane.' So she caught the train and I met her in Brisbane. It was near Christmas time, so I was coming home anyway, and she came with me. When we got to Darwin, I stayed with the Randalls for the holidays and she stayed with one of her older sisters who was living in Darwin. We'd meet up and you would've sworn we were twins, Rita and I. We dressed the same. She'd come and say, 'What are you wearing tonight?' And I'd tell her what I was wearing. 'Don't you wear the same as me!' I'd say, and she'd come to my house and we'd be the same.

When I trained as a teacher, we had to train as a mothercraft nurses at first. We had a big kindergarten nursery in the City Hall in Brisbane, up the top floor, and that's where we trained, me and a lot of other girls. I had to do the preschool teacher training at nighttime. I went to night studies at Kelvin Grove College to get my preschool degree. That's where I became friends with Gail, she and her parents lived at Holland Park in Brisbane. On the weekends, we would meet up, the three of us with Jocelyn. Gail and I became friends for life. We communicate to this day. In 2010 all the teachers who trained with me and after my training met at a reunion. I was the first Aboriginal teacher who trained at Kelvin Grove; a couple of years later, some women from the Torres Strait Islands trained there. Afterwards they went back to their communities to teach. It was great to meet all of them at the reunion and to exchange news of what we were doing to this day. Most of the women from the Torres Strait Islands were still teaching or working at the schools with children. And my Gail, my best mate, came to the reunion.

When I was training at the City Hall nursery, a lady came in to drop her child off. She must have worked at one of those fashion houses. She saw me and said to Ms Henderson, the supervisor, 'Do you think Eileen would like to model our clothes?' Then they asked me if I was interested. I looked at her and I thought, What the hell is modelling? One of the girls said, 'Eileen, they want you to dress up in their clothes and walk in a parade. And then a lot of women will come to those to look at the clothes and then choose them to buy.' I said, 'They want me to do it? Why me?' and the girls said, 'Well, they must think you look all right.' I was asking silly questions, and they were explaining to me what modelling is and Jocelyn was laughing at me. I said, 'Well, I don't know.' I was worried because the Church might be against it because I was still in the Methodist Training College. In the end, I was allowed to do it, so I modelled for them. I was quite a looker at that age, I suppose, and I walked really well, because of my mother. I have the same stature as my mother. I was the only Aboriginal girl in the group. I did it every now and again for the time I was down there, weekends or whenever they ran a fashion show. I think they asked if I wanted money or clothes and I said 'clothes', because I really loved clothes at that age, I loved looking in shops. I came back with some really beautiful clothes from there. So I did that on and off, not as a future job, just because I liked being at these events, I liked the clothes, I liked looking at things. It was a new excitement, a new enjoyment for me. It gave me confidence, it built my self-esteem, which I needed, I suppose. I was in a different Country, nobody around me, no family. And I loved the way they train you, how to walk and all of that, they were really lovely people. So I did it for me, for my own self-satisfaction and for my own development, not for anybody else.

When I completed my training, I taught at St Lucia Preschool for six months, that's where the university is, then at Indooroopilly Preschool for six months, as a teaching practicum. That was in '63. When I was working at Indooroopilly Preschool, there was a little fella, his nickname was Spanky. He was a gorgeous little boy, little round thing he was. His parents owned a bakery and every Friday he would get us, the staff, buns and cakes and whatever for morning tea. He'd come in and bring us all of those lovely things and then he'd say to me, 'Ms Smith, I'm getting my mum and dad to take me to the beach on the weekend. When I come back on Monday, I'll be as brown as you.' Colour was nothing to him!

I said, 'Oh really, Jeffrey?'

'Yeah. And when I grow up, I'm going to marry you.'

'Oh, truly, darling,' I said, 'I'll be an old woman by the time you grow up,' because he was only four or five.

The other teacher would say to him, 'How come you're going to marry Ms Smith?'

'Because I love Ms Smith,' he'd say. Oh, he was a gorgeous

little boy. Colour meant nothing to my little preschoolers; children only see people, not what colour they are.

Brisbane, that was my first time living in a place of mostly white people. Often, I was the only black person on the bus. And I didn't know about racism and all of those things, I'd just hear comments. A little boy said to his mother, 'There's a black lady over there.' Well, he did call me a lady! And I looked at him and gave him a smile and looked the other way. I thought to myself, Well, according to him, I'm a lady, so that's not too bad, I suppose! But there was no real racist comments. I did have a few odd looks on the buses – maybe because I looked different, I don't know. I was well dressed, I was dressed to go to college and training. I took no notice. I just jumped on the bus like everybody else. I was shy at that time, too. There were comments and that, but I never put my head down or anything. I always held my head high and thought, Oh well if they want to carry on, they can, but that's not going to shame me. I'm going to stay here.

When I was 21, I came home to Darwin. I taught at Parap Preschool for two years, my first teaching job, and lived in a government hostel on Cavenagh Street. Where the ABC now stands in Darwin, there was a hostel for government workers, teachers and others. A car picked us up every morning to take us to the schools, a big black car of some kind, belonging to the government, Commonwealth plates on. At that time we were employed under the Commonwealth. They'd drop me at work every day, pick me up in the afternoon, take me back to the hostel. So I lived in the hostel for the first part of my years, and then I moved to Mum and Dad Randall's house.

Parap was the first school with 60 children. It was a double preschool, they called it, with 30 children there and 30 children over here. We had one main teacher, she was head of the school, and then myself and two other workers underneath her. We'd swap; I'd be with these children for one week and with those other 30 children the next week. I loved teaching the children in the preschools and the kindergartens. It was enjoyable and rewarding work and the children were amazing. We happened to see a documentary called *The History of Darwin* or something a few years ago when we were out with all the Stolen Generations mob. Then, all of a sudden, 'Eileen, that's you!' It's a picture of when I was teaching at Parap and I was walking in the yard, putting up planks or doing something with the children. All the group saw me, all the old ladies, 'Eileen, that's you!'

I was the only Aboriginal at the school, the rest of the staff were white. I don't think I really knew at the time that I was the first qualified Aboriginal teacher in the Northern Territory. They started to write about it and all that. The *Courier Mail* would do stories. But I just never really talked about it, I suppose. I'd just go to Parap Preschool every day, teaching. A lot of the doctors and lawyers lived in Fannie Bay and their children came to my preschool. I didn't think a lot about being Aboriginal, when I was teaching, I don't think I did. And the children accepted me. I think there were no Aboriginal teachers before me because nobody from our mob wanted to do teaching. And then after that came Kathy Nichols, she came into the high schools, and Isabel Adams was another preschool teacher. They were after me.

I met a man in Darwin and was going out with him and fell pregnant. He went back to play football in Perth and wanted me to go with him to Perth, but I wouldn't go. I took off and I went to Adelaide. I said, 'No, I'm going to Lorky.' That's the first place I ran to, Lorky. Because I wasn't married, I was a single mother. And Lorraine said, 'Come down here,' because of course she wanted to look after me again. She was always like that, our Lorky. I think I felt her, the protection, and I felt good. I just wanted to be there with her. At first, while I was pregnant, I was working in a nursing home. But I couldn't do that for long because of the weight thing, because it was a handicapped home, I couldn't lift anymore.

My daughter Raelene was born in '66. I had a bad birth, I was really ill. I was in the hospital for three months, because I had trouble with my kidneys. What do you call it? I had really bad kidneys[25] so they wouldn't let me out of the hospital. But after three months, they let me go home because Lorky came up there and said, 'Look, I want to take Eileen home, I can look after her.' So I went home with her and John and stayed with them until I got back on my feet. Lorky had married a Dutchman, Uncle John Siwes, and she was pregnant with Phillip. Phillip was born when Raelene was nearly six months old, so Phillip and Raelene were together as little babies. He was in the bassinet and she was in the cot next to him, standing up talking to him. Uncle John was a huge man. We had some really good laughs with him. He'd take Raelene in the truck, 'I'm taking her for a ride!' Him and Lorky would go down to the shops, take her with them and I'd be home by myself resting because I was still recovering, I guess. So it was a good time for me to get back my strength, to get back on track again. After three or four months, I was able to do things myself. So I started looking for jobs.

Lorky found a flat for me. One of her workmates had a little granny flat at the back of their house in Glenelg. So she gave me that. I paid rent, but not much. It was just a one-bedroom place for me and Raelene, but it was comfortable. And I was close to work and close to Lorky still. She could come down and see me, it was only about 10 or 15 minutes away from one of those boys' homes where she was working. She checked on me just about every second day. It was lovely having her with me.

And then I went back into the preschool nurseries, because one day, Lorky and I was down looking at this kindergarten nursery on ANZAC Highway and I said, 'That's what I used to do, cuz.' She said, 'All right, we'll go and have a look.' We met Val, the owner, and I said, 'I was looking to get into one of these places so I can work again.' She said, 'Oh, I'm looking for somebody to run this place.' She owned one there on ANZAC Highway and one at Marion nearby. So I put my resume in, didn't think much of it. A couple of days later she rang me and said, 'Eileen, you want the job?' So I went to work and took Raelene with me. That's why I wanted to do it, I wanted my baby with me. I didn't want her put somewhere where I wasn't going to see her all day. The preschool was half kindergarten and half nursery. We'd take children and babies from people who'd come to town for the day to shop. I had a couple of girls working in the nursery and a couple working with me in the kindergarten. So I ran the whole place with about five staff. And then Val said, 'Oh, what about you running the brand new one we got at Marion?' Again, we had 30 preschoolers and the rest was made up of children from out of town, from farms and all those rural areas. The mothers would come into town for the day and go shopping and drop their children off at the day care. I was the only black person there, there were no black staff or kids, but I didn't think anything, really, about me being Aboriginal and having white staff and running a kindergarten.

There was one handicapped boy there. He gave them such a hard time, the staff said, he would just go around screaming. But once I got him, he started to participate in kindergarten because by that time he was about four, five years old. I was the only one that ever got him to participate in kindergarten. And he loved it, he ran around with the kids and try to talk. He was a lovely boy. He played and participated with all the children. The thing is, I sat down and talked to him like he was one of the children. I think I spent more time nurturing him, helping him to adjust, and he settled down and started participating in the play groups. I didn't want him to feel left out. The staff used to medicate him all the time, but I didn't want him medicated. I didn't like that medication business. Then the boy's father approached me and said he was happy with his son's progress. He was a big businessman, really rich, with two children and I learnt that his wife had left him. His other child was older and going to school. He'd make sure the children would attend school and creche and he would pick the boys up every day. One day the boy's father spoke to me, 'Eileen, ever since you'd been with him, he's been so good. We don't have trouble with him at home. He goes in his bath, has his dinner and goes to bed.' He said to me, 'Eileen, can you come and work for me? You'll have your own unit, you'll have a car, you'll be well paid, but you have to look after him 24/7.' I didn't want to, or even consider this because I felt uneasy. You know how men are when we're young; they might think they can own you. I was thinking along the lines that women were often used in that way and I didn't want to be. But it wasn't like that at all, it was a straightforward job offer, he wanted to make a contract for me to work for him, be his boy's carer. This was a generous job offer, but I longed to be home in Darwin, that was in the back of my mind. So I turned down the job and returned to Darwin.

I had a very good little setup in Adelaide and I would've been comfortable there for the rest of my life, but I wanted to come home and see my mother before she died and take my daughter back to my Country. And Dad Randall was pestering me, too. He'd ring and ring me and say, 'Eileen, when are you coming home and bringing our granddaughter back to us?' So I came home then. Raelene was just over one, I think. We lived at the Randalls' house and Dad was really happy, because Raelene was his first grandchild. Alan, Johnny, Dorothy and Anita just loved her and Mum and Dad did, too. She was their little baby.

I had met Ray[26] when we were younger. He was a boxer

with Dad Randall's boxing troupe, and he was good friends with all the Croker boys because they boxed together. Ray was part of that crowd. When I came back from Adelaide, I saw him again, and after a while we started to see each other. He said, 'Eileen, you want to come and live with me? I'll look after you and Raelene.' And I said, 'Well, I don't know if I want to live with anybody.' I'd become quite independent, I had done all of this on my own – with the help of Lorky, of course. I'd never forget her help. She was always there as my support mechanism. But I got the jobs on my own and I'd brought Raelene up, and I didn't really want anybody, I thought I could do it all on my own. Ray kept saying, 'I'll look after you.' In the end I went and lived with him, not far from Mum and Dad Randall, just down the road. I went to Mum and Dad's all the time when Ray was at work; Raelene almost grew up in their house.

I had Shelly in 1968. Michelle – but I always called her Shelly. And Sheena in 1970. I didn't marry Ray until after Sheena was born. I married him in 1970, before the cyclone. So Ray and I weren't married, but we were living together and a priest would come to our house trying to convert me to Catholicism because Ray was Catholic. I didn't like it at all. Ray said, 'Well, Eileen, you know we are living in sin,' and I said, 'Well, I don't care if I'm living in sin. This is my choice and I'm not becoming a Catholic.' I said, 'I'm a Methodist, I belong to the Methodist church.' But the priest kept telling Ray and I that we have to get married, and I kept saying, 'No, no, no.' The reason we eventually got married was because Housing wanted to give us a house. In those days, in the 60s and 70s, you had to be married before they gave you a house. So we just went and got married at the registry office. It wasn't because I wanted to. He wasn't the love of my life, the love of my life was Raelene's father, but it never eventuated. I didn't want to go with him to Perth. But Ray and I, we were all right and the kids were all right. He loved Raelene, she was his daughter as far as he was concerned. And we all got along quite well. Those years, they were happy times.

When the kids were little, I stayed home and took care of them and gave private childcare at home to parents shopping or playing sport. The whole idea of me staying at home with them, with Raelene, and then Shelly and Sheena, was that I didn't want my children taken from me. Welfare were taking a lot of other children from Croker Island women in Darwin and they used to come to Mum and Dad Randall's house to see how their kids were. When I was young, I always felt that that's what they might do. And then this Catholic priest kept badgering me to get married. And I was thinking, Well, if I don't get married, I won't keep my kids. They won't give me a house. Where am I going to live? All those sorts of questions kept coming up. Once we'd left the mission, all of us feared that our children would be removed in the same way from us. That we had to behave, we couldn't do the wrong things. We had to be good mothers, we had to have a proper home. All those things came up in our minds, that the government could come and take our children. So that fear was always there, it never went away. All Stolen Generations children have that fear.

While I was doing private childcare at home Ray worked for Transport and Works, with the government. There was a big depot that ran all the buses and all the government cars, and he was working as a mechanic with the buses and cars. Before that, he was working on the railways, he was a guard on the railways. Sheena was a baby then, I think. Ray had to go on the trains from here to Larrimah and back again. And some mornings I'd go in about one o'clock in the morning to pick him up down near the wharf, because that's where the trains pulled up.

When the railways stopped, he went to Transport and

Works. We'd go fishing and swimming every Sunday. I remember this one time at Mickett Creek, it was Mother's Day and Ray was determined to get me a big fish to celebrate. While he concentrated on fishing, the girls and I collected periwinkles and shellfish in the mangroves to cook. Ray had caught a blowfish and he threw it up on the bank and told the children, 'Don't touch that fish.' But Michelle paid no heed and decided to poke and prod the fish with a small stick. Suddenly she was screaming and running around with Raelene in hot pursuit. The fish had latched onto Michelle's hand between her thumb and pointer finger. Ray ran up from his fishing and grabbed Michelle's hand and prised the fish free. Michelle was left shaking and with a bruised hand. So she learnt never to play with blowfishes again!

Never will I forget Cyclone Tracy on Christmas 1974.[27] Raelene was eight, Michelle six and Sheena four years old. The wind was roaring and on the floor of our house, there was water a foot deep. I put the children in the hallway wardrobe. Ray and I sat in chairs all night, and his brother Keith and his family were with us, come to shelter after a tree fell on their caravan. We watched our roof lift several times and I said to Ray, 'Please let's go out to the car.' Thank goodness he refused. We would have been killed, because a big thick pole pierced the car from the windscreen to the back. The next day we looked outside and saw the roof from next door on our back lawn. The roof came off the house behind us. The only walls still there were for the bathroom, where the family had sheltered under mattresses. Some of our rooms were smashed, and the entire house was waterlogged. The children were very quiet as we huddled in the hallway. It was such a terrifying experience for all of us. Afterwards, Michelle had the shakes every time we had storms. Raelene took it all in her usual stride and took Sheena under her wing, who didn't say much for a while. She was always a chatterbox, but this really affected her. After that none of us liked storms and I always worried in the wet season we would get another cyclone.

We drove around in Keith's car and checked on friends and family. Everybody was okay but there was so much damage, the destruction was unbelievable. That afternoon, Ray took us to the bus depot where he worked and we slept on new mattresses and in the morning went to the airport to catch a flight to Adelaide. All adults had a child on their lap and every seat was full. I managed to grab a few clothes in a garbage bag. Many of us had no baggage but a few plastic bags with our important papers and a change of dry clothes for the children. We flew to Adelaide and stayed with Lorky for a few weeks until our house was repaired.

5

Reconnecting with Family and Country

After they took me away as a child, I never really forgot my family, but I was still under Native Affairs until 18. I wasn't allowed to go see them until I was 18. And then I was training in Brisbane, so I couldn't go back and look for my mother then. I always knew I had other people, my mother and my people. I knew I had them somewhere, and someday I was going to go and find them. It was always in the back of my mind that would happen. But you know how you've lost something and you've never been able to find it, or get back to it? That was my life. I'd lost my mother and I lost my people, and it was hard to think about going back.

But old Jack McKay always wanted to get me back there; I think he'd always wanted me to reconnect with my mother at some stage. When I was on Croker, he would write to Native Affairs and say, 'I want to come in and get Eileen and bring her back to Mainoru so she can see her mother' and her people. But they wouldn't let me. He did that every year from the time I left there until I was ready to go to Brisbane. But I didn't know that until later in life. It was only when I started to get to know Heather Dodd, his niece, that she started to tell me everything about her uncle. She said, 'You know, that old man came in every Christmas. He wanted to take you home to see your mother and your people.' Those roads are really terrible at Christmas time because of the rain and weather. But I didn't know that until I had grown up and Heather told me. Even Aunty Nelly said something and one day Mum said something about this, too. Later, Jack would write to the Randalls to see how I was, so he could tell Mum. That's how he found out that I was going to go to Brisbane, when I was 17, and he came into Darwin and I met him again and he got Sandy to take me shopping. Then when I started to go to school in Brisbane, the *Courier Mail* would do stories about me with photos and old Jack, because he was from Queensland originally, he got all those newspapers. He might've got it months or weeks later because he was out in the bush, but he always got it. Anything that came up about me, he'd show to Mum. But I don't think Mum realised that was me. Maybe I'd changed too much, I don't know. He'd show Mum, say, 'This is your daughter now, but she's in Brisbane. Brisbane is a long way from here.' But Mum wouldn't have known where it was.

Then I was 19 and back from Brisbane for a holiday, a break from school, and Jack brought Mum into the Royal Darwin Hospital at Myilly Point. She had TB.[28] Old Jack said, 'I've got to go and find Eileen so we can take her to see her mother.' He came and got me at the Randall's, where I was staying. I think he had contacted Dad Randall beforehand and Dad said it was okay. He was really happy about it because he was always encouraging us removed children to go and meet our mothers again. When Jack came and picked me up he said, 'Do you want to come and see your mother?' and he took me up to the hospital to see Mum. That was the first time I saw her, after they'd removed me from her.

When I saw her, old Jack said, 'You know who this is, Eileen?' and I said, 'I think it might be my mother.' That's what I said. And he said 'Yes. That is your mother.' He said hello to Mum, and then he said, 'Eileen, I'm going to leave you with your mother. Is that okay?' I said, 'Yes,' and off he went. I don't know where he went, he might've just gone for coffee somewhere. He didn't like coming to Darwin, he was a real bushman. I sat down and Mum started crying. She didn't speak. She was crying, just sitting there crying. And I said, 'Mum, you remember me?' She said, 'Yes, you are my daughter, Eileen, that they stole from me.' Those was her exact words. There were a lot of other women there with her in the ward and then she rattled off language to the women who were sitting there. They must've been women from Arnhem Land, too. But she rattled off some language and they understood it because they're going, 'Oh, oh,' like that. I think they were feeling sorry for us.

When I first saw her again, I felt that she didn't want me, but I could see the tears running down her face. And I knew that it must have hurt her because she always said they stole me from her. That's why I think Jack always made sure that she knew what was happening to me. I don't think she could take it all in properly until she actually saw me again. Then when she saw me again, I came back as a woman, not as a child. And I think that sort of threw her a bit. And I was expecting, you know, love and affection and all that, that she'd jump up and grab me and hug me and kiss me and all of that, but that's not the Aboriginal way. So I felt a little let down. When I thought about it later on I realised that's not the Aboriginal way. There is a cultural difference and I have to accept the way she behaved. But I could hear her talking in language to the women. And telling them I was her daughter. So I knew then: well, she's acknowledging me, she's telling them about me.

I think by this time my memory of her also had sort of faded. I remembered being there with her because I used to run in and out of the kitchen when she was cooking. I remembered her making damper and johnny cakes for me. I remembered Mum walking around, this big tall woman, sort of regal looking. She walked with her head held high and she had a good posture, I remember her like that. And I remember when I was on Croker, I used to chase this older girl all the time, Gladys, because she reminded me so much of my mother. Because she walked the same, she was tall and sort of regal looking. Then I found out later in life that Gladys was from Ngukurr, her mother was from Ngukurr. So she's some relation to my mother. They removed us all from all our connections but deep down they were still there. But if you asked me then what my mother looked like, I wouldn't have been able to tell you. All I could remember was this big, tall, slender woman; that was my mother.

I sat with her for probably half an hour, and we were talking about all sorts of stuff. I just wanted to talk to her and see if she remembered me and see how everybody else was. I asked her about my grandparents, and she said they'd passed. I asked about my uncles and aunties, and she said, 'They still all there.' That's my Uncle Dick and Uncle Larry and all their families. Another thing Mum and I spoke about was the two of my cousins who had left Mainoru as babies, cousins who were also fathered by white men and taken by them and raised interstate. Mum said that Jack made this happen, he didn't want any more children removed by Native Affairs. At least the children had one parent they knew.

After I had returned to Brisbane, I sent Jack a couple of letters, to see how Mum was and to tell him that I wanted to come home. He always told her what was happening to me, but he never responded. Later in life, I said to Heather, 'Well, I did try and write to him a couple of times, but he never responded.' And she said, 'Yeah, but he never forgot you, Eileen, because he always came in to try and take you home at Christmas.' After I first saw Mum in the hospital, I used to see them a bit in town because Mum had to come back for check-ups, and old Jack would bring her up to Darwin. Sometimes she'd been flown in by the medical service. A year or two later, after first seeing Mum, I ran into the girls, my cousins. I was playing softball with Mum Randall when I was back from Brisbane. She was playing in the Ramblers, the nurses and teachers team, and she said, 'Eileen, you're coming to play with me because you're a teacher here.' So I started to play softball with her and the Ramblers, and we looked like prisoners because we were in green-and-white-striped uniforms. One day, we were playing softball and one of the girls from the other team came up and said, 'You are Eileen. You are our cousin.' I looked at her and said, 'And how?' She said, 'Your mother Florrie is my father's sister.' That was Uncle Larry, and the girls were Annette and Susan, my cousins. I didn't remember them, but then I realised that they may not have been born until after I'd gone or they might've been babies when I'd left. All I remembered was my older cousins. But Annette knew me straight away. I could see them looking at me, but I didn't know why they were looking at me. And then she came up and said, 'You are my cousin.' Annette told me this, and I was so excited to have a link to my mother and my people. They had come into Kormilda College, the boarding house for people from remote communities who came to secondary school in Darwin. Annette was playing for Kormilda College because they had a team in the competition and they would come into Gardens Oval to play softball every Saturday.

After having my girls, Ray said to me one day, 'Eileen, you want to go out and see your mother? You always talk about going home. You want to go home.' He sort of understood because he was taken off his mother, but only briefly. I think his mother, when she moved from Tennant Creek to Darwin, she had all her children but had nowhere to live. She was working for this big trucking company and they gave her a little hut next to the transport depot. But I think Welfare wasn't happy with that arrangement because in those days they controlled our lives. The Native Affairs and Welfare, they controlled Aboriginal people's lives, and whether you thought you were doing fine or not, they always wanted to remove the children. So she had to let them go. Ray's older sisters, Janet and Nanette, went to St Mary's Home, another Stolen Generations home in Alice Springs. Ray, his older brother, Joseph and sister Lillian and toddler brother Henry were sent to Garden Point Mission, a Catholic mission, but he never really talked about it. I knew he had a lot of connections with the Garden Point people, but I didn't realise for a long time that he'd been taken there as a child as well. I think he spent about five years at Garden Point Mission, because his mother had nowhere to live at that time. So my husband was very supportive. He might've been a bastard later in life, but at that time he was really supportive, he wanted me to go home and see everybody.

I said, 'Yeah, I'd like to go and see Mum. I'd like to go there.' So Ray said, 'We'll go back to Mainoru and see your mother.' This was during the June school holidays. Raelene was at school, I think. She would've been about five or six, and Shelly was about two or three. Sheena was about 18 months old. So I must've been 28, around that time. We didn't have a four-wheel drive in those days, we just had an ordinary car, a Ford Falcon station wagon. And we had to go through the rivers and soft sands and everything, it was quite an experience. We pushed the car a lot of the time and finally got back to Mainoru, but Mum and the family had moved from there to Bulman. They moved from Mainoru to Bulman station when old Jack had sold up when he got too old. He died in 1966 when I was in Adelaide having Raelene. But I met other families at Mainoru that I had known as a child. There was a lot of other families and they were saying, 'You remember me?' And I would look at them and say, 'Yes,' because I remembered playing with them as a child, but I couldn't remember their names or anything. It was wonderful the way their children played with my children. It was as if I had never left.

So we came back to Darwin and, soon after, Ray said,

'Come on, we'll go again.' The trip to Bulman is over 600 km, at least eight hours from Darwin. We still didn't have a four-wheel drive and we hadn't travelled that way before so we were not aware of the road conditions. When we arrived at Flying Fox River, we had to find a way to cross the water away from the road. The Flying Fox is before the Wilton River, and before they had the bridges, it used to flood. We had to push the car through the sand to get to the other side. Ray drove off through the paper bark trees into the soft sand and we pushed the car across the bad parts back to the main road. The kids thought it was great fun, and I let them have a swim to cool down. As we were driving along, I started to recognise plants and the way the country looked. We finally arrived at Mum's camp and the family was overjoyed to meet us. Uncle Larry was still alive, Uncle Dick was still alive, her brothers. And Mummy Lucy was still there. And old Dad, that's when I saw Dad Jugaduk again. We stayed for two weeks with the family. On the first trip back, Mum and them weren't living at the station. They were living at a little living area away from the cattle station, and that's where we all camped. It wasn't a house, we were camping near the river. We went fishing and hunting, we were eating bush foods and fresh beef and damper, sitting around the campfire. But I missed out on seeing my grandparents, which really broke me up because they were my carers when Mum was working. I loved my grandparents, and I never saw them again. That was the saddest part about going back to Bulman and seeing Mum. But it was good to see Mum and the family and all my cousins. The kids felt at home straight away, running around with all the other kids.

When I came back that first time, I felt that my mum didn't want me. You know how when you see somebody, you run up to them and give them a cuddle? All the aunties and uncles were doing that, running to me and hugging me and picking up the kids, but Mum didn't. I looked at her and I could see tears running out of her eyes and I said, 'Mum, aren't you happy that I'm here?' She says, 'Yeah. Them birds been telling me you're coming,' that's what she said. This is Aboriginal way. I think it was cockatoos, this big mob of cockatoos was there. And I said, 'Mum, you are happy we came?' 'I'm glad you brought my grandchildren home.' That's all she kept saying; that's all she seemed to be worrying about, the grandchildren, but not me. That's as much as saying you don't matter, you know? I really felt that she didn't want me, that first time. But then I thought about it for a while and it suddenly hit me: she'd seen me as a child going away. Here I am with kids in tow, and who's this woman? That must be what it was. It wasn't that she didn't want to see me. It was she couldn't actually take in the fact that when I left, I was a child. And here I was, a grown woman, and different from her. She had to understand that this is still her daughter; she had to process it. And when I asked her if she's happy to see me, she just said, 'Yeah,' nodded her head, and tears were streaming down her face. Poor old Mum. I think she found it really difficult, you know, until I started going there every holiday and spending two weeks at a time. So we'd go out there and spend that time with her and Dad. It took her a while to get comfortable with us.

At the time I went back to see Mum, most of my family was there, except for my brother Ronnie who was working in Darwin for the Health Department. Ronnie was born in 1946, so I was still with Mum when he was born, but as children we didn't spend much time together as I was removed in 1948. The family and the people at home would say, 'Why didn't you remember Ronnie?' because he would've been a baby and I would've been playing with him, being the big sister. But I can't remember him as a baby. Why did I forget him? When he was born, I would've been about three. Why don't I remember that? I didn't meet Ronnie again until after I first went back to

Mum. After that, I found out where he was living and I'd go and visit him and his family and take my children to see him. But by that time I'd been married and had my kids, and he was married to Christine and had all their kids. So we spent a bit of time at his house and he'd come and visit me and Ray and the children. He was living and working near East Arm, he had a house not far from the leprosarium hospital at East Arm. They were living not far from the mud flats and when I'd visit them, Christine and I went down looking for long bums and periwinkles. And that's also when I met Heather Dodd, daughter of Mr and Mrs Dodd, old Jack's niece. Ronnie was the one that told me about her, he said, 'You have to come and meet Heather,' because he'd grown up with Heather at Mainoru and she kept in contact with all the Mainoru kids. Heather always said, 'I grew up with all of them.' She used to speak the language. Ronnie named his daughter Heather after her. He had five children, Peter, Lorretta, Margo – I call her Margo, not Margaret – Heather and Desmond, five of them. But the kids were only little, that's when I would've met him again and we reconnected.

Ronnie had come to Darwin to work for the Health Department, working with Dr Hargrave[29] in tropical medicine at East Arm Hospital. He got involved with health because Dr Hargrave used to go out to the communities to check who had leprosy, and that's where he picked up Ronnie. Ronnie would've been in his teens, and he became his laboratory technician. And then he travelled the world with Dr Hargrave studying tropical medicine. They had a memorial for Dr Hargrave a few years ago, but my brother had passed, poor thing. He passed away Australia Day 2015. I went to the function and they remembered Ronnie well, a lot of the Health Department lot still talk about him. He did really well for himself. He finished high school and then started to work with Dr Hargrave. He did all the tests. He was quite brainy, that brother of mine.

I was really proud of him. It was amazing, he'd lost one of his legs from the knee down because he ended up getting leprosy as well. So Ronnie had one of those prosthetic legs, but when I first saw him again, I didn't know he had it because I used to see him walking and driving and I never realised he had one leg because he moved so well. Then one day, I was visiting him, and he was sitting on the bed and he told one of his kids to bring his leg to him, and she brought it. I looked and I said, 'You mean to tell me you've had one leg all this time?' And we just burst out laughing. I think he'd lost it when he was about 19 or something. He stayed in Darwin for quite some time, about 10 years, I suppose. I think he, Christine and the children went back around 1980 to Bulman because he wanted to be close to Mum and Dad. I think Dad must've been getting sick then, but Mum was still firing fit. He said to the Health Department that he wanted to go back to Bulman. So he went back to work at the health clinic there.

So, I've got a biological brother, that's Ronnie, but all my cousins are also my brothers – because of the Aboriginal system, the children of all my mother's brothers and sisters are my brothers and sisters too. But actually, when I first started going back to Bulman, I thought all of the boys were my brothers, but Ronnie was my only biological brother. The others were my cousin-brothers. I said to Mum, 'How come you've got all these boys?' Mum did look after a lot of children. She and Dad, they took in a lot of kids. Aunty Alice, who was Dad Jugaduk's sister, was married to Uncle Dick Murray, Mum's brother, but she ran away and left all the kids there. So Mum took over Uncle Dick's children, and she grew up Bruce and Kenneth, and Abie was the girl. With Ronnie, he was only little. And she grew up Rex Campion, because his father was Jugaduk's brother. 'Well, I've been grow them all up, my girl,' she said, like that. In other words, I grew them up, so they're my kids. But really, Ronnie and I were her only biological children. She just brought up kids all around her, the children of hers or Dad's brothers, because she didn't want them to be picked up and taken. She didn't want to leave them kids on their own, because I had been taken away from her. That's Lesley, Ewen and Scott from Mummy Lucy, Roland from Uncle Larry, Bruce, Kenneth and Abie from Uncle Dick. And Lincoln, Spencer and Stuart are Mummy Nelly's nephews. Bruce and I were really close when he was alive and my kids just loved him. He was a really funny man, and a real big man, big and really black and they just loved him. Bruce and I were so close. When I started going back there, that was the brother I always was with, Bruce. Because Ronnie wasn't there at Bulman at the time, remember? Lesley was Mummy Lucy's son whose father was a coloured man. Lesley's father, Billy Moore, was one of the head stockmen at Mainoru station and was with Mommy Lucy at the beginning. Lesley was picked up after me and he went to Retta Dixon. I didn't even know he was there because I went to Croker Island, but by the time I started going back to visit Mum, Lesley had gone back to Bulman and was working and living there. He was a horseman. He worked with his father at Mountain Valley station and Mainoru station. He worked at quite a few other cattle stations, including Elizabeth Downs station at Daly River, Roper River station, Victoria River station and Bradshaw station near Timber Creek.

After that first time we went back to Bulman, we returned every holidays because I wanted to reconnect with my family properly, and that was the only way to do it, to go out and be on Country with them. I'd take the children out every June, July, because up here we had six weeks holiday in the middle of the year. Now they changed it to four weeks, but that's the best time to go bush because the roads aren't flooded and it's dry season and it's cool, really cold it used to get at nighttime. Wet season's no good, you end up getting bogged. So I always tried to go out in June or July so that I could spend a couple of weeks out on Country with Mum and Dad and all my cousins and aunties and uncles – all the family. It was something I'd look forward to. The children looked forward to it, too. By this time, they had houses out at Bulman that had been built for them. Mum and Dad had their own little place. Once Ronnie and Christine moved back to Bulman, we'd stay with them in their house. I spent a lot of time with him, and I started to get to know him better. We had a wonderful brother-sister relationship, in the end. I'd drive myself all the way out to Bulman, just with the kids, and Mum would worry about me. She'd send all the boys when it got to sunset, 'Go, find your sister.' And we would meet them past Weemol,[30] on the road near the airstrip, and I would say, 'What you lot coming for?' They'd reckon, 'Ahh, that old woman, she sent us.'

When I took my children back there, it was like we'd never left home. We'd just be back as part of this big happy family. The children loved it. Raelene and Shelly and Sheena, they loved going out there. And later, my grandchildren were the same. The kids, they'd go off running everywhere. The boys would get them the horses so that they could ride and we'd go down the river, swimming, fishing, hunting, gathering bush tucker, all sorts of things. They had the best time. But when I first started to take the children back, I used to get a bit panicky because they would run off to the river, and Mum would just move her hand like that, flat and parallel to the floor. She wouldn't talk, she'd just go like that. In other words, 'Eileen, be quiet, they can go.' She never growled at me or never said I couldn't do anything when she didn't think something was right, she'd just go like that with her hand. But I would get panicky and think the kids might drown or something. There were older children there with them to look out for them but I had been brought up in the white system, so I had to learn the Aboriginal system all over again.

There was a spring there, next to Weemol, with clear running water. The kids loved the spring and we would take them there swimming, and down to Bulman River to get yabbies and freshwater crayfish. One day my cousin Kenny said, 'Let's get the freshwater crayfish out of the river.' He wrapped his hand with a cloth and stuck it under the rock. I was scared because I wasn't sure what was there, might be a snake. Before I could say anything, Kenny had his hand out with this big crayfish clinging to the cloth, a nice big freshwater crayfish. He said, 'I told you everything would be fine.' The children made a big fire and proceeded to cook the crayfish and the fish we had caught and the mussels we collected. I went back to the river to fish, thinking the children would call out when all was cooked. Half an hour later, Christine and I came back from fishing to find only the shells and bones left. I was really disappointed because I loved eating food from the rivers but having a dozen children there to feed, I guess that was to be expected. Christine and I then cooked damper and johnny cakes, which were gone as quickly as they were cooked. We had a cup of tea from the billy and ate damper and syrup with the children. We'd do all sorts of things. My cousin Bruce, when he was still alive, he'd take us everywhere on the back of the truck and we'd go swimming, fishing and turtle hunting with him. Sometimes when we came to different parts of the Country, Mum and Mummy Lucy would start singing in the back of the truck, singing as we were getting closer to our destination. And one of the kids, I think it was Raelene, she said, 'Mummy, what Nana doing?' And I said, 'Oh, she's singing to our ancestors because we are coming into Country.' That was something the kids would learn: When we approach a different part of the Country, you sing to the ancestors to let them know you're coming.

At nighttime, if we weren't there for a ceremony, we'd just sit around the campfire. It was always important to have that campfire because that was like a meeting place. People sat around it and talked and told stories and did things together, so the campfire was always a good place to be at. And Mum and Mummy Lucy made fresh damper for us every night. We had fresh damper and johnny cakes with our meals, and Christine and my cousin Lesley as well, they were great cooks with the camp oven. Lesley was a really good cook; he did some real good cooking for us in the camp oven, beautiful stews and stuff. And we always had beef. I used to laugh, because later when I sent the boys back to stay there for the holidays with Ewen and Ronnie, they'd say, 'Nana, we had beef for breakfast, beef for dinner, beef for tea.' I said, 'Well, did you eat any vegetables?' 'Yeah, but we didn't really want that. We wanted rib bones.' They loved the rib bones. We always had fresh beef when we went home because the boys would go out and get a killer and then we'd have fresh beef all week, it was a constant part of the daily menu – morning, noon and night. And Mum had nanny goats too, she had her own herd. She loved nanny goats, she got milk from them. If they didn't have beef, or when she didn't want to eat more beef, she'd kill one of her goats so she could have goat meat.

All the kids would play there around the campfire. One day, my kids were playing marbles with the other kids. I called Raelene to come and help me with something and her response was, 'Wait, Mum, I'm playing marbles.' Then my cousin called her children, and they came straight away. Well, this was a lesson from my traditional life. The kids in the community listened to their mothers and immediately did what was asked of them, but my children had been raised in white society and told me to wait before doing what they were asked to do. You could see the difference in how I was raising them and how our people were raising their children. That was something I learnt from watching my mob and how they were doing things. You never ever saw my cousins raise their voices, but when they called the children, they came, whereas I'd get upset with the kids. The difference was that my children were being raised in the white system. It was a learning curve for both the children and me in how our people did things. Now we've got all this violence and abuse, but if you went and sat at a group camp with your family, you'd see the beauty of the Aboriginal way of doing things. It was lovely to see because at that time we didn't have alcohol and all of that other abuse.

We always had a wonderful time at Bulman. And you know this actor? Chris Hemsworth, he's out of Bulman – Chris and Liam. They grew up at Bulman because when they were children, they used to go and stay with their uncle and aunty out there because their uncle was doing the buffalo catching. They were there for six weeks of the year, for holidays, and they would be gone off fishing and hunting with all the rest of the kids. With all the mob of children, no matter what colour, creed, or background they come from, they'd all run off and play together. So Chris especially, he still goes out there and sees the family.

When I first started going back to Mum, I longed to reconnect with her, but it did take time. I had to wait because I wanted to get to know her, I didn't want to come in there like a bulldozer and start questioning her. I had to get to know her and to understand where she was coming from because Mum rarely spoke. She'd sit there and wouldn't say very much. I know her English wasn't that good, but I think she was still trying to get her head around that I left her as a child and now I'm a woman. And I had to understand that, too. That's why I couldn't barge in there. Around that time I started working with the Education Department in Bagot and Belyuen[31] and I started to understand the ways of our women. I knew that I couldn't just go in hell to leather. Working with the women there taught me how to approach my people and how

I should behave, and for me to understand my Aboriginal background, because they removed all of that from me as a child and brought me up in a white system.

I had to work my way back, and the way I worked my way back was learning through the women in the communities that I worked with. They were helping me to understand my Aboriginality, my background, my people, and the best way to approach them. Because a lot of people I know go back into their communities and because they've been educated, they think that they can just take over. I had to learn the right way to do it. I had to understand the customs again because I was removed from it. Working with the women throughout the Northern Territory helped me greatly to understand that better.

So I was able to sit, and often just sit with Mum. We'd sit around the campfire or at the river and there wasn't much talking at first. For the first few times, we never spoke much. She just kept saying, 'I'm glad you brought my grandchildren back. I'm glad you brought my grandchildren back.' Not once did she say, 'I'm glad to see you,' but that's the white system. So I had to learn how to relate to mum and how to talk to her because she wasn't from the white system, she was from the Aboriginal system. She was happy to see me, but she didn't say that. She'd just sit there silently and wouldn't say much, whereas my aunties were all over me, and my uncles and my cousins. I got the feeling that 'Yes, I belong here' because of them. But it was very difficult for Mum and me to get to that point.

I was happy to see my mother, because I'd longed for my mother for such a long time. But then getting there and feeling that disconnection, I felt sort of lost. But she did care, and I always sort of knew she cared; it was just our communication. She might've worked with Jack McKay on the station, but her Aboriginal system was very strong in her, and she wanted me to learn that. Sometimes I'd be talking about work and Darwin and she'd say to me, 'Stop talking like that now. Leave that behind, you back home now.' And I'd just crack up laughing. She was so funny, she'd bring you back to earth, you know. She wanted to make sure that I was back there with them wholeheartedly, not just coming and going. She wanted me to be part of that whole system again, because she knew I'd lost so much. So she put in place a way to reconnect me to all of that by putting me through ceremony and by making sure I went back and understood the Aboriginal system and the Aboriginal customs so I could settle back into my life as an Aboriginal woman. She could see what the white system had done for me, and she didn't want me to remain only in the white system. Mum wanted to ensure that me and my children had the benefits of being back with family and with her. So Mum and Aunty Nelly, they talked to me about different things but I think mostly Mum wanted me to learn not by talking, but by watching and being part of that group.

After a while, when I got to know her better, I started to ask her questions. She used to say, 'So I don't know why they took you. I wasn't a bad mother, I was a good mother. You had a good home. I worked all my life. Your grandparents looked after you.'

I said, 'Mum, that's not the point. Look at this colour here—' and she looked at my skin colour '—that's why they took me. For this colour. I've got different colour to you and they wanted to teach me white man business.'

And she'd reckon, 'Ohh, I always wondered why they took you, my girl, because I've been work hard all my life.' Poor thing, she always maintained she was a good mother. I had a really happy life as a kid, and that's why Mum could never understand why they took me away.

I kept saying, 'Mum, because it was the government law, they make laws with the government and that was a law. They had to pick us all up as kids because we had white fathers and black mothers. And they said that they wanted to—' I couldn't say 'assimilate', so I said '—they wanted to make us more like a white person,' and she'd understand that. I couldn't say 'assimilation'[32] because she wouldn't have known what that word was. I'd say to Mum, 'Because they wanted me to grow up like a white kid.'

'But why? You're black fella,' she'd reckon.

I said, 'Yes, I know I'm black fella. But that's what the government wanted because they didn't think I'd have the proper education out home here.' Because she thought they took me because she was a bad mother, she had to live with that guilt. What a heavy burden to carry for such a long time. It really broke her, I think, because she didn't know how to work with the pain or how to cope with it. Mum just wouldn't talk about it. Another time, I asked her about my father, and that's when she said, 'Him finish.' So I never found out who my father was because she wouldn't tell me.

'Him finish now,' she said.

'Is he dead?'

She just looked at me. 'No. I don't know. But him finish.' She didn't want to remember this part of her history, and I thought I better leave it because the memory was too painful.

Mum and I would talk a lot once we got to that point, but everything was so short and clipped, her responses, because she wasn't really fluent in English. And I had lost the language and wasn't really versed at Kriol. But I remember when I first went back to Mum, she was rattling off language, I think to Dad, and I answered her. She almost fell over because she realised that I'd heard and understood her. She said, 'You remember?' and I said, 'Little bit.' I could understand what she was saying and I responded to her, but I couldn't really speak it. By listening to it, I must've been able to pick it up again, because Lorky sort of kept our language alive for us when we were on Croker. But I didn't speak the language, then. If I'd spoken the language, Mum and me would've been rattling off language. Raelene speaks the language fluently, and Kriol as well, because she had a lot to do with her grandparents, she just loved her grandmother and grandfather. Raelene started to go out there on her own and she'd stay with them. Something funny happened one day. Mum walked down the road and this old woman sang out to her, 'Who that munanga kid with you?' – talking about Raelene, you know. 'Don't you call my granddaughter munanga!' Mum said. 'She's not a munanga, she's same as me and you,' she reckon. Uncle Tex told me the story; he reckoned Mum was going to have a fight because this woman called Raelene 'munanga'. And I just cracked up laughing to think my dear old mum was protecting my daughter. That would be Florrie! Later on in life, Raelene started going out that way for work, and whenever she went down to Bulman, she'd stay with them, with Mum and Dad. My mother spoke pretty clear Kriol, and that's where Raelene picked it up, from them. Kriol is a version of English and it's how the tribal groups around the Territory talk to each other, because a lot of our people don't speak the language as much as they used to. Mum was always teaching Raelene our languages, Rembarrnga and Ngalakan. And Raelene learnt well and came back speaking the language quite fluently.

When the kids were little, Mum got Ronnie to ring me one day. She said, 'You gotta come to the land claim.'

I said, 'What land claim?'

She said, 'Roper River.'

'Why, Mum? That's not our Country.'

'Yes, it's your grandfather's Country. Him Ngalakan,' she reckon.

I said, 'Oh. This is where grandpa comes from? But he wasn't there. He was with me at Mainarou,' and she said, 'Yeah, we all come there to work.' That's when she told me about the family coming up to Mainoru from Urapunga, down the Wilton River. She showed me, 'This is the way we come back from Urapunga.'

I said, 'Well, Mum, why didn't you tell me about grandfather?' because Mum never talked about it. I had always thought that only Bulman was my Country. Baghetti[33] is the Murray's tribal land at Bulman, that's where Mummy Lucy was born, at Lucy Creek not far from the outstation. But then I found out that Ngukurr is our traditional lands from our granddad. My grandmother was Rembarrnga, but my grandfather was the eldest of all the Ngalakan leaders. He was head of the tribal group, in charge of ceremonies and all of that, and he had five brothers. But he was the eldest of the brothers. I never knew that he was from that way because Mum never ever said that. By the time I got back from the mission and tried to reconnect with Mum and them, Grandpa and Nana had died.

We went back there for the land claim, the Roper Bar land claim. Mum took me. I went with her and my aunties and my uncles. She wanted me there with the children and she actually put all the kids' names down with her, my name and my brother Ronnie, and my children and his children. This would've been 1980. We went out and we sat on the banks of the Roper River where we had the land claim, and they talked about the Country and everything. Then the anthropologist showed me a genealogy with my grandparents on it and Mum and her siblings. I had always assumed that my grandpa was from where we were, at Bulman. I didn't know that Ngukurr was my Country. So we've had to claim the Ngalakan side. We always thought we's just Rembarrnga until Mum reckoned, 'Come on. We're going land claim.' So I am Rembarrnga, but I'm Ngalakan too. After that, I went to all the meetings in Ngukurr to see our relations. And I've taught Malcolm[34] the same. So when he's at the football in Queensland or Sydney he says in his talk he's Rembarrnga/Ngalakan and from central Arnhem Land. All my children, grandchildren and great-grandchildren know where their Country is.

I also had to go back through all those ceremonies again. When they took me as a child, I lost all of that. Mum was a ceremonial person. She ran the ceremonies for women before Aunty Nelly took over. She taught Aunty Nelly, and Aunty Nelly took over – that's what Aunty Nelly told me. And Dad was also quite high up in his ceremony, because of Grandpa. But when I first started going back to Mum and Dad, I didn't realise they were going to all these ceremonies. When Mum was younger, she travelled to those ceremonies with my grandfather, because Grandpa had to run them, he was the ceremonial man for Arnhem Land. That's why Mum knew all those languages across Arnhem Land. Whenever we met with people, she'd rattle off different languages with them. And I said, 'But how do you remember them, Mum?' She said, 'Because I talked to all of them.' When Mum and Dad were older, they went to all these different places for ceremonies, and to Lajamanu and Yuendemu in the centre. Ronnie would ring me – by that time, Ronnie had moved back to Bulman because he was worried about our parents getting old. But they didn't stop; they kept going everywhere. He said to me, 'When you going out to Yuendemu? Mum and Dad going that way.'

I said, 'I went out there last week. What they going for?'

'Oh, for ceremony. Dad has to do ceremony.' I could see all that land, but I didn't know it was connected in any way to our Country because Arnhem Land's big, but ceremonies went right through and Mum and Dad always went to them. When you're doing ceremonies, you've got responsibility for another Country within our Aboriginal structure. It mightn't be your Country, but you've got responsibility to do ceremony there. That's why we are all so interconnected.

Dad reckon, 'What you think, serpent dreaming is just

only up here? It goes all the way down to the centre. That big snake,' he reckon 'all the way down.'

I said, 'And what, you follow it?'

'Well, I have to go to ceremonies'. So me and Dad sat down and talked about it one day, old Jugaduk. Because to me he was my dad, he grew me up. When I was going out to these communities for work, that's how a lot of people knew me, because of my parents. They'd say, 'We know who you are, Eileen, your mum and dad are Florrie and Jugaduk.' It was amazing. It was a way for me to connect with all the other communities around the Territory, because of the footpath Mum and Dad built between where we lived and all the other communities when they attended ceremonies. I often thought if I'd stayed with Mum and Dad as a child, I would've done those trips with them. But they took me away from them as a child. To this day that is something that really breaks me up.

Some of the ceremonies I went to were beautiful. I took the girls with me. They'd sit down with all the women, and I'd go with the older women up to the ceremony ground. The ceremonies were held out in the bush, past Bulman, and we'd camp on the Bulman River near the ceremonial grounds. We were on the side of the river camping, with a big campfire going all the time. One night, we camped down there and we were all sitting around the campfire, eating our dinner and talking. Suddenly, a herd of buffalos came through the camp and everybody was screaming and running this way and that way and Mum just said, 'Get in the car, Eileen.' Thank goodness. The kids were already sleeping in the back of the truck, so I jumped in with them. And Mum, Mummy Lucy and Dad were sitting down next to the campfire, they were just sitting there and everybody else was running around, trying to get out of the way of the buffalos.

One ceremony I went to was really special. I was in my late 30s, I think it was. This was a big ceremony for all of us. We camped in Bulman down near the river and we had to walk for nearly a mile up the hill. The men went one way and the women went the other. All the men were there in the background, but we never saw them. We just saw the torches in the background and could hear the singing and dancing, the didgeridoo and the clapsticks and everything going. We had to walk from there to the women's business ground. All those women walked with Mummy Nelly leading. My mum was there but she couldn't walk right up to the ceremony. She and Mummy Lucy sat down at the camp, where everybody else was sitting around a big fire. All the aunties, all those women in that age group, they were all there. And my kids. Mummy Nelly and all the younger and middle-aged women and me, we all walked up to the ceremonial grounds. It was magical because we're coming down and all you could see was these torchlights. Not really torchlights, but the burnt top of the pandanus palms. There were burning pandanus trees all around the block, it was quite a big square. They had torches at each end of the square and fires next to each of those dugouts. They were like a bed, but sunken into the ground. There was about six of them. And Mummy Nelly said, 'We got to sit down there now, in the dugouts.' I just did what she told me and followed her. About five of us went into each of those dugouts, dug out of the sand, and we're sitting there and Mummy Nelly starts singing and talking and whatever she had to do because she was the leader. We weren't even allowed to look around. We had to just look on the ground and stay where we were. It went for nearly two hours.

After the ceremony in that circle, we went down to the camping ground to the people in the camp around a big fire. When we arrived back, Raelene said, 'Mum, it was so pretty when you were coming down the hill with all the women,' because she could see the lights. Raelene would have been about 13 years old. Mummy Nelly really wanted to take

Raelene with us, you know, but my mum said, 'No.' I said, 'But she's nearly a young woman now,' and she reckon, 'No, no, not this time.' Afterwards, I said to Mum, 'What's this for?' She said, 'For you. Because you missed out on all of this when you were little. They took you away. This is for you.' That's why she wouldn't let Raelene come with me. It was some way of bringing me back to the tribe, bringing me home. You could feel it, you know. Mum hadn't told me anything beforehand. She just called me and said, 'You gotta come back to Bulman.' When I got there she reckon, 'Oh, tomorrow night you're going to go with Nelly and the women. And you're gonna go up there to the ceremony ground.' I couldn't ever get it out of my mind. It was just the most beautiful thing. This is the way my family brought me home. I felt whole and I felt amazing. It made me feel different, maybe because this was accepting me back home. It was a way of bringing me back into everything I'd lost, I guess, as a child. She did that for me, Mum, made sure I got that. I've been to all the other ceremonies but that was so special. I can't ever forget it. It was pitch black. All you could see was the fire glow; I can still see those fires in my memory. Sometimes I lie down and I can see it all over again.

People don't realise that I've been to a lot of ceremonies. Then one day, one of the Croker girls blurted out, 'Eileen, you're more lucky than us. You've had everything.' I said, 'Only because of my people. If my mother wasn't still alive, I would have missed out.' I did go back to Country and I was accepted into Country because my family just accepted me when I came home. They took me back. Mum and the family never refused me. Then they took Raelene through ceremony. Later, Raelene was being initiated into women's business with Mummy Nelly; Mummy Nelly was training her and teaching her. She said, 'Your mum taught me everything. That's why I'm doing it now and I'm teaching Raelene.'

There is another example in my family of reconnecting through ceremony. There was another sister of mum's, Njayjay. Her English name was Ivy, but we called her Njayjay, that was her nickname. I didn't meet her till years later. Mum never talked about her, so I didn't find out until later in life that Mum had this older sister, who belonged to grandpa's other wife. Nana Ivy lived at Bringun just outside Roper River station, a little outstation off the Roper River highway, opposite the Roper River station turnoff. Raelene went through that Country one day, she was working for Katherine Yolgnu Association and she went through there to drop off food and mail to the outstations. And that old girl just ran up to her and grabbed her and started crying. Raelene got the shock because she didn't know her. The old girl is singing out my name, calling her 'Eileen', and Raelene reckons, 'No, no, old woman. That's my mum. My mum is Eileen and her mother is Florrie. I'm her granddaughter.' 'Well, your grandmother is Florrie, that's my sister,' she reckoned to Raelene. 'Mine sister is Florrie and Lucy,' she said. And she was crying, crying, hitting her head and carrying on and Raelene didn't know what to do. Then she rings me up when she gets to Roper and she said, 'Mum, you got an aunty called Ivy?' And I said, 'No,' because Mum never talked about her.

The next time I went to Bulman for holidays, me and the kids, I said, 'Mum, you got another sister?'

She reckons, 'Oh yeah. Not let talk. No good one, that one.'

I said, 'What she do? She couldn't have done something that bad.'

'Yeah, she been married the wrong way and your grandfather real upset,' she reckons. 'Your grandfather real upset.'

'So what did he do?'

'Oh, we left her behind.'

I said, 'But that's cruel, Mum. You left one sister behind.' But she reckon, 'She had her husband, she had wrong way husband.' So I found out what had happened. Mum and I sat down and talked about it. My grandfather was married to two women, and Ivy was from his other wife. Mummy Ivy married the wrong way, wrong skin, and grandfather just took off and left her there. He picked up Mum and her brothers and moved them to Mainoru, to the cattle station. That happened before I was born and Mum never talked about it. So the customs were still very strong when that happened, the Aboriginal customs. If you did wrong, you got punished for it. So they banned Mummy Ivy from the tribe, but they wouldn't kill her or they wouldn't kill her husband because of grandpa's status, because he was head of the Ngalakan tribe.

Then we finally met her, Mummy Ivy. Dad Jugaduk died in '85, and she came to Bulman for his funeral. We all went out there for Dad's funeral and I'm sitting down with all my mummies, sitting there, and we were all talking. Next minute, Mummy Ivy come flying up on her truck, and then she got out of the truck and she was sitting there on the ground crying. Mum was there and Mummy Lucy and, next minute, they got these little skinny sticks, really skinny, like the twigs you use to make fires. And they were hitting her, hitting her with them little sticks. And I'm saying, 'Mum, what you doing? Mum, Mum, stop it!' trying to stop her. Because I hadn't been brought up in the Aboriginal way. Then I realised it must have been some sort of punishment to Aunty Ivy, so I better shut up. It's got nothing to do with me; I can't say anything. I thought, Eileen, you've got to let them do this, it's their cultural way. Mum explained it to me afterwards, but I knew already that they were welcoming her back to the family. They were accepting her back, hitting her to say, 'This is your punishment, now we can take you back.' Those skinny little sticks couldn't hurt anybody. They could have done it with the nulla-nulla,[35] but they didn't. They were just hitting her and old girl crying, and they're rattling off language to her, and she's responding. She's sitting there and taking it all, crying and saying, 'Sorry,' but getting a hiding. It was the funniest thing, because I'm sitting there, you know, grown woman, watching my two mothers flogging another woman. And Raelene looking at them, too. She's saying, 'Mum, what are they doing?' I said, 'It's all right. They're just welcoming nana back again. That's all.' They stopped and they hugged, the three sisters, and it was finished, and they went off to the funeral. This is the way they accepted her back. And they were really good after that. That was the interesting thing about meeting Mummy Ivy.

After I met Mummy Ivy at that funeral, every time I went to Ngukurr I'd stop off and see her at the outstation, once I found out she was my aunt mummy. Every time I went out to Roper, I would stop in to see her and take her things, a blanket and food, because I didn't want to go there empty handed. Mummy Ivy died not long after, but Barney, her son, was really close with Raelene and me. Barney ended up taking on the ceremonial rights of grandpa, because grandpa was in charge of Ngalakan, and he went back and trained Barney. So Barney became one of the big ceremony men for our lands at Roper, because Barney was living on Country. They had moved from Urapunga to Minyerri, that's where Barney lived most of his life. I think Grandpa hadn't forgiven his daughter, but when Barney came along, he was the only son of the right age and Grandpa didn't want the ceremony to go to anybody else. Because by that time, Bruce and them were all too young. Bruce and the siblings at Bulman didn't get that teaching until Dad Jugaduk taught them. So Barney became the one that grandpa trained and taught. And Barney, he had all the attributes of Grandpa, he understood the ceremonies through and through. He was also like a medicine man; he could heal people., Barney inherited all the things that Grandpa had. So regardless of what happened between

Mummy Ivy and Grandpa, he didn't leave his grandson out. Raelene and Barney became quite close, and he'd often ring to see how Mum was and see how the family was at Bulman. And whenever he came to town, we'd see him. Barney always had his eye over the family to make sure nothing happened to us, because that was his responsibility from Grandpa.

I have a sister, Mai Katona. Our mothers worked in the cattle industry, like many of our people. Working as cooks, working in gardens, tending goats, working cattle and horses on the cattle stations. Her aunt Clara actually grew Mai up, and then Mai got picked up from Pine Creek. They took her off Aunty Clara and she was sent to Retta Dixon. I think it was Clara that told Mai the story later on in life and told her that she may have a little sister somewhere in Arnhem Land because that old man went that way, to Mainoru and Elsey, and Clara thought there was another kid. So Mai started to dig through the mission records and found records and thought that it was me. We met for the first time in the 80s, I think. She was living in Tasmania, but she brought a group of Aboriginal kids back to the Territory for a visit, it was like an exchange thing with those children from Tasmania and our children from up here. I had heard about her before, because she always told the Retta Dixon people that I was her sister. When we finally met, she would come and visit me at my house, and she told me what Aunty Clara had told her. And then we had that sister connection. Whenever my kids went down for sport, they'd stay with her in Tasmania. And ever since she moved back to the Territory, we were always together. I got her to come and work with me, she worked at Chief Minister's with me.

All our lives we believed we were sisters, but we did nothing to really check. Recently we had a test and it shows that we don't have the same father. So I was right with my assumptions all these years. She always believed I was her sister through our father. I never believed it, but I thought there was something. Our mothers are related, so we think the resemblance is through our mothers. But I didn't realise how close Mai's mother and her people were to my mother and my people until she started to look it all up. When you look at it, there's a system called the Skin. So we are related through Skin, right across the whole of Arnhem Land. My mother is part of that, and so am I. And when people saw Mai and me together, they thought we were proper sisters because we do look alike. Now we find out that had nothing to do with our father, it must be through our mothers.

We always thought that one day we'd have to be tested, but we said: we will remain sisters, no matter what. Over the years we have developed a close relationship and our children have a close bond. Regardless of who our father was, we believe we are sisters and we are very close. After the test, she said, 'I don't care what that says, Eileen, we're still sisters,' – because our mothers are related in some shape or form. And when I explained this to the children, they said, 'We don't care, Aunty Mai is our Aunty Mai,' and that's it, because my children have been taught in the Aboriginal system about family. A lot of the children in the institutions, we call each other brothers and sisters, and they're not really our brothers and sisters. But because we grew up in the mission system, that was the only families we had.

When I started going out there, to Bulman and Ngukurr, they never ever called me 'Eileen'. Some of them called me by my skin, which was Gaman. But once I got to my 50s, a lot of the younger people call me 'Olgaman'. That's what they call you when you get to a certain age. It's like 'old woman', but they say Olgaman. It's part of the Aboriginal system, it's showing you respect because of your age. At first I wasn't sure I liked it, because I still thought I was pretty young! I was still playing softball and everything else at the time. And to me,

'Olgaman' would've been an old granny, and I was probably 50. But by that time I was a grandmother anyway, so it didn't really matter. It was a way to show where I fit in that structure of the Aboriginal system.

Going back to Country was really important to me, I wanted that reconnection with my family, with my people, with my customs, and I didn't want my children to miss out on it either. That's why I took the children out all the time. My kids always had a wonderful time back home at Bulman, because it's away from towns and centres. They learnt about their own Aboriginal culture, and the way things were being done through family. After that, the children have been going out there themselves. Then the grandchildren. That's why they've got such a strong relationship with our mob, they wouldn't have learned that if they had grown up only in Darwin. Now when my children mix up with the family from out there, you can see the wonderful relationship they've got and the understanding they have of our people. We'd also come down when we had ceremonies and for the funerals, my grandchildren as well as my children. So they were part of that as well. They could experience ceremonies even though they weren't allowed to participate in everything. Children are always at ceremonies no matter how old they are, and they participate in the way the women want them to. The children loved being around that campfire at ceremonies and they could hear, and even when we were sitting there at nighttime and there was a ceremony going on, they could hear the clap sticks and the music. It was important for them to be part of it; I didn't want them to miss out, like I had.

So my children have been more fortunate than a lot of children who have grown up in Darwin. They've had both worlds. Mum and Dad helped in that. And even Ray, they both loved Ray and often Dad took Ray off and was talking to him and helping him to understand, because Ray's from a different Country. He was talking to Ray about our customs. Ray and Dad spent quite a few days together. They just wandered off together talking. It was wonderful that my dad did that for Raymond as well.

My brothers and their families look after my family; they're the ones that have been teaching them everything about our customs. My daughters were taught by Mummy Nelly, Christine, Jill and other women, and my granddaughters by Ronnie's daughters. They had teachings about our people, customs, ceremony and bush life. My grandsons were sent out and stayed with my brothers so that they could learn as well. My brothers helped to reconnect my grandsons. When they got a little older – and at first that was Raymond and Gavon, my oldest grandsons – they went out on their own to spend the holidays with my brothers Ronnie and Ewen at Bulman. The boys were staying with Ewen in the single men's quarters with his sons, Ronnie's son Desmond and a few other boys. The boys had such a great time, they didn't want to come home and eventually Ronnie and Ewen had to send them home. My grandson Gavon caught his first fish on the Bulman River, and my brothers talked to them about the customs and the traditions and the ceremonies. They'd take them through that ceremonial track. So from very young, they made sure the boys understood where they were coming from. When my grandson Yowane got into trouble, he went out and spent time with Ewen. So my children and grannies had the opportunity to connect with family and our customs. They've got a family that'll take them in forever, so we try to keep that family connection going. I don't want to lose it. It was hard enough getting it back.

When I finally had all those years with Mum before she died, it was the most fulfilling time of my life. Dad got sick and died in 1985, and Mum died in 1992. Gee, she lived a little bit longer, didn't she? Maybe that's why I'm such a cheeky old bugger and still alive, because of Mum! We had beautiful times out there when Mum was still alive. I had many years with her, and not many people had that, other people from Stolen Generations. This is what annoys me. They took us away from our mothers, from our people and everything. But even when we turned 18, they never tried to reconnect us to our Country. We've been denied our own people because no way in the world were they going to help us to get back. But in the last 10 years, they put in this thing called Link-Up service, a way to reconnect us to Country and to our people, the Stolen Generations run that. And Raelene actually runs the Link-Up service for NT Stolen Generations in Darwin. People have been reconnecting with Country, but a lot of them have found that their mothers and their old people have died. It's hard to reconnect, but at least they meet up with some of their family. But what's the point now – because we're all adults, but we were removed as children, and they never helped us reconnect when we were younger. In all that time, Native Affairs and that system never ever tried to reconnect us with our people.

We had to find our own way to reconnect, and many of us didn't have that capacity. The older children didn't get back in time to meet their mothers. Others didn't feel they could. A lot of them felt it wouldn't work because of the way they changed their lives. When I asked some of the older ones why they didn't want to go back, they said, 'Because they won't want us.' I think they were frightened they'd be denied their right when they went back to Country and to their people. I never felt that because Jack McKay made sure I knew about my mother, and because I actually went and saw my mum when I was 19. A lot of the older people felt that if they went back there, they'd be denied. And they didn't want to feel that. I suppose a lot of us, because we were removed, didn't want to go through something like that again. Being shut out of your family. A lot of the old mothers never forgot us. They remembered who we were, and it was up to us to try and get back there, because the government never in all their years tried to help us to do that. They took us out of our Country, away from our mothers, away from our people, but they never, ever tried to help us go back. And that's the saddest part about the removal policy. What was the purpose of us being removed? They say it was to educate us and to assimilate us. But did it really do that? I don't think so. In many instances it made our people go the wrong way because they lost hope. If I didn't have that hope, I think I'd be there too. But I always had hope, Lorraine instilled that in us, that we could reunite with our family and our people without feeling lost and gone forever. And Dad Randall was always encouraging that, he wanted all of us Croker people to be able to go back to Country to see our people, to meet our mothers again. Yes, they grew us up in the white system, but that doesn't mean you're not Aboriginal anymore. You're still Aboriginal and your people are still there. But if you wanted to do that, you had to do it on your own. That's what my husband and I did, but a lot of the others sort of lost hope and just lost the will to do it.

Like Hal. He's one of the boys that grew up with me on Croker and then they sent him down to Adelaide when Lorky went with that group of kids. Hal ended up living in Adelaide and running a farm out at Victor Harbor. So he's lived most of his life down there and came back when he was 60, back to the Territory. And he said, 'You know what, Eileen. My mother didn't even really know me.' He said it was a really strange reunion with his mother. He said, 'I felt really hurt.' Whereas I never had that. Yeah, my mum didn't talk much, but I could see that my mother loved me and I could see that my people loved me. But with Hal's mother, it was like, 'Who are you?' Like he wasn't her son anymore. That's how he felt, he said.

It was really sad. When he first went down to Pine Creek to see her he said it was like meeting a stranger, 'She didn't even make me feel like I was wanted. It was the strangest experience I've ever had, Eileen.' I felt sorry for him. So often when he's talking about Stolen Gen, he gets really upset. I think that's the way many of us feel not being reconnected to our mothers and our people, we feel hurt and loneliness.

So myself and Lorraine and Rita, Tarni and a lot of people from my Croker Island mob, we all went back to Country. The mob that I related to most closely were the people that actually went back to Country. Lorky, every year without fail, as soon as the kids got old enough, she'd travel to the Territory, stay at Barunga with the people and visit Beswick. She'd stay in Katherine with her sister and then come back to Darwin to spend time with Rita, Tarni and me. She'd do it every year, Lorky. One day, she said, 'You know what, Eileen, for the first time in my life, you know that big black hole we always had there.' This is what she called it, a big black hole. She said, 'Once I came back to Country and saw everybody again, that big hole closed.' That's how she explained it to me. That we'd lost everything and all we had was a big black hole. We didn't have our mothers, we didn't have our family, we didn't have language, we didn't have Country, we didn't have anything.

But I was fortunate enough to go back to Country and meet my mother. And not many Stolen Generations people have had that opportunity. Some of the people used to say, 'Eileen, but you are lucky,' but it's not luck. I went out and did that because I wanted to reconnect with Mum and all my people. And my family never forgot me, they didn't want to forget me, they didn't want to leave me out of the family circle. My mother and my family made sure the reconnection did happen. That's why my grandchildren and my children are enriched. What I'd missed out on as a child, my brothers and family reinstated in my children and my grandchildren.

That's why I'd like to tell my story, to show people that even though we were disconnected as children from our family, our mothers, our Country and our culture, there is a way of reconnecting.

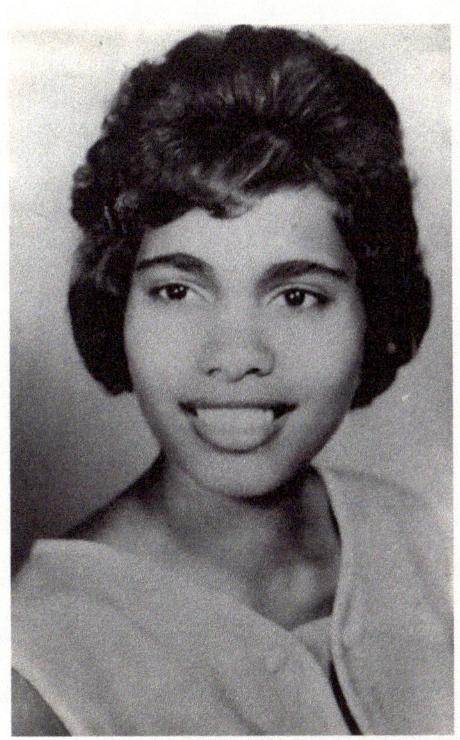

Left: 4.1 Eileen Cummings, c. 1960

Above: 4.2 Darwin High School softball team, 1960 (*Darwin Highschool Magazine* 1960)

Bottom: 4.3 Eileen Cummings, pre-school teaching in Brisbane, c. 1961

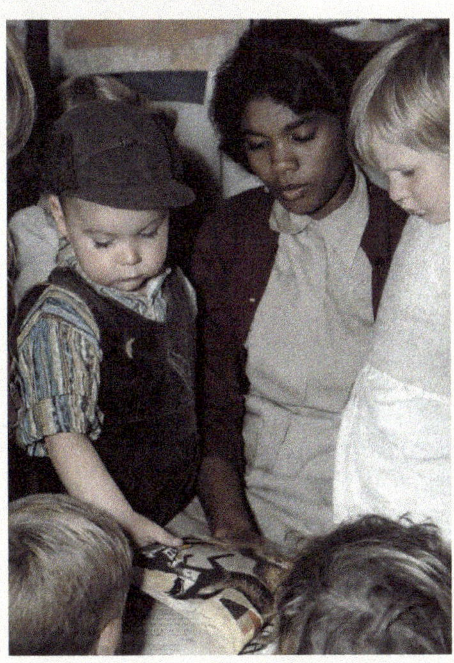

Right: 4.4 Newspaper article about Eileen, with photo of Eileen Cummings (Smith) and Gail Peters, 1964

Below left: 4.5 Raelene at the kindergarden–nursery in Adelaide

Below right: 4.6 Raelene and Michelle as children

Above: 5.1 Florrie Lindsay with Eileen Cummings' brothers, Ronnie and Rex, and other family members

Left: 5.2 Ronnie Lindsay

Below: 5.3 Eileen Cummings, Mai Katona and Mai Govan

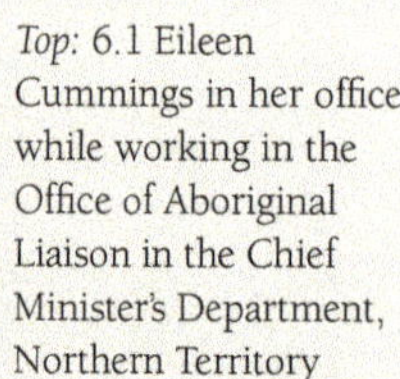

Top: 6.1 Eileen Cummings in her office while working in the Office of Aboriginal Liaison in the Chief Minister's Department, Northern Territory

Middle: 6.2 Eileen Cummings at a meeting of the Northern Territory Office of Women's Policy, 1980s

Below left: 6.3 Eileen Cummings with her grandchildren Grace and Shania and Chief Minister Shane Stone

Below right:
6.4 Eileen Cummings representing the Office of Women's Policy at the International Women's Conference, New Zealand, 1990s

Above: 6.5 Eileen Cummings and the NT representative group at a national Women's Forum in Adelaide, 1990s

Below: 6.6 Eileen Cummings speaking at the 2nd National Child Protection forum, Darwin, 2019

Above: 7.1 Stolen Generations Memorial, Darwin Botanic Gardens. The memorial was dedicated in 2005

Below: 7.2 Women from the NT Stolen Generations Aboriginal Corporation viewing Harold Thomas' painting, ***Tribal Abduction***

Top: 7.3 Eileen Cummings with Senator Malarndirri McCarthy, Darwin, NAIDOC Ball, Darwin, 2018

Above: 7.4 Tenth Anniversary of the National Apology, 2018

Above: 8.1 Eileen Cummings doing a NT Stolen Generation Corporation presentation for the Flinders University Northern Territory Medical Program, 2017

Left: 8.2 Eileen Cummings at the ceremony for her honorary doctorate at Charles Darwin University, with her daughters Raelene and Sheena, niece Melissa and granddaughter Grace, 2023

6

Working in the Northern Territory Government

In 1975, after Cyclone Tracy, I put in for a job in Aboriginal Adult Education in the Education Department. They advertised the position, Aboriginal liaison with Education, and I got the position, and then this bloke appealed it. He was a white fella and he kicked up a stink. He said he'd been working in Aboriginal Affairs for 10 years, or something, and I had never worked out in remote communities. He said I wasn't experienced, had never worked for the government before, so why should I get the job? But, of course, he didn't mean that. I think he meant because I was black. That's the point of it. I was a black woman and how could I have the education to do what he'd been doing for the last 10 years?

So this public servant said to me, 'Eileen, you got to fight. I know you don't like fighting, but you got to fight for this position.'

And I said, 'Why? If I don't get it, I don't get it.' That's how I looked at it.

'We want you in that position,' he said, 'so you've got to fight for it. You've got to come up with a fighting strategy. Or just tell them why you think you should have the job.' When we got to the meeting I explained why I wanted the job. I said, 'Well, for one, I'm Aboriginal. This position is for an Aboriginal person. I've been in the system since I was born, in the Aboriginal Affairs system. Maybe I haven't lived at the remote communities, but I'm from a remote community, and

I go back there all the time to see my mother and my people. I've got family there.' And I said, 'Who's better equipped to work with her own people?' That's all I said, I didn't really want to carry on about it, because we've never been brought up to push ourselves forward; that's not the Aboriginal way. Anyway, I got the job and I was happy.

I found the job very exciting, teaching adult education. I was based in the Bagot Adult Education Centre and, once a week, my colleague and I would go out to Belyuen community near Mandora across the bay from Darwin. I used to take a Telstra boat across the harbour, before they started the ferry service, because Telstra had all the poles and things over there in Cox Peninsula, and they had to go back there every day to look after them and see if they were working. We'd spend the day there at the health clinic working with the health workers. We would do classes with the health workers in literacy and numeracy at both health clinics, in Bagot and Belyuen. You couldn't take all the health workers away at the same time, so you'd have two or three in the classes and somebody else was on duty. We were up skilling them in their jobs, improving literacy to make sure they could read properly, because you have to look at medications and all of that as health workers. We were working with the council[36] as well because they had to be equipped to read and understand all things under the local government. I had to do some training to get into that area. I did a Diploma in Adult Education and Community Services at Darwin Community College so I could work in adult education with my people. I was a teacher by profession, but a preschool teacher, not an adult educator.

We had women's groups there, too, at Bagot and Belyuen. They used to come and do arts and crafts. I also taught out at Humpty Doo community. I taught them screen-printing, all that sort of stuff. We had good fun and talked about all the issues while doing the arts and crafts. Then some of the women said, 'We want to know how to manage money.' We started to work on finance management, and when they went shopping, what sort of groceries they're going to get and what is healthy and good for the family. We had a big shop at Bagot, on the community, but the women said, 'No, it is too costly here.' What used to kill them was the meat, because the meat cost quite a bit in the stores on the communities, even though they tried to eat less. I said, 'So where are you going to go? To Woollies? Or to Coles?' So they were learning about stores, they could see that it was cheaper and they could get stuff from there. They were happy with that. That was part of the adult education program, giving people the skills and confidence to do things outside of the community.

Whenever they wanted something done, we'd try and fit it into the adult education program. We taught the parents about the school environment because although they'd send the children to school, they often avoided contact with the school. They would say, 'We don't want to go talk to them munanga.' They only had the preschool at Bagot, but after that the kids went to school outside the community, to Ludmilla Primary and then to high schools. Some of the people would say, 'Oh, we never went to school for that long and school's not really important to us.' I would say, 'Well, how do you think they're going to live in this world? It's important that the children get that schooling; the children need your support. You can't expect them to go to school and you have nothing to do with that school.'

I had experienced that myself, it was the only time I got upset about racism. Raelene was at Ludmilla Primary School and she was doing something in the library. Raelene's fairer than my other two girls, because she doesn't belong to Raymond. But he grew her up from a baby, from a two-year-old. A teacher got really angry with Raelene and hit her. She might've been in one of those moods and she just slapped her.

So Raelene ran out of the room. The liaison officer rang and said, 'Eileen, I think you better come and get Raelene. She's quite upset.' I asked Raelene, 'Were you giving Ms so and so cheek?' She said, 'No, Mummy, I didn't. I was stacking books and she told me to go and sit down,' and Raelene looked at her and then the teacher hit her. She was an older teacher and maybe she had enough of all the children that day, but she had no right to hit her. So Raymond went and saw the principal and the teacher and he said to the teacher, 'I want you to apologise to my daughter because she did nothing to you. You had no right to hit her.' I think they were a bit tough with the Aboriginal kids, you know, they would sometimes get treated differently. I don't think the teacher would have hit her if Raelene was a white girl.

So I went to all their teacher and parent nights. I made sure I went to those, because a lot of our parents wouldn't go. I encouraged the Bagot women to go too, to Ludmilla, and I'd go with them. I'd say, 'If you don't front up, they'll think you're not interested in your kids.' So we took the women up to Ludmilla Primary School for parent and teacher night, we started that through the adult education program. Our people didn't like going to those sort of things, it made them uncomfortable, but my colleague Joy and I talked the women into it. Some of the fathers came, too, because we said, 'You've got to hear what they say at these meetings.'

I worked for a while with Education, going to remote communities and working with the people there, and then I started to train our own people so we had Aboriginal adult educators in the communities rather than people coming in all the time to do the teaching. We set up a course at Batchelor College[37] so they could train as adult educators. I helped to establish the Adult Educator course, and the Early Childhood course at Batchelor College for our remote students. A woman called Joy was working with us, and she went to Batchelor

College. She became our first trained Aboriginal adult educator and she ran the adult education program in Bagot. When we set up the Batchelor College training, we got people from different places, different communities, coming into the college to train as adult educators. But Joy was the first one, in the 80s. I was there as a mentor and trainer as they did on-the-job training and attended lectures at Batchelor College, and it was a good learning curve for me as well.

In the communities I learned how I could work with my own people again, how you communicate with them, the way you do things so that it wasn't coming from the white system. Because they brought me up in a white system, I didn't really know enough about my people and I had to learn through the people I worked with – and the women were the backbone of that, the women in the communities. Working at Bagot and Belyuen with Joy, and all the women there, it taught me how to approach my people. If I hadn't had that, I don't think I would've got very far. A lot of people I know go back into their communities and because they've been educated, they think they can just take over. I had to learn the right way to do it. Joy and the women at Bagot taught me: 'You sit and listen, Eileen, and when they want you to talk, they'll let you know.' It was two-way learning. If I hadn't had that, I wouldn't have been able, later, to go to all the communities around the Territory and work with them. I knew when to listen and when to talk. You can't just come in spouting off and saying what you want to say. Lots of time I wanted to do that. I needed to understand where they were coming from so we could ensure that programs were the right ones for each community.

I was with Education for around five years, and then a job came up in the Chief Minister's Department. They wanted a liaison officer in the Office of Aboriginal Affairs. That was in '79. So I put in for that job, got the job, moved to Chief

Minister's and stayed with them forever, except for one stint at Conservation. Through that time, I worked with a lot of the chief ministers. I started under Paul Everingham, then Ian Tuxworth, Steve Hatton, Marshall Perron, Shane Stone, Denis Burke, and briefly with Claire Martin. She'd only just started when I decided to retire. I had good relationships with all of them. Most of those ministers were under the Liberal government, because they were there for 26 years.

When I started, I was in the Aboriginal Affairs and Land Claim Unit. Sometimes I went to the land claim hearings with the department. I'd go out with the officers to sit with the people to talk about the land claims they had. But most times, my work was in community liaison. We had to look at development in communities,[38] to make sure they were working well with government workers, because we had Health and Education out on the communities all the time. We had local government going to look at the councils, because in the old times, the councils were run by the community. They didn't have other people coming in, they had their own community council, and they ran the communities themselves.[39] I really loved that work, talking and liaising with my people and government. I was giving policy advice to chief ministers, but I was doing liaison as well. I had to visit communities to liaise, see that the health and education facilities the government put on the communities were working, and assist with their problem solving. I did that a lot, translate information from the government back into the Aboriginal context so they could understand what it was about.

An example of my work as a liaison officer was when the Retta Dixon home survivors found out that the land in Darwin they once lived on as children was to be called Queen Elizabeth Park. I was confronted by angry past residents who said, 'Why should the park be named after the Queen? That was where our home was, why would you want to put Elizabeth's name on it?' Marshall[40] sent me out to see them. They said they want to meet with the Chief Minister, so I requested a meeting and brought the people in to meet him, there were about six of them. They said they felt the name was not suitable. They questioned what the Queen did for them when the removal policy of Aboriginal children was in place from the early 1900s to 1967. They wanted to give the park an Aboriginal name. They explained to Marshall that 'karu' was an Aboriginal word meaning child and so they wanted it to be named Karu Park. Marshall listened and said he would pass their selected name onto the board that decided names. It was a good meeting and the group left feeling happy they had been heard. The park remains Karu Park to this day; where Karu is now, that is where the old Retta Dixon home was sitting.

On another occasion, Marshall said to me, 'Eileen, I want you to go and talk to your mob about gambling.' Our Aboriginal people were openly playing cards down at Mindal beach where tourist visited, and he was getting complaints. Marshall wanted me to find out where they wanted to sit; they were going to have one place to go to, not gambling everywhere, and not in public. He was prepared to put them somewhere where they were comfortable, and he wasn't trying to stop them from playing cards. So I went down to see them, there were about 20 people there, but they weren't from one Country, they were from everywhere. From Tiwi, Larrakia, all the different tribes. I sat with them and informed them about the complaint and asked their thoughts. I said, 'You mob not supposed to be gambling here.' They reckon, 'Well, we're not doing anything wrong, we're just sitting and gambling.' I said, 'But gambling's illegal.' That's how I was, just talked to them straight out. They explained to me that this was a way to sit and socialise away from their homes and alcohol. They had their own rules within that group, like no alcohol, drunks or violence. If anybody was drunk and came to the groups, they'd send them away. They had their own system in place, it was marvellous, and they had two people – a male and a female – to ensure the rules were followed. These were people with a strong status in their own community as well as here in Darwin; in other words, the two people had been selected because they were senior in men's and women's business. As far as I could see, the rules were always listened to, so the group really was no trouble. They were happy to move if I had an alternative, and we ended up at the old Fannie Bay oval near bush land. They had toilets there, they had water from a tap, whatever they needed. A van brought food to purchase. And Marshall never sent out the police. He told his police to stop going and harassing them. When I reported to him, he knew both senior Elders and was satisfied with the outcome. This was the beginning of a new way forward for my people, being part of discussions and responses to their well-being.

We also had a media and video unit in Aboriginal Affairs. It doesn't exist anymore, but back then it did all the videos for our media outlet. We called it the video magazine. We'd go to communities, recording community programs and development, and I had some wonderful trips to remote regions in the Northern Territory. We ended up having about 20 videos, and copies were given to the communities to be viewed in their school libraries. On occasion we attended land claims and videoed these events. Often we would be on the land claim site for a week, camping or staying in community visitors' accommodation.

I really liked the senior staff at the media unit, and we had a few young Aboriginal guys training in film and video recording. Young Steven McGregor worked on the cameras and now he produces his own films. If you ever saw *Sweet Country*, he produced that. So we had him, and Mango – we used to call him Mango – Richard Anderson. He ended up with the ABC and worked there for a long time. I knew somebody who worked at the ABC and he said, 'Eileen, I'm looking for a young person to come and work for us.' At the ABC, Richard filmed the football, and a few stories on Aboriginal people. So the media unit provided training and I am proud to say the men did really well after they completed their training.

When Tina Turner came up here, she came into our office and we filmed her with our people. She came to sing at the NRL Grand Final in Sydney in 1993. We asked her if she was interested in coming to the Territory, and she jumped at it. I loved her; she was really down to earth. She got beaten by her husband all her life, it was terrible, so she understood what we were trying to do on the communities with violence. She travelled with a film crew to the communities, and she loved it. She overcame the beatings. She became her own person, her own manager, she did everything herself in the end. She raised her sons by herself. It was good for our people to see somebody else, from another country, in our films. The other film we used was *Once Were Warriors*, a film about family violence in New Zealand. It was really sad, but we used that a lot because the people wanted to see it. So whenever they asked for that film, we would show them.

Out of all the chief ministers I worked for, Marshall Perron was my favourite. He understood me and my people. He felt it was time the Aboriginal voice was heard. It was a new way of working with him, with the government, to give Aboriginal people the opportunity to speak on their issues and develop programs for the health and well-being of their communities. It was to work in partnership: whatever strategies were developed for the community, our people will be participating at all levels to ensure the programs were by the people, for the people. Not the government putting programs in communities that they planned and developed because they thought they knew best. He had the vision to do that, he and his government, and that's why he later pulled me into the Office of Women's Policy. Later he allowed me to go to Conservation to help the management committees at the parks, because he wanted the Traditional Owners involved. He wanted all Territorians to have a voice and be listened to. Marshall Perron knew that if we could hear from the people, he'd know where to best put the funds and the best way they could be used. I think I had a little to do with that, because I was always saying that to him: 'You have to listen to the people.' Not many politicians think that way. I loved working with him. I felt privileged to be part of this new way of thinking and working with my people and communities. That's when we started to make things happen, when Aboriginal people's voices were being heard.

I think he was like that because he was a Territorian. He's born and bred up here. He knew all lot of the Aboriginal mob because he went to Darwin High School with some of us. He knew what our people have gone through all our lives because he'd been raised with us. I remember one meeting with our mob. 'Hello, Chief Minister', all nice and calm. Then we'd get into the discussions and they'd say, 'Now, Marshall, you have to listen!' And he'd say, 'Roseanne, I'm listening.' But they'd argue and fight with him and carry on. It was because they knew him from school, they tended to forget he was now the chief, the head of government. I liked Marshall, I liked working with him. He allowed me freedom to do things. And we used to have some really good laughs, me and him.

Marshall Perron moved me to the Office of Women's Policy, which was part of the Chief Minister's Department. He brought me in to make sure that Aboriginal women's voices were heard. I had to go and meet women in remote communities and bring back whatever they wanted to be said to him and his government. He had an inkling that the old system wasn't working because he said, 'How come we are not hearing what the women are saying?' We had local government going out to communities all the time to look at the councils. The councils had men *and* women on them, because you've got a law in the women's business as well as the men's business. But it was only men coming to the meetings with the government workers. I said to Marshall, 'You're sending white men out there, the officers are all white men. You've got no women, black or white, going out to the communities. The women are not going to talk to the men. So you got to change your system. You have to have women workers, particularly Aboriginal workers.' Marshall wanted to know women's issues, how to work with them in partnership, how to develop programs with them for their communities.

Every time I went to the remote communities, it was for a week. I said to Marshall and the other chief ministers, 'I'm not just popping in one day and popping out again like all the other government workers do. That's not my kind of talking with my people. I need more time.' The first day was about giving them the information. On the second day, we would go over that again and I would ask how they felt about it all. On the third day we would start to plan. So you kind of had to go for 4 or 5 days to get the full picture from the community. It was good that the government and the communities allowed me to do that.

On several visits I attended women's law gatherings where I shared some great moments with the Elders in ceremony and discussions. At such events, the Elders taught women's culture and responsibilities to their groups, what women's rights were and how to seek assistance under women's business. The Elders told stories and enacted role-plays of women in crisis, and how to resolve incidents affecting women. They taught women's lore. The role-plays were powerful and exciting and full of laughter. Other occasions we sat on the riverbanks and discussed their concerns; their feelings about the violence, the excess of alcohol and how to develop programs to assist women, families and communities. Women were the backbone of these communities.

This work was really exciting for me; I never tired of working with our women, especially the Elders of the Territory. They shared so much knowledge, and showed strength and resilience. I had lost so much about my Aboriginal life due to the removal policy, and this was a great opportunity for me to learn and share with my women. Wider Australia didn't see what these wonderful women were doing in remote Australia for years. My job was to bring this to the government, to make sure our women's voices were heard and listened to through my reports and evaluations of their programs. In Aboriginal society, both men's business and women's business play an integral part in their communities and cannot be ignored, especially when working, talking and developing programs for the communities. It was a big job, but the women I had working with me made it quite easy because they supported and directed me.

After Marshall built up the public service to work better with Aboriginal women, more women came out to the communities. For example, Centrelink had used all men before, and that didn't work well with our women. Some of the women started to work in the health system as health workers. We even started to get women interested in being part of the councils. I supported women to understand that they could be councillors and how to become one, so they had a voice in decision-making on their communities. Women applied to be on women's councils, education councils and their local government councils. They had a voice and were being heard.

I also encouraged them to come into the Office of Women's Policy. I was trying to get our women involved in the Women's Advisory Board. By the time I'd finished with Women's Policy, I had Aboriginal women as members of the Women's Board.

We had a woman from Katherine, we had a woman from Yirrkala, I think we had a woman from Maningrida. All the different places: Groote Eylandt, Lajamanu, Yuendemu. Joy came from Bagot. This process opened their eyes to how government works and showed them how to be involved. Marshall wanted me to set up a system that could be passed down to other workers within the communities.

When working in the Chief Minister's Office of Women's Policy, I attended many conferences on women's affairs – local, interstate, national and worldwide – presenting papers on community issues and our women's responses in the Northern Territory. Remember how, as a child on Croker, I wanted to see the world? How we'd sit there in school and spin that globe around and point to different countries. When I started working for the Chief Minister, I got the opportunity to visit all these countries. To go to the international women's conference[41] in Beijing with 5000 women from all over the world was the most exciting thing I've ever done. To see them, all the Indigenous people dressed in their traditional clothes, was just amazing. We had about 300 Australian women and about 30 Aboriginal women, and I was the NT government's representative. What a sight, all these women dressed in their traditional dress speaking about their issues and concerns. I made many lifelong friends and exchanged information about the work we're all doing, programs working with our women on social issues, health, abuse. Even Hillary Clinton attended; she came to Beijing and spoke. She was really into all these women's issues and the rights of women. But you should have seen all the security around her; you couldn't go anywhere near her because they had so much security. And why? We women were too busy meeting each other to attack her. It was just so wonderful to meet all the other women from other countries, and the ambassador for Australia invited us, all the Australians, back to his residence.

That was the first international conference I attended. The next one was in New Zealand. I went to New Zealand three times, I think, on behalf of the Chief Minister's Office of Women's Policy. We went back to the Maori women's traditional houses. We went back to their meeting places, the wharenui, and they gave us the biggest feast and performed the *haka* for us. This was special to me. I attended similar conferences in America, talking about Indigenous women's programs and community development. All these conferences were educational and fulfilling. State conferences also gave me an insight into programs and projects in the remote communities of the Territory. Then going back to my own Elders' law gatherings, we had some wonderful times there too. Listening and learning from my women Elders at these gatherings showed me the importance of our women and their family connections and women's business. I will cherish this for the rest of my life. There was a lot of laughter, tears and great enjoyment. I was fortunate to be part of this. Working with my people brought me so much joy, and love of my Aboriginal heritage. Conferences allowed us to discuss women's concerns and plan and develop programs that were culturally appropriate for our communities.

In the early 90s, I was seconded from the Chief Minister's to NT Conservation Commission. Conservation actually asked. 'We want to set up our boards in conjunction with the Traditional Owners of the land. So can we have Eileen for six months.' In the end, I was there for two years, until Marshall rang and said, 'I want Eileen back!' Conservation wanted to set up joint management committees on the parks so Traditional Owners had a say in decision-making. I had to set up boards that incorporated the Traditional Owners and Conservation to ensure Traditional Owners had a say in the running of the parks on their lands. I had to meet the Traditional Owners, talk and plan with them, and develop a joint committee. We held regular meetings to discuss any concerns and develop a plan about parks endorsed by both parties. This was a new approach and it wasn't always easy. I spent many challenging hours working with Conservation and Traditional Owners, travelling with Conservation to the parks and the communities. I was encouraging the women to come too, so they were developing and attending meetings with me, and they became part of the management committees.

We did one big trip with Traditional Owners, because Nitmiluk (Katherine Gorge Park) had to decide whether they wanted to go under the federal Parks and Wildlife or stay under NT Conservation. The real push came from the Nitmiluk mob. They were feeling left out; Conservation was running the park, and they wanted more control. Should they move to National Parks? The Nitmiluk mob said, 'Well, how are we supposed to make a choice? We don't know anything. We only know NT Conservation. We don't know anything about National Parks.' They're the Jawoyn people, the Traditional Owners of that Country. To assist the Jawoyn to make a decision, we decided to take them to see how the parks in the Territory were managed, the Northern Land Council, NT Conservation, six Jawoyn Elders and myself, we made the trip. We went to Cobourg, Kakadu, Keep River, back to Darwin. Then we went to Yulara for them to look at Uluru. They were trying to make up their mind, whether they wanted to stay with NT Conservation or go national. We met and talked with the Traditional Owners and the parks staff and observed the management. At Cobourg Park, the rangers took us out to do some fishing. Some of the Jawoyn people had never been on the sea.

When we went to Uluru, the Jawoyn men stayed at Mutitjulu, the community there. But it wasn't right for me to stay with the men. So I stayed in town, in Yulara, with the rest of the staff. One day, the woman from NLC, she came running out and said, 'Eileen, you got to talk to the men. They've gone off drinking and they're not supposed to be drinking. We brought them down here for a special reason, so they shouldn't be drinking.'

I replied, 'And you expect me to go there and tell them that? I'm only a little kid to them. These old men will tell me where to go.' But of course I did talk to them, I talked to them quietly and said, 'What you mob did last night?'

'Oh, you know what, we had a couple of drinks.'

I said, 'Were you silly?'

'No, we just had a few drinks.'

'Did you give it to anybody else?'

'No, we just sat here and drank ourselves.' They didn't drink at Mutitjulu, they drank in Yulara and then went home.

I said, 'So what happened when you got home?'

'Oh, we've been too buggered, we went to sleep.' That's all they said. It was like having a drink after work, but that non-Indigenous woman felt they shouldn't.

On another day, one of the old men reckoned, 'Eileen, we want to go and look at the rock,' Uluru. I said, 'Okay, we'll go and have a look at it.' That same worker, she was trying to growl at the men and tell them they couldn't go to the rock. But they weren't going to climb it; they just wanted to have a look. She was going on and carrying on and she was screaming at them old men. I said, 'What's going on?' and the old men reckoned, 'That munanga trying to tell us what we are going to do.' I said to the worker, 'You don't speak like that to these men. They're senior men. They're ceremonial men. You can't talk to them like that. They want to go and look. They're not going to climb it. They know what a sacred site is.' In the end, the Conservation mob from there took us up in the helicopter to show us the rock from the top. The men were happy about that because they could see down on the top of the rock. So in the end, we had a really good trip.

Kakadu and Yulara were under National Parks and Keep River and Cobourg were under NT Conservation. I had actually helped the Traditional Owners establish the co-management board at Keep River, under Conservation. National Conservation had a lot more money, so I was saying to them, 'Maybe if you went under them, they could do a lot for you.' But when I took them down to Mutitjulu and Kakadu, the Nitmiluk mob weren't impressed. At Mutitjulu, you have to pay a lot of money to get in. They felt with Mutitjulu that the park gets all that money for the rock and the Aboriginal community's not really that good. It might be better now, but when we went there at the time, the housing and standards weren't good. You could see humpies on the hill. At Kakadu, the places where the Traditional Owners lived looked all right, but also weren't great. The housing is supposed to be provided by the Commonwealth government. The Jawoyn took one look at it and said, 'No.' They didn't like how the Traditional Owners lived. In Cobourg, the houses built by Northern Territory Conservation were much better. The Jawoyn felt the Traditional Owners were better cared for by NT Conservation than National Parks so when they came back, they said 'We're not going with them.' They wanted to stay with the NT Conservation Commission. I said, 'Well don't tell me! You have to talk to your mob. When we have that big meeting with Conservation, then you say what you really want for your park.'

In the end, the Nitmiluk set up houses at Werenbun near Edith Falls, which were very comfortable. The other one was Gorge Camp, set up just five to 10 minutes from Nitmiluk, so the Traditional Owners could live there. It wouldn't be on the park as such, but close enough. They still had access to the park and were still part of the park. So that was a good decision. I was so fortunate to have experienced so many ways the NT government liaised and worked with Aboriginal

Territorians in so many fields and departments. To my knowledge the management committees are still functioning at the NT Parks.

After the stint at Conservation, Marshall pulled me back into the Chief Minister's Department to run the domestic violence unit. This was in the mid-90s. He wanted me there to liaise and work with the women, because he wanted it to be by Aboriginal people, for Aboriginal people, so it would benefit them and their communities. That's how we developed the Aboriginal Family Violence strategy. I was working in that area and directly with the Chief Minister. He had that vision, and I could talk to him about anything. If I didn't agree with something, he'd listen. Like, when he said, 'Eileen, I'll give you six months to go around and do the family violence strategy.' I said, 'Oh, don't be funny. You want me to go around the whole of the Northern Territory? That won't take six months, it'll take two years.' 'Well, however you want to do it,' he said. When you think about the Northern Territory and how many communities I had to visit, right around the Territory from the top to the bottom, that was a fair distance to travel.

I went all over the Territory, to every community: Alice Springs, Ntaria, Yuendumu, Lajamanu, Docker River, Areyonga, Utopia, Papunya, Borroloola, Barunga, Yirrkala, Bagot, Belyuen and East Arnhem, the Barkly region, and Ali Curung. I wrote to the councils, because in those days the council ran the show and the women had their own groups. So I'd write to them, tell them what I'm coming for, and how long. Then I'd go and spend a week in each community. We drove out there in these Landcruisers. One time Margaret and I were going out to Numbulwar, that's 20 km from Ngukurr. We had to cross the main river before the community, which was a little frightening as I had to drive across a floating pontoon to get to the other side of the river. We had a satellite phone. I was to ring in every morning and every night so the department knew where I was and that I was okay. Then at every community, the police station knew where I was. So if the Chief Minister wanted me, they'd ring the police station and say, 'Can you find Eileen? Where is she?' and they'd come and find me. I worked closely with the police because they were trying to do all this family violence stuff as well. They had offices in their department working in family violence in those days. Often I did these trips to the remote communities, but it didn't faze me. I loved travelling.

The policy was to be for Aboriginal people from Aboriginal people so in the communities I'd sit with them, run workshops, get their views on how they wanted it. The strategy was theirs, the first time they ever did that with government. When I ran the workshops, I normally took a male and female Aboriginal staff member with me from our unit. I didn't have any white staff with me. We'd get them together on the first day, explain it to them as a group. Then I would say, 'Well, the government wants me to write a strategy for family violence for you mob, but it has to come from you. I'm going to sit with the women now. Jerry, one of the male staff and one of the health workers will sit down with the men and we'll talk to the children later, but we're going to do this now with the women.' So we'd sit and talk to them and find out what the issues were in their community. I'd explain what the government wanted to do; and how do you feel; and how do you want to deal with this in your community? They'd tell me, and we'd write it up on big whiteboards and put down everything they wanted. We talked separately with each of the groups, the women, the men, the Elders, and the children and young people – because the major concern in the communities at that time was the children. Everything was around those children. If we don't fix it, who are we going to have here to lead this community? Because we can't help our children if we can't help ourselves.

During the last two days, we'd bring them all together and we'd say, 'This is what the women spoke about.' I would get one of the women to come up, help to present. 'This is what the men spoke about,' and get the men to talk about it. Then we'd get one of the two Elders, man and woman, to come out to talk for the Elders. We'd have young people talk about their issues and how they were going to try and make it better for the community. Then we'd talk about all the things they raised and how they would like the information given to the government. We'd bring them all together so they could hear what they'd said. Nothing was hidden. We'd write it all down so they could see what each group wanted for the community.

The first time I went out there, I took the green domestic violence folder, which is done by the government. When I got to Papunya, one old girl reckon, 'We don't understand that one. Chuck it out!'

I said, 'I can't chuck it out. But we could write one that suits you and your community. I'm showing you what the government has done. Now it's our turn to tell the government what we want.'

She said, 'Oh, okay. Because we don't want to use that. That's not ours.' That was the white system in there. Nothing to do with Aboriginal people.

'Well, I know it isn't,' I said. 'Reason I'm here to help you do your own. We are going to develop something that comes from you and from the community so it's yours.' All the old girls thought that was funny. We had a good laugh and went to work.

The heading on the folder was 'Domestic violence', and the women said, 'We don't know what that is.'

I said, 'Well, when you get beaten up by your husband, what's that?'

'Oh, that family violence. It's between us, the family. We don't know what that domestic violence is.' That's how they looked at it, and that's the term we ended up using, family violence, because it came from the communities. The white system was saying 'domestic violence' and our communities were saying, 'What's that?' and I said, 'Well, you mob fighting.' It might be between sisters, or two wives, sometimes two wives would fight over their husband, so it was all family violence. That's why I introduced that to the National Domestic Violence Unit, but it came from here, from the Aboriginal women of the Territory.

We had really good workshops all around the Territory. I drove to just about every community in the Territory and we'd have these discussions. In every community, I found a real strong women's group, but they had never participated in anything before because they didn't want to talk to the male staff that was coming out. Our approach was different. We changed it to suit the community. We sat on the riverbanks and discussed their concerns, their feelings about the violence and excess of alcohol and how to develop programs to assist women, families and communities. Women were in the front line talking about their issues and how to improve the life and health of their women, families and communities. They marched against alcohol abuse and violence.

They were tired, the women were tired of being beaten. They said a lot of it was alcohol, because the man would come home drunk and want to fight them for more money to go and drink. And the women wouldn't give it to them. So the violence became part of their lives. They had to fight because they wanted the money to feed their kids. It was a no-win situation for them. Many women got beaten anyway, even though they ended up giving the men money, they still got beaten. It was a really violent situation, that's why they marched through Alice Springs, to say they wanted alcohol banned on their communities because of the violence.

It was the women who made that family violence strategy

possible, but I always had support from the men in the communities. One Elder at Ntaria said to me, 'Eileen, we just letting the women do it. That woman's business.'

I said, 'And where do you think the problem comes from?' and he looked at me and he said, 'The men.'

I said, 'Yeah. So what, do you just want the women to do this all on their own?'

He looked at me, 'Oh you cheeky girl,' he reckoned. We sat there with the council and told them what we were trying to do. Then he gave us the go ahead. So where difficult situations came up, I was able to smooth it over a bit. I was able to talk to the men like I talked to the women, not with disrespect – but no nonsense. We met with the women, then we got some of the health workers from Ntaria, men, to set up the men's groups as well. I had a couple of staff, male staff from town that came with me, couldn't speak a word of language, but it didn't matter because we had an interpreter there, one of the health workers talked in language. This was the first time I had this acknowledged by one of our leaders in the community, that family violence affects us all. I was overjoyed because now the message was getting to everyone. Our communities, both men and women, were working so hard to make things better and were willing to work with us.

When I got back, I wrote it all up as a strategy to address domestic violence, or family violence. Then before it became the strategy for the government, I took it back to them, to the communities, and I said, 'This is what I've written up now. This is the new strategy that we're going to use and this came from you mob, so I want you to look at it now and tell me if it's okay and whether we should change it or whatever.' We'd workshop that to make sure it was the right thing coming from their communities. They were all happy with it, the family violence strategy that I developed. So they were part of the process from the beginning, from the time I started to the finished product. I went back to Chief Minister Marshall and he was happy with it. Then I went ahead and finalised the strategy.

People didn't realise, I'd never really talk about my husband and his violence when under the influence of alcohol. When we were first together, Ray and I, we were all right and the kids were all right. He loved Raelene, she was his daughter as far as he was concerned. Then we had Shelly and Sheena, and we all grew up quite well. I was doing private childcare at home and Ray worked for Transport and Works, with the government. So those years, they were happy times. The children remember going fishing and swimming every Sunday. When I married Ray, he used to drink weekends sometimes, if he didn't take us out somewhere. But when the children were younger, we used to go camping and fishing. But as the years got on and the kids got into sports and I was taking them to sports all the time, then Ray would work all Saturday, come home and start drinking. Friday, Saturday, he'd go to the pub and play pool with all the fellas. I'd have to go and pick him up from the pub, and I didn't like that at all. But how else was he going to get home? Me and the children would pick him up and bring him home. He'd still be drunk and sometimes go to sleep in the lounge. So I'd roll him onto a blanket and drag him into the room and the kids would help me, they'd help me drag him into the bedroom. Because I didn't want him drunk out in the lounge. I'd drag him on the blanket all the way to the room, but he was quite a heavy man.

I used to run away every weekend, I even taught Raelene how to drive, chucked her in the front seat, told her to take her sisters around the corner, and I'd get out of the house, meet her, and then we'd go to my cousin Rita's[42] place for the weekend to get away from the violence. I was getting her to drive the car when she was about 10, out of the yard and down the road so I could run out to meet her. Raelene, she was the only one who really knew about it because I put the other two girls to sleep and wouldn't let them hear it. But Raelene always heard it and understood. We sort of shielded the other two, I guess. I didn't want my children to see it. When the police came, they would say, 'Well, we can take you to a woman's shelter.' And I said, 'No, I'm okay. I'll drive myself to my cousin's.' I laugh now because Tasha, one of my cousin's children, she used to say, 'Yeah, I remember, Aunty Eileen, when you used to come to our house and the girls would just lie down on the floor with us and watch TV. They'd slip back in like nothing was wrong.' Tasha would say, 'All those years, Aunty Eileen, I thought you were just coming to spend the weekend with us. I used to love my cousins coming to stay with me for the weekend.' Then one day, when Tasha grew up, Rita and I told her what we were doing all that time. My kids knew about it because they used to say, 'Mum, I remember we used to run away to Aunty Rita's every weekend.' And I'd say, 'Yes, and you know why?' So I ended up telling them why and they said, 'Yeah, Dad used to be really nasty.' Children always know, you can't hide things from children – but I thought I was. They remember those parts, but of course that was their dad, and they didn't want to think of him in the worst way. Children don't, do they? Ray would never hurt his children, but he used to hurt me. The kids were a bit upset when I spoke about it, but I said, 'But it's part of our life, darling,' and Raelene would say, 'Yes, I know it's part of our life.' Raelene was aware of it all. So I told them eventually, but I haven't really spoken to them about it.

Eventually, I was ready to leave him and then he ended up getting cancer, that was in 83. After all those years, I was ready to take off and I packed up the house. My children were down at sports; they all represented the Territory. Raelene and Shelly were in Tasmania playing softball. Sheena was playing softball in Queensland. I packed the house up ready to leave, and then we found out he had cancer. What a blow it was to me. I thought, I can't kick a dog when it's down. I have to stay and help him. I felt it was my responsibility, that I had to stay. So I did, I took him down to Adelaide, and he stayed at the Royal Adelaide Hospital and had all those operations. When he came back, I still took care of him because I didn't feel that I had the right to abandon him. Once he got sick, all the violence stopped, didn't it? Once he got sick, I knew he wouldn't be violent again. I was able then to concentrate on my women and the best way forward.

I didn't talk much about it, but I did say it to my workers, to Emma and the others, that my husband was quite violent when he drank. So I had the experience and understanding of women who had been beaten. I grew up with it. It was part of my marriage. That's why I got into the area of family and domestic violence, to help my community because I came from that background. I knew what it was like; it was the alcohol, always the alcohol. A lot of our men have had those issues. When I worked with the women at Bagot on adult education, one of my colleagues had been going through it; she had some horrific experiences. She was a self-assured woman, but still her husband was beating her. Trying to help her and the women was something I felt I had to do. We became real close sisters, and I said, 'Well, do you want to stay with him?' She goes, 'Well, I haven't really got a choice. I've got to go back to Daly River and talk to the women there and the Elders.' When you're married under traditional law, the children have responsibilities under their parents' laws; they're slotted into areas where they have a responsibility. If you took a child away from the father, they'd lose their rights under his laws. So she said, 'But if I go, my children won't have anything.' You cut them off from the lines of the family. And she didn't want them to be cut off. I said, 'So what do you want to do?' She said, 'Well, I've got to go back to Country first to talk to the lore women and men to work it out.' She went home to sit down with them because she didn't want the children to miss out on their lineage, the lines within the tribal structure. They said, 'Yes, you can go for security and safety, the children are fine. We still got them there.' She moved into her own place and she was all right then. She finally left her husband, but she had to do it under traditional law and it took us almost a year, because she had to go back through women's business and the men's business for her to be allowed to leave so the children wouldn't lose their rights under their father.

That's why I felt I'd be a good person to write that strategy, I was able to understand it better coming from the experiences I'd had. It was a motivation to make sure that our women were safe and didn't have to go through that violence. I wanted to be there to help the women so that they could have better lives for themselves and their children.

We had a really good team working in the Chief Minister's Department; I met amazing people through work and made some good friends. There were support people like Ann Ellis and Toni Greenwood. Toni used to be our secretary at the Chief Minister's Office. When she had her baby, she was allowed to bring him into the office days when she didn't have anybody to look after him. As Adam grew up, she told him I was his grandmother. They live in Queensland now, but they came back for holidays a few years back with Adam, now six foot tall. Adam said, 'Oh, I always told everybody, Eileen, that you was my other grandmother, my black grandmother from the Territory.' Lovely people they were.

There were wonderful women in charge of the units I worked in, like Jenni Zeik, Pam Griffith, Emma Williams. Pam worked with me in Women's Policy with the women in remote communities. Mai, my sister Mai, also came to work with family violence. I also had a good working relationship with many NT police officers, like Lorraine Carlon, and a few others. Working in family violence, I had to work with all the agencies to ensure the service understood our community women and their needs. Once a fortnight, Lorraine, Pam, Mai and I would meet up at the Nightcliff cliffs near the jetty and have some laughs and talk about anything and everything happening in our lives. I thoroughly enjoyed those times together. Emma became a good friend of mine. We worked in the family violence area for some years, first in government and then at Charles Darwin University. I spent many happy hours with her and her husband Adam. They live in Perth now, but we still visit each other.

We wrote the Northern Territory Aboriginal Family Violence Strategy. The community program to implement it commenced in 1995 and I became program manager of the Aboriginal Family Violence Program. Emma and I were running all the family violence programs in the communities around the Territory. One big part of it was setting up safe houses in the communities, because the community didn't want their women coming to the towns and cities, like Katherine and Darwin. They wanted them to stay in their community so their families were able to see them. The women felt the same way, and they didn't want their men to go to prison. They wanted to work out programs in the community so their men wouldn't go to prison. The women wouldn't leave the communities. The idea behind the safe houses was to build something there, so the women could feel safe and secure until it was sorted out. It was better for them to be on the community where they could see their families and their children could go to school.

So the safe houses were for families affected by family violence, not so much by sexual abuse, but by family violence. It was safe; nobody could go there. There were police, and the community people did night patrols. Most of the safe houses were a little distance from the community, up near the police station. The one at Ngukurr is near the police station, so the police can just look down; they got high fences. The communities run them and the security is by the night patrols and the police, ensuring everybody's safe.

The women can go there with their babies and young children and stay at the safe house. But there was a certain age, the children had to be small. Teenage children had to stay at home with their grandparents or aunties and uncles. The women who work at the safe houses will talk with the women to plan the best approach to deal with these issues. If the women want to see their husbands, the staff would arrange that. And if the husband was in the men's safe house, it would be worked out between the two groups to find the best way to do it. Because as I said, we've got Aboriginal systems in place where children come under these Aboriginal laws and if they're not under that structure, they lose their identity, they lose their traditional responsibilities. That was one of the biggest reasons our Aboriginal women didn't want to leave, they didn't want to be cut off by the husband's family, and their families, too. The white system couldn't understand that.

When I was working on the National Family Domestic Violence Committee from Canberra, I had to explain to them that our women have a traditional way they do things. They can't just get up and go. They had obligations to their tribal group. Aboriginal women are culturally dependent on not just one person, but the whole tribal group, because it's all interconnected. The kids had their own skin names, they had their own Aboriginal names, but if the mother broke that lineage, that would affect the children. That was their biggest fear, the Aboriginal women. It's changed a bit since then, now some of the Aboriginal women move when they're ready. Back then, traditions were stronger. To ensure the family connections continued, the men in the men's safe houses and the women in the safe houses, they work together with the families to come up with the best solution.

When we started putting up the women's safe houses, the men asked for a place for themselves. The men said, 'How can we change when all you're doing is working for the women?' So I said, 'Well, when I was coming out doing this family violence thing, you didn't talk about that.' They had told me that programs have to be there for men, but they didn't say how they wanted them. When they saw us building safe houses for the women, they said, 'When the men start playing up, we can put them into that safe place and work with them to change their attitude.' One of the first men's safe houses we set up was at Ngukurr, at the other end of the community from the women's safe house. If the men were fighting with their wives, they could go there and the men working at the house could work with them. They did that at the Tiwi Islands as well. The communities didn't want their men to be charged and taken to prison, they wanted to deal with them there through the Aboriginal system, to help them to work on their issues about family violence. The women were telling us they didn't want their husbands to go to jail, they just wanted to them to sort out their lives.

So the men's safe houses were a cooling down spot, but also about teaching them how to behave towards the women. They'd have somebody to talk to and work out why they're doing that. Most times it's alcohol. The staff would say, 'Once upon a time you used to take your family fishing and swimming and hunting. Well, why aren't you doing that any more? Why are you running off to find grog and come home and beat your wife?' The men's safe houses worked in conjunction with the women's safe houses, the workers there would be the liaison and they would work those things out in the community, the best way forward because we got our own laws in relationships and marriage. Our senior people can work out some solution instead of taking the people away from the community. In the legal system, white legal system, they do take them away. They fly them into the safe houses in town or Katherine, Alice Springs, Nhulunbuy or Tennant Creek. But how are you going to sort things out if you haven't got all your kids with you? How can you rebuild your family? Anyway, that worked really well, it's a good system the communities worked out. They decided how they were going to do it, not us and not the government. But it was up to the government to support it, support that decision-making through the community. Emma and I helped to negotiate and establish that.

We ran the program and trained our staff in the communities. I ended up having about 30 people in the remote communities, about four or five in each community. We got one woman to run the women's safe house, one man to run the men's safe house, and they had two or three men and women working with them. Those were paid jobs. I was training them, talking about family violence, how it affects the family. We'd run workshops right around the Territory for all of them to get together, so we didn't leave them on their own. We got that established and up and running, and they were going really well. After we'd done that, we evaluated the program to make sure the communities were getting the full benefits out of the program, and that it was running how they wanted it. We'd go and spend time at each shelter. Not just one day, we'd be there a week with each group. That kept me busy for nearly six years.

Another of my roles was to travel through the Territory and other states to talk about family violence. On one such trip, my colleague Margaret and I were invited to go to Balgo in Western Australia. First night we were staying in a demountable next door to the nuns' accommodation and there was a most scary attack by a man wielding an axe on his partner and one of the nuns. He was trying to get at the woman who was sheltered in the nuns' quarters, chopping at the door. But that was steel meshed, so he couldn't get in, thank goodness. I yelled at the man who dropped the axe and took off. Poor Margaret was petrified. The nuns, Margaret and I calmed the woman down and the sister dressed her wounds. The next night the community council asked me to run a workshop and show films about violence and abuse. It was a great night and the community council said they were preparing to put a women's shelter in their community. Discussions had been going on for several months, but the holdup was where to put the shelter. Most of the women wanted it on the women's ceremonial grounds, but some of the men weren't happy about that. Several months later the council chair wrote me saying they had finally made a decision that the shelter would be near the nuns' accommodation. It was built and run by the women Elders and the nuns were able to work with the women. The council chair also started a program to work with their men.

I also wrote papers on our family violence strategy and addressed conferences in the other states and Canberra on family violence, what it means to our people and what structures our remote people had in place to keep the women and children safe. I was also on the National Women's Policy Unit. I used to go down to Canberra quite a bit, because I was on the Domestic and Family Violence Advisory group, and I had to do a lot of talks about how our women saw family violence in their communities and how they dealt with it. That's why the governments started to take us more seriously, because all the programs they funded before were for white women, not Aboriginal women. It was a wonderful experience being with all the women and talking about the best approaches to deal with family violence.

By that time, Claire Martin mob[43] came in and they moved the family violence unit from Chief Minister's to Health. I didn't like it there. We always thought that family violence should have stayed in Chief Minister's, I seemed to have more control from the Chief Minister's than from Health. I stayed and ran it for a while but I just didn't like how Health Department was running it. I'd had enough, and I just wanted to move on. They asked me to stay. I said, 'No, I've trained enough staff to do that. They can do it.' And then as soon as I left, they started making changes. It was sad. I didn't like the changes they were making. Emma was still there, so she was trying to keep everything in place. A few years later, the Intervention[44] came in and that buggered up everything anyway, because it took away all those structures we had worked so hard for.[45]

So I retired from Health Department in 2002, and then I thought I'd retire altogether, but that didn't take place because I got called back to Education. Raelene says, 'You retired six times, Mum. One minute you're retiring, next minute, you're going back to work. When are you going to retire?' But I went back to Education. There was a job going in the remote education unit and I thought it'd be nice, to do something different. So I worked there for a while. Remember how I helped set up the training courses for Aboriginal people at Batchelor College in the 80s? Well, when I went back to Education, it was to make sure that our people, like our teachers – that were trained through Batchelor and had gone back to communities – that they were still okay within the system. A lot of Aboriginal teachers came out of Batchelor College, and a lot of them were running the schools back in their communities. Not only in adult education, but through the schools, because we had primary school teachers going back and high school teachers going back too. So I was going out to see them and ensure they were okay in their jobs in the communities. I went back to Education as a policy liaison officer, working in the remote areas to ensure the teachers were supported on their communities. We didn't want to lose them. We wanted to make sure our people hadn't fallen through the cracks, I suppose. We were also looking at how they were training our Aboriginal teachers, because a lot of them stopped training once they had completed Batchelor College. We wanted to make sure they had the opportunities for more education to give them a higher-level job. So we set up things in the remote areas so they could have better training to expand their work experience and their knowledge. I enjoyed that. I met a lot of the teachers in the communities.

Also, I was writing policies again and working with FEPPI, the Aboriginal advisory board to the Education Department, made up of our people from remote areas all over the Territory. *Feppi* was an Aboriginal word from the Yirrkala region; I think it meant 'education', but I'm not sure. I organised meetings, things like that. There was talk about having secondary schools in the remote communities. They wanted the education system there to do just as good a job as in the towns so the children didn't have to come into the cities for school. Our people out bush were getting fed up. They reckon the kids were coming back different, losing their responsibility as part of their family. They wanted them home where they could see them and they could be educated in their Country.

Finally I retired altogether from the government in 2007, to spend more time with my family but also to work in other areas. I can't go anywhere without running into people I know from work. The grannies get really fed up, 'Oh Nana, can you stop stopping?' But I can't just walk past them. You can't be rude; you've got to talk to people. Usually they're pretty good, like my great-grandson Fabian. 'Oh Grandma, everybody knows you,' and I say, 'Yes, my darling,' and give him a big cuddle. And we keep going.

7

Justice for the Northern Territory Stolen Generations

In the beginning, the Stolen Generations people in Darwin used to 'just' meet, most of them Croker Island people. We are still really close; we call each other brothers and sisters. The Croker Island mob were the ones pushing all the time, pushing for acknowledgement and compensation. We wanted this from the Commonwealth government from the beginning; this was in the early 90s. At first, I was too busy with work, but I'd go to meetings every now and again at nighttime after work. We'd meet at someone's place and we'd talk about all the different issues and how to push the government to actually recognise us, and really take us seriously. There was a couple of the men, they passed away now, but they were the ones keeping the fight going. The Stolen Generations people established all these Aboriginal organisations in Darwin, from legal aid to the health services. Many of our Stolen Generations group had good jobs. They were working in government jobs, they could give talks, they could do everything. They had the skills. But in the end, we had to fight the Commonwealth government for 30 years to get recognition and compensation.

When the *Bringing Them Home* conference[46] happened in 1994, I went with all our Stolen Generations people, from Alice Springs, from everywhere. I was working at the time, but I asked the department if I could have a couple of days off, so I went to Kormilda College to be with the mob. All the Croker Island people came up from Adelaide, so it was a good reunion for all the institutions. Barbara pulled that together, the conference, her and young Jackie Katona. Barbara Cummings had been working with Stolen Generations for a long time. Jackie is my sister Mai's daughter, she had moved back here from Tasmania and she started to work with Barbara, because Barbara was at the Retta Dixon home with Mai. They worked on having a conference for all of us, and so all the NT Stolen Generations people went to Kormilda College in 94. It was really good being with everybody. People from all the seven institutions were there, because people were still alive then. But after that, even though we'd all met, everything sort of went silent. We ended up establishing an office in Darwin for the Stolen Generations. But we had no funds, really – I don't remember where we got the money from to work the office. Barbara and some others were running that office in the city. I was still working for the government, so I didn't really have time to do anything else because I was travelling all the time with my job.

After the conference, Mick Dodson was doing the Inquiry with Wilson, I think his name was.[47] Mick came up and told us he'd like to talk to some of the Stolen Generations people. We agreed to meet with him, some of the members of Stolen Gen and the board. Mick and Mr Wilson wanted to know what we wanted to do about the issues we had raised at the *Bringing Them Home* conference at Kormilda College. We said, 'We've been going for a long time and many of us are getting older. We really want the Commonwealth government to do something about addressing Stolen Gen.' Mick started to take our stories and that's when the government established the Healing Foundation. Mick's work was really good. He talked to individuals because he wanted to get the true stories from the Stolen Generations people. Mick got really emotional, too, poor dear. By the time of that Inquiry with Mr Wilson, Mick said, 'I'd like to talk to some of you individually, but can I also meet with the board?' So he came to talk to the NT Stolen Generation board first, to tell us what he was doing and whether we could help him to get some of the members to talk to him. He followed the right procedures, so we were really happy to see him.

Mostly we'd just sit under trees or in people's houses and meet. Most times, each institution had their own little group to meet with. Croker Island had their little committee, so did Retta Dixon and Garden Point. We were separated in our own little institutional groups. When we started to talk to everybody, we said, 'We won't get any support, because we are all separate little groups, we need to combine our committees if we want to be heard.' After working for years with the government and seeing how they worked with communities and organisations, I made the suggestion to combine our forces. It was important we combine our institutions as one, so the Commonwealth government would take notice and listen to us. They're not going to fund us separately. The more of us together, the more likely they would listen to us. From that time onward, we got more serious in contacting the Commonwealth government. We had a big meeting with the Stolen Generations members and we told them the only way forward is as a combined force. There's not enough people in the small groups, because a lot of our people were passing away.

The Stolen Generations people then decided to become the one big corporation, the Northern Territory Stolen Generation Aboriginal Corporation (NTSGAC) – that was in 1998. The seven institutions as a group, all together as one. Alice Springs got a little upset at first. They had their own office running in Alice Springs and they didn't like us being called the NT Stolen Generation because they thought we were leaving them out. I said, 'How can we leave you out when your people are members of our organisation?' We just wanted everybody to be together, because we thought the government would listen. That's when the government did start to listen.

Throughout the 90s and 2000s, we also had reunions and went back to Croker Island. I had actually gone back to Croker a few times, I went back there for work with Chief Minister's, because I had to go to every community to talk to people about their issues and report back to the government. It was lovely to go back to the island home. I met old Mick and Medic and Hazel and Timothy when I went back there, and it was lovely to see them all again. I would ask, 'Do you remember me?' 'Yeah, you're Eileen Smith,' they'd say, the old people. With Stolen Gen, we actually had reunions. People went to Garden Point for a reunion, Croker Island people went back to Croker Island, but we didn't actually run the reunion for Croker. It was run from Nunkuwarrin in Adelaide, the Aboriginal Health Service there, they had a Stolen Gen office in their service building. So they liaised with our Stolen Generations up here, brought the Croker Island people living in Adelaide up to Darwin.

Many of these people are deceased now, there's hardly any of them left. But that was a really good reunion. Very sad we have lost so many. Prior to losing so many of our people, we had another reunion in Darwin, and many of the Adelaide people came up for that. One day they all flew out to Croker Island to see the old mission site. Quite a few of the people who were sent as children to Adelaide never really got the opportunity to go back to Croker Island. Those of us living here could still go back if we wanted to. Of course, a lot of us didn't. I did it because I had to go back there for work, and it was good to see the island again and all of the people I had once lived with. The most recent time I went back there was when we had to bury Mary Yarmia, a girl who grew up with us. She was Uncle Mick and Aunty Medic's daughter. Not the eldest one, that was Daisy, who was like a sister to me. Mary was younger and had died from cancer, so we flew out there, a couple of the Croker people. The mission didn't look the same anymore. The people now operating the community had to knock down all the old mission houses. And you know what? All those houses we grew up in had asbestos. It's a wonder we're not all dead, but a few of us did get some sort of cancer. And you know who supervised that work of knocking down the old houses? One of the boys, Halpin, who'd grown up on Croker with us. He happened to be there for a holiday, and got asked whether he could supervise the work. It was his job to knock down those houses we used to live in. Halpin said it was sad watching the houses come down.

I asked, 'What were you thinking when you were knocking them down?'

'I was feeling really sad, I felt like crying,' because those were the houses we had grown up in.

In 2001, the NT Stolen Generations group took the Commonwealth to court. Barbara Cummings and her colleagues were pushing it all. We had Uncle Peter Gunner and Aunty Lorna Cubillo as the plaintiffs. And do you know who was one of our lawyers at that time to get compensation for us children? None other than Mr Dreyfus, who is now the attorney-general in the Labor government.[48] He came up with another lawyer from Melbourne and we had the court case up here.[49] One day I popped over to attend. It was in the federal court and I was working in NT House at the time, so I went over for a little while. My sister and all the other mob were there every day. Uncle Peter and Aunty Lorna are part of the Stolen Generations group, but we weren't given a choice in who they were putting up. We were a bit disappointed because we thought maybe the case would have been successful if they could have selected other people with better stories, but the lawyers chose them with the help of Barbara and her committee. And that court case wasn't successful. The government had all the records claiming the clients weren't really impacted much by their removal. You know, they were trying to tell us that we didn't have a bad life where we were placed; we had all the things to have a good life. They were trying to make it look really good. Did they forget our stories how we lost our mothers? We lost our Country, we lost our people, we lost our culture, we lost our language, we weren't allowed to speak our own languages. So we lost the court case and Prime Minister John Howard and his government refused to compensate or apologise, or to acknowledge what had happened and the effects this had on us. We were really disappointed and we just sort of gave up.

Then the NT government issued an apology to the Stolen Generations people in the Northern Territory. That came out of that Inquiry about Stolen Gen,[50] but they took a long time. The other states did it years earlier, but the Territory only in 2001. It was sort of good, but a lot of us didn't think much about apologies, we didn't like apologies. Many of our people were still angry about what the Commonwealth had done. Even today, many of them don't want personal apologies. Later on, when we got an apology from the church for Croker Island, some of the old people weren't happy about it. I said, 'Well, let's accept it for what it's meant to be. But you don't have to participate if you don't want to.' A lot of them are still very angry. I think because they haven't had the reconnection to mother, Country and kin. For me, I was able to go back to Mum. I was able to go back to my people. I was able to do all of my reconnections to Country. Whereas a lot of our Stolen Generations people haven't had that opportunity, they haven't gone back. So they're still angry with the government. And I said, 'Yeah, but I haven't got the energy to be angry. My energy wants to be focused on what we can do.' When I was younger, I was very angry about what happened to us as children, because I missed out on being with my mother and my people. But as I grew older and the reconnection to Mum and Country began to happen, I thought I'll put all my energy into fighting against the Commonwealth government rather than being angry because they removed me.

Our Stolen Generations people, I don't know how many times we went down to Canberra for meetings. We went all the time. And we kept telling the Commonwealth what we wanted and they kept saying no. John Howard[51] actually said, 'We'll never pay you, and we won't apologise.' We were there in the sittings in Parliament House one day and he said, 'We can't pay you.' He said, 'It was part of the laws of the day, it was government policy to remove you as children. So we don't owe you nothing.' So Maurie Ryan turned his back on him in Parliament. Maurie was part of our committee, the Stolen Gen board. I think he was chairman at the time. What happened was, some of us went down to Canberra for another meeting about Stolen Generations, and the government were in parliament and Maurie turned his back on Howard in Parliament House. Howard, he didn't want to listen to us at all. I think they sent up security to take Maurie out, but he just walked out himself. 'Maurie!' I said when I heard that. 'You can't do that!' But it was too late. He had already done it.

Kevin Rudd, who came after Howard, did the National Apology.[52] I went down to Canberra for that, but I was a little bit annoyed about that whole process because in the end, only a few people were contacted from the NT Stolen Generations group. The organisers didn't really talk to the NT Stolen Generations group as such. I said, 'Well, they better include the Elders,' like Aunty Connie, Aunty Netta, Aunty Florrie and Aunty Lorna Cubillo. 'You need to get these Elders down there.' By the time we heard about the airfares and accommodation for our people, there was none left for us. So Tarni and I went and saw the Fred Hollows Foundation. We asked, 'Will you help us with our air fares and accommodation?' They were able to assist three of us, Tarni, Raelene and myself. We travelled to Canberra, because Fred Hollows Foundation assisted us. Raelene had flown to Sydney by herself and got a lift by car to Canberra. We all went to Parliament House the next day. We were waiting outside, and then this young fellow who was working for the Labor government up here in Darwin, Mr Garner, he knew me from work and he saw me standing outside and he says, 'Aunty Eileen, what are you doing?' I said, 'Well, we don't know if we are allowed to go into the foyer' – or to where the announcement's going to be made – 'because they didn't include us on their invitation list.' He said, 'Well, don't worry about that, Aunty. I'll take you in.' So he just took us in, me, Raelene and Tarni and a couple of other women. He took us in and sat us down in the front row there. It was a big place, Parliament House and its foyer. Rudd was above us and we were looking up at him making the announcement. But if that young fellow from the government hadn't seen me, I would've been still waiting outside with all the other people. I was really upset with the people in Canberra. I said, 'How dare you leave the NT Stolen Generations group out.' I then specifically asked that they make sure our Elders were there. So in the end they did have about 10 of our Elders there and I was happy about that. Dad Randall was also there, he came, but I didn't actually see him because it was a big place and he was part of the official group and somewhere up high in the room, in the gallery.

Hearing Rudd make the National Apology was very emotional because, at long last, one of the Commonwealth governments acknowledged what had happened to us and was apologising for it. Because John Howard and his government didn't get the gist of it. They couldn't apologise, that's why we kept on fighting. When Kevin Rudd became prime minister, he made the National Apology, but no government,

Labor or Liberal, would even consider paying compensation to the Stolen Generations people.

As soon as I retired from the government in 2007, I really got stuck into Stolen Gen, the compensation and all of that. I had the time to concentrate on it, but still not full time. I didn't become the chair until later. At first, I made sure that the Northern Territory Stolen Generations people would meet the Commonwealth government. Sometimes we had nowhere to sit because we had no office, Stolen Gen had no office. So we'd sit under a tree or at somebody's yard talking about our issues and how we're going to go about it and where we'd get money to go and talk to the Commonwealth and all of that. There was about 10 or 15 of us, the survivors of the Northern Territory Stolen Generations, but most people on the committee were from Croker Island. At first we'd get funds from little bits and pieces of grants to run functions and travel to meetings. We'd go to different organisations and ask for money so we could travel. The Fred Hollows Foundation gave us money that one time to travel to the National Apology in Canberra. We also used to do our own fundraising. We did all sorts of things, we did arts and craft to sell, we held raffles, a lot of raffles. We used to have functions and sell food, some of the boys did paintings and we sold the paintings. We had to fundraise to get money because we weren't getting money from the government. We had a little room down at Coconut Grove where we used to meet, but it was so small we could hardly fit. I think the people that owned it gave us that room. We didn't use it on a regular basis, we only used it when we wanted to hold meetings. So they'd give it to us for the day we wanted to use it, so we didn't have to pay for a building.

Then we had a little office in the city in Cavenagh Street, that's where Barbara mob was working from. I don't remember where we got the money from, but Barbara Cummings and her group were running that office. Then we lost that office. We then used the building down in Coconut Grove for meetings. We didn't have funds or an office until we wrote up that submission for Link-Up. One of us had seen an ad in the paper saying they were taking applications for the Link-Up program. We then sat down one night – Cynthia, Sidney, Halpin, myself, and about 12 other Stolen Generations members – and wrote up a submission so we could get the Link-Up Service funds from the Commonwealth government and place it into our Northern Territory Stolen Generation Corporation. We knew that Danila Dilba, the biggest Aboriginal health service in Darwin, they wanted the money for the Link-Up service. But we thought that Link-Up is better situated within the Stolen Generation office, not in some health organisation. That's why we put in a submission for it. We sat down and wrote up a really good submission, but that was our small group of 15 people, sitting in the backyard of Cynthia's place because we didn't have an office. We'd all take a dish or plate of something to eat and worked on that for a few nights. And on the last day, we found somebody who knew how to write up submissions. We asked the young woman who had worked for the Stolen Generation office in Queensland to assist us with the submission. She was up here, listening and meeting with us for several weeks and we had a real good relationship. She helped us write the submission and we sent it off to the Commonwealth government. And we were successful – we ended up getting the funding! So it's been at Stolen Gen since 2012 and will remain there until 2028.

Link-Up provides a service to link families of the Stolen Generations people. It works with our Stolen Generations people so they can connect to family, Country and the communities from which they were removed. Link-Up is now our core business, but we do other programs like family kinships, and Elders well-being programs. That's how Northern

Territory Stolen Generation Corporation is operating now. The funding comes from NIAA to the NTSGAC for the Link-Up service. And then when the Healing Foundation[53] was established, they helped with a lot of small grants because they had the funding to assist. Often the CEO Maisie[54] would go to Healing Foundation, and also to the NT government, applying for funds. We do get small amounts of funding from Healing Foundation when we want to run the workshops, community gatherings and healing programs, but Stolen Gen has to put in a submission or applications for funding every time. We get funding from the Territory government for little functions, but we have to put in for that as well. It's a lot of work; fundraising can be really draining. That is a big job for our CEOs, seeking funding. All the work the board directors and members do is unpaid work; it's all volunteering.

When our board went to the state government asking for help – we need a building, we need this, we need that – the Chief Ministers said, 'Eileen, you really need to go to the Commonwealth. It's not the state's responsibility.' I said, 'I know that, but surely you can do something. We're Territorians. We live here. This is our country too.' So they started to help. Some of the Chief Ministers helped with small grants. They'd give us funds and then once we'd won the funding through Link-Up, the last Chief Minister, Michael Gunner,[55] decided to assist us with a building – the building that NTSGAC now occupies. He said, 'Okay, if you find a building, the NT government will refurbish it for you, and then you can move in.' Michael Gunner started to support us because his uncle was one of the plaintiffs in our first court case against the Commonwealth. He helped us get that building because we were in a building already at Casuarina, but it was too small, we needed a bigger space because we had more staff on Link-Up. So they refurbished a building in Malak, maybe even paid the first month's rent, I think, and put us in. That's the building we now use, it's up the road from me. That's why it was easy for me to go to work there every day when I was on the board and doing all the work for compensation. It's a beautiful building, but now it's leaking and we want to move out again because there is no proper up-keep. We're trying to get the Commonwealth to help with a building to house the NT Stolen Generation Aboriginal Corporation. A building we can call home.

I then became the chairperson of Stolen Gen, which made it easier for me to really do something. This was when I'd stopped working properly, because I was still running around with CDU[56] before that. I'd come on the NTSGAC board in 2014 and became chair in 2019. That's when I really took it on properly: the board was behind me because many of the board directors were Stolen Generations members and survivors. After that, the younger people, our descendants, started joining the board. But at that time, most of the board was Stolen Generations survivors, people who had been removed and placed in missions and institutions by Native Affairs. I had a whole group of my own mob working with me, the committee was behind me and we were able to push our case forward to the Commonwealth government. We were fighting for recognition and compensation. I remember being there for at least three or four stints as the board chair; I kept putting in my applications year after year because I didn't want to stop working for the compensation issue. The board and corporation gave me a computer and an office and I'd sit up there and do all the work, Bernadette, Halpin[57] and me. A few of the others, like Maxine, would come in every now and again. We worked for quite a while together. I suppose we worked on it for five or six years, but in the last two years, that's when things really started to happen, after we'd been looking at that issue for 30 years, fronting the Commonwealth about our compensation, apology and an acknowledgement.

Being the chair of Stolen Gen, I had to go to Alice Springs and meet several times with the Alice Springs survivors, to see what their thoughts were, work out what they wanted. I found they wanted exactly the same that we wanted up here. So we put all our matters forward to the Commonwealth.

Another action I had to do as the chair of the board was to write to all the politicians. We just continued meeting and talking and talking, the board, and then I said, 'Well, this isn't getting us anywhere. What do you suggest?' They said, 'Well, we will have to write to them.' So I started writing letters, to all the prime ministers, to the senators, the ministers, the opposition, to the members of parliament, to the state people, everybody. Then we found out that Mr Dreyfus was attorney-general, so I sent him a letter too, because he was one of our lawyers when we went against the Commonwealth years earlier. We also met with politicians whenever we could, but the letters reached more people. When I started writing those letters, they had to listen because the letters went directly to them. I just wrote, wrote, wrote all the time. I think three prime ministers, all the senators, all the ministers in government, and all the ministers in the opposition and the opposition leader, everybody. So we just kept going, from that time on. We were writing letters to the government for a long time before that, the Croker Island people were. I noticed when I was given the files for Croker Island, there was a lot of letters that they'd written to the Commonwealth government and to some ministers. They were writing to these people for a long time, and I think they did get some response, but they never followed through with it. The Croker Island committee didn't follow it up, which was sad. Whereas when I started to write letters, me and our working group would ring the offices, then we'd wait for their responses.

In the letters, I would say, 'I want you to acknowledge what you did to the Stolen Generations people of the

Northern Territory and take responsibility'. At that time, I wasn't looking for money, although everybody else was – but in all the letters, I didn't talk about monetary gain. I spoke about the loss to our people. We lost our mothers, we lost our Country, we lost our language. We lost all our traditions and our spirituality and our culture because they removed us and put us elsewhere, far from our own Country, mothers and families. Those were the issues I focused on. I said, 'All I want you to do is to acknowledge what you did to us children and take responsibility.' I wrote that in the letter and I signed it off as the chairperson of Stolen Generation. The board was behind me, but they let me do the writing. I'd write the letters and then I'd present it to the board, and there might've been a few little changes in the wording sometimes, but most times they were all good and the letters were endorsed by the board and then sent. The board said, 'You just sign it, Eileen, but if they want to talk to us, we'll talk to them.' It was a lot of hard work as volunteers. In the early days, David Dalrymple was our lawyer for Stolen Gen, he was really good working with us. He helped with a lot of our letters to make sure that people would listen, legal sort of stuff, but I'd write the letters and I'd show him to get his advice.

Some of them responded. We got a letter from Morrison, the Prime Minister,[58] we got it from the chief ministers in the Northern Territory, because we sent them letters as well. Malarndirri[59] always responded and so did Ken Wyatt.[60] I was quite surprised Ken Wyatt responded. He came and met with us, we had a few talks with him. People were asking why we were meeting with him I said, 'Well, at the moment he's the Indigenous Affairs minister, so we'll talk to him. Maybe he can push for us.' The other person always pushing was Senator Malarndirri. She was behind it all the way and whenever we couldn't get anything through, we would talk to her. Today she's still there for us. She was there all the time for us; she came to meetings with us, talking to us all the time. We really appreciated her support and assistance.

I just kept writing to everybody, and we'd meet them whenever we could. We were under the Commonwealth government, because the Territory is a self-governing body, and we couldn't be compensated like the states. We talked about the seven institutions in the Northern Territory, we'd tell them our story. One day we said to the Commonwealth government, 'You're talking to all the Aboriginal organisations, but you didn't once come to Stolen Generation to talk to us. Why can't you front the NT Stolen Generations members? We're the ones affected. We're the survivors. We need you to come and talk to us, not everyone else, about our situation.'

We met with anybody who came to the Territory. We were never refused, particularly by the Labor government. The Labor government always met and talked to us. We'd go and meet with them at any opportunity we had, a few of the board directors. There were several prime ministers during this time. We had Gillard,[61] she came up here with her minister who had the Indigenous portfolio, Jenny Macklin.[62] A few of the board directors from Stolen Gen went and met Gillard and told her what we wanted. At that time, Mai and a couple of other people were on the board, so they went to meet with the prime minister. That was before I'd retired. But Gillard listened to Mai and them when they met with her, and then made arrangements for them to meet and talk to Jenny Macklin.

We then wrote to Penny Wong[63] through our lawyer, through David Dalrymple, who was our lawyer at the time, and told her our situation. We wrote her a long letter. She couldn't meet us, but she sent us a beautiful long letter and then she put us in touch with the finance minister, Mr Gray.[64] He had worked in the Northern Territory government years before he'd gone back to Perth, and then he was in the West

Australian government. So we went and met Mr Gray in Perth, Halpin Hart, Maxine Kunde and I. We flew to Perth to meet him in his office and we put our case to him, he listened intently and he was really good. He was going to do something to help us, but then the government changed and it went back to the Liberals. So it was just chopping and changing from one government to the other, but we didn't give up then. Whoever we could meet, we grabbed them all, we'd arrange meetings with them, talk to them. So it was a slow process, a long process. We went to Canberra a few times when we were invited to meet with politicians. Once Healing Foundation was established, that gave us the leverage to get to meetings in Canberra because they helped with the funding. Other times we had to scrimp and save and look for funding from elsewhere because Stolen Gen has never had any money of their own.

The first thing that happened with compensation was the National Redress for abuse, but this wasn't really Stolen Generations. They started to do the compensation for the National Redress for sexual abuse in the institutions, but that was not just for Aboriginal children, but for all children.[65] The National Redress group, they've got an office here in Darwin. They rang me from their office and said that they'd like to meet and talk to some of our Stolen Generations members. I said, 'Well, you know that sexual abuse is something that's really difficult for them to talk about?' They replied, 'Yes, Eileen, but we'll have one officer talking to them so it won't be a big open meeting. We'll see them individually and everything is confidential.' So I came back to the board and said, 'The National Redress wants to speak to some of the people,' and they agreed. They had a really good team of people, the Redress office. I invited them to the board so they could let us know what their role and function was. The Redress people came and told us what they were doing.

We told our members if they wanted to go and see the people from the National Redress, we would pass on their names and phone numbers. Some of our members ended up going to them, but it took them a long time to get there. Many of them did get compensated through that scheme, but it was very difficult for them to talk about what had happened to them, because they still felt it was their fault. And I'm saying to them, 'No, it's not your fault. You were only a child. So just go and listen to them and tell them your story if you want to.' They had really good staff there at the Redress and I'd often talk to the staff there when somebody wanted to go and see them. When any of our Stolen Generations people came to me and said that they wanted to go there, I'd ring National Redress and say, 'So-and-so would like to come and see you. This is their number. Can you get in contact with them please?' It was more confidential, people didn't want other people to know why they were going to the National Redress. So we as Stolen Generation were involved in how people sought that service. They even employed a couple of Aboriginal people from Darwin that we knew. They were putting everything in place quite well, and we were happy with what they were doing, but I said to the Redress team, 'It might take some of them time to come to see you, but if I keep reassuring them that you'll see them individually and everything's confidential, I think they'll start.' So that was our role, to liaise with the Redress teams and our Stolen Generations members.

It wasn't easy for our people to talk about the abuse. We all knew that things were happening in the missions, but a lot of the things that happened to us, we never let anybody else know about it, not even when talking between ourselves. That's why it was very hard for our people to go to the National Redress. I didn't know that my best mate from Croker Island mission had been abused, she never spoke about it. She didn't talk about it to me until she was a grandmother. I used to go to Adelaide and visit her all the time, but she never told me what happened to her. When all the Croker Island Stolen Generations people came up for the conference in 94, the *Bringing Them Home* conference, she talked to me about it then, but that was years later. She said, 'I always felt it was my fault.' I said, 'My dear, you were a child. It wasn't your fault. Those carers shouldn't have done that to you. The adult is at fault, not you.' She was abused by her foster family, but she didn't talk about it until after 1994. I used to go down to Adelaide all the time for holidays, stay with Lorky and visit my friend – but not once did she talk about that abuse.

One day when I was visiting her, she and I were sitting down talking after she was beaten by her husband again. I said, 'Why do you put up with this man? He's beating you. Get rid of him. Don't live with him anymore.' I said, 'I used to put up with that treatment from my husband. He used to beat me too, and I tried to put my foot down.' So my dear friend, she said, 'Well, Eileen, I don't know what else to do.' It was because she felt she wasn't worth anything. But it wasn't from her husband so much, it was because of what had happened to her as a child in her foster home. She'd grown up feeling that she wasn't worth anything to anybody. It was sad. I felt really sorry for her. I helped her to get into services so she could talk about it and get help, and she finally left her husband. Working with the Office of Women's Policy gave me the understanding and empathy to work with my women and discuss family violence and all these sorts of abuse. I suppose it's because of my work with family violence and sexual abuse, I was able to get the services there to talk to our people. But for the longest time, we didn't have any avenues for our people to talk about such things. So in Stolen Gen, we started to open up areas where our people could start having that conversation and deal with their family concerns.

Over the years, Stolen Gen has also worked on establishing

memorials. They put one in the Darwin Botanic Gardens. I went there when they presented it in 2005. Karu Park, where Retta Dixon was – there is a plaque there. There's one up in Myilly Point where the Kahlin Compound used to be, but they're now putting in something much bigger, like a memorial garden. We are trying to get one established in Pine Creek where the Pine Creek home once stood. We've been negotiating with Heritage and the people in Pine Creek. This new Territory government now wants to get rid of the heritage office, so we want to meet and talk to them about that. In Alice Springs, where the Bungalow home was, that's a tourist attraction now. They've got the history of the Stolen Generations there. The Bungalow home's gone, but where the home was, near the top of the Todd River, there's a museum. There are photos and videos talking about Stolen Generations.

Every year for some time now, the schools write or ring Stolen Gen office and ask if someone can go to their schools and talk to the children. The children's ages range from little tiny ones, primary schools, right up to high school. This was done through the board. So me and a couple of other board directors often went to the schools to talk to the students about Stolen Generations history, about our lives as children who lived on the missions. Raelene's been doing a lot of that lately. The little children, some of them didn't know about Stolen Gen. So we were highlighting the history of the Stolen Generations. I remember a young boy said one day, 'When you were growing up, did you have houses?' They wanted to know if we had houses on the mission. I said, 'Yes, we lived in houses and we went to school and went to church and we did all these other things like swimming and fishing and everything on the island.' But the saddest part, I would say to the children, was not being able to be with my mother and my family, so they could understand. One little boy from a Catholic church school said, 'You know what, Aunty Eileen?

My mother's the same as you, but my father is not Aboriginal.' I asked him, 'Okay, and are you all right?' and he said, 'Yes. We go home to Mum's Country all the time for holidays.' It was lovely hearing one of the children interact that way. It's a good time; it's a learning time for ourselves and for the students.

The Healing Foundation wanted to do a study about what happened to us growing up in a mission, and our removal from mother, Country and family, the intergenerational trauma. They were doing case studies, and they wanted to talk to two people in the NT Stolen Gen, a man and a woman. When Maisie, our CEO, received the letter from the Healing Foundation, she came to me. This was in 2020. I was really excited about it when Maisie came and told me about the case studies for the Healing Foundation. She said, 'Eileen, would you do it?' and I said I would. Maisie asked in front of her staff and one of them, who's never been through Stolen Generations, said, 'Why do you want to do Eileen? She's got everything, she's made good with her life, it doesn't seem to have affected her.' Raelene, my daughter, was there with the staff and said, 'How do you know what affected my mother?' She was sitting there because she's the head of the Link-Up Service caseworkers, the team leader there. She said, 'Mum never even talked to us about it. So how do you know what my mother went through and how she is feeling?'

A couple of women came to talk to me and they seemed all right, but then, later on, Maisie said, 'Eileen, are you okay with them?' I said, 'Yeah, sort of.' She said, 'Because Matthew[66] can come back and talk to you if you want him to.' I felt real comfortable with Matthew, because I had done other work with him years ago. He had been doing the timeline for the Health Department for how Aboriginal people were part of that whole process all the way through, from way back, as health workers, and how they worked in different areas of the department. He did stories with me for this big timeline.

When Maisie suggested Matthew do the case study, I thought it would be great, because Matthew's been here with me before. So he did interviews with me and put it all together for the Healing Foundation. Their project aimed to see the effects it had on us being removed from our mothers and our Country.[67] Lance Stott also participated in the study, he had been at the Retta Dixon Home from an early age.

We, the NT Stolen Generations, for many years were writing letters and meeting politicians. We just kept on talking, talking, but a few of the politicians we met were useless, they never did anything for us. Halpin had a fight with one of them one day. We went to Snowden, a Labor senator, at his office. Halpin said to him, 'Well, you've been in the government all this time out west in the Territory, but what have you really done? You haven't done anything for Stolen Gen. I really haven't seen any changes yet. We've had so many meetings with you and what have you done for us?' The senator got quite angry and asked us to leave. Another time we were meeting one of the prime ministers, and I said, 'You are waiting for us to all die, aren't you?' He replied, 'No, I'm not, Eileen.' I said, 'Yes, you are, because we're all in our 70s, 80s, 90s now.' We really felt and believed this, the NT Stolen Generations people. At that time, Stolen Generations people in New South Wales were getting money from the New South Wales government,[68] but we weren't, because we were under the Commonwealth.

And finally, the Commonwealth started to listen. I think the reason why it was pushed so quickly was because, having worked for the chief ministers and the Territory government, I understood the way governments worked and their systems. I also understood the Commonwealth system and the state system so I was able to write to the governments and negotiate with them on behalf of the NT Stolen Generations. People were trying to do it all the time, but they never came up with the right solution. I said, 'We have to front them and we have to meet with them and we have to write them letters. Nobody's going to listen to us if we are just going to sit back. We have to face them.'

Morrison was really good. When we met with him, he sat and listened. Some of the Stolen Gen group went down to Canberra and met with Prime Minister Morrison. Maisie Austin, our CEO, and a couple of the board members were in Canberra for some other meeting with Healing Foundation, I think. At that time I was so busy with my court case with Shine Lawyers that I couldn't go. Maisie and the board asked to see Prime Minister Morrison and they met with him. Maisie came back from Canberra and said, 'Oh, the PM listened, Eileen!' I said, 'Yeah, but did he say anything?' She said, 'No, but he listened and was very interested.'

The final push was the class action suit, because it was ready to go to court then. Shine Lawyers was taking our issues as a class action to court. I was the first plaintiff; it was my case they'd put forward.[69] Shine Lawyers did all the work on the case; I had a wonderful relationship with them. They were going to take the Commonwealth government to court for me. I was the lead plaintiff on that class action, so if my case got through, then we could put in all the rest of the NT Stolen Generations people. It took two or three years to put together my case, a long time. And then just as we were ready to go to court, the Commonwealth decided, 'We are going to pay them.' The Commonwealth said, 'We'll give each of the survivors $75,000 and $7000 for healing.' Up to then, the Commonwealth government kept saying, 'Children were removed because of this policy.' Shine Lawyers said, 'No, Eileen and the NT Stolen Generations lost their mothers, their families, their culture, their language, their land.' They had a really good case, mind you, and the lawyers were looking at a large sum of money for me. The Stolen Generations from the

Territory, from the time they started to take us in the early 1900s to 1967, they took 2000 children away. We are talking just about the Territory. Out of that 2000 people, when I counted up our people a few years ago, there would've been more than 300 still alive. Now, of course, there's hardly any of us left. But if the class action case had gone through, it would've been a large amount of money in compensation for each person. Can you imagine that cost to the Commonwealth?

We had these numbers because I listed all the people who went through the seven institutions in the Northern Territory. For Shine Lawyers, for the court case. We had seven institutions in the Northern Territory and in those seven institutions there were around 2000 children removed and put into those homes. For each institution I found records, listings of children online. I made up lists of all the children removed from their homes to missions and gave the lists to the lawyers, all the names from the seven institutions, the people still alive. So there were seven institutions: Bungalow and Kahlin Compound were the two old ones. The Bungalow in Alice Springs was like Kahlin Compound up here in Darwin, they were the holding places. The Commonwealth government put the children there before they sent them to other missions and institutions. There was the Retta Dixon home in Darwin, run by the Inland Missions. Then we had the Methodist mission on Croker Island; the Anglican mission on Groote Eylandt; and then the Catholic mission on Melville Island, which was at Garden Point; and Saint Mary's Home in Alice Springs. Seven homes, seven institutions.

I worked just about every day at Stolen Gen on the computer, putting it all together. It took me ages, I worked two years straight on all of that. I had the support of the Stolen Generation board and office because they allowed me to do it on the computer there. Maxine Kunde helped a bit, as did Bernadette Shields and Halpin Hart. They were really good, working tirelessly for Stolen Gen, helping with the lists and liaising with our people. But most of the work on the lists I had to do because I was computer literate, whereas they weren't as much. Whenever I had finished a list, I'd ask the other Stolen Gen people to check it, to make sure that these were the right people. I had Maxine working with Garden Point; Valerie and Audrey with Retta Dixon; me, Hal and Emily with Croker Island. Anne Blitner worked from Groote Eylandt and we had people like Wendy Espy, my cousin from Ngukurr. Her mother's related to my mother. She did a lot of the work with the Groote Eylandt lists. And we had people from Kahlin Compound. I had all these people to help me check the lists I provided. They'd say, 'Eileen, you left out so and so.' So we'd include them.

To work on the St Mary's lists, Maisie and I went to Alice Springs to meet with the Stolen Generations people down there. We met with Harold Furber, Ann Ronberg and some of the Elders. We'd talk about the compensation, and they would tell me if I had left anyone off the list. When the names were included we would agree the lists were okay. Wendy helped with the St Mary's one as well because she was put in there for school. There was a team of about 15 of us working on the lists for the lawyers. Then when the Commonwealth decided they were going to pay us, they sent a message to Maisie and said, 'We'd like all the lists that Eileen provided to the lawyers.' So I sent the lists to them as well. That's how they knew about us all. The lists became the basis for the compensation.

When Morrison finally said he was going to pay us, we nearly fell over. Maisie got a call from Andrea Kelly, an Alice Springs girl in charge of NIAA, the National Indigenous Australians Agency. They rang our office at Stolen Gen and said, 'We've got some good news. The Prime Minister is going to make an announcement at such and such a time. We'll

Zoom you in so you can watch it.' Andrea Kelly said, 'Aunty Eileen, we want you to watch it.' So we gathered all the Elders we could. We had quite a big group of people there watching the announcement at Stolen Gen, we put it up on the screen, on the big TV. We all sat around the big TV and watched the Prime Minister Morrison make the announcement.[70] The ABC came around to Stolen Generation office to interview me. We were happy about it, very emotional. We were sitting there and crying. When I was doing the work with Stolen Gen, I was getting really tired. My daughters kept saying, 'Mum, you gotta stop.' I said, 'I'm not stopping until I get what I want.' So I kept going. Then finally, when Morrison agreed to pay us, I was just so relieved. Just take responsibility and acknowledge what you did to us as children. There were babies. We were little children. I was so young. There were four-year-olds, two-year-olds. Some little ones were still being breastfed when the patrol officers picked them up and removed them.

Watching the announcement, we were really happy. We thought, Well, they finally listened to us after 30 years. That was the response from all of us watching the coverage, we finally got the Commonwealth government to listen to us and they're going to give us something. But the whole time I was writing and talking to them, I was saying, 'All I want you to do is acknowledge that you did this to us, to all of us as children. Please accept what you've done, acknowledge us, take responsibility. If there's compensation in any form, fine, give it to us.' But really it was the acknowledgement. We wanted them to acknowledge what they'd done to us as children and take responsibility. It was a lot of hard work, but when it was all over, a lot of people came and thanked me. They were really happy about what I'd achieved. We were getting phone calls from everywhere. I think Ken Wyatt even rang us.

We sat there listening to the prime minister and thinking, Okay, that's all they're going to give us, about $82,000 for each of the survivors. If I'd gone to court and won my class action, I would have received quite a large amount of compensation, just for my case alone. I was a little disappointed, but I had to think about everybody else. I couldn't be selfish, I had to think about the rest of my Stolen Generations people and what was best for us all. Shine Lawyers said, 'Eileen, so we're going to stop your court case?' I said, 'Yes, because our people don't want to fight anymore. They want to just accept what's been offered.' I didn't want to go against my people. Might be I'd end up with all that money and they'd have nothing. That was my choice. It wasn't much money, but to me it was. We shared it with our children, and I bought everything I wanted for my house.

Some of our people wanted more. I had to go and talk to all the old people, all the Elders. I said, 'They've offered us this amount for compensation,' and I told them how much it was. 'Do you want what the Commonwealth is offering or do you want to keep on fighting?' They said, 'No, Eileen, we've had enough. We don't want to keep on fighting, 30 years was long enough fighting. We're tired, we're all too old. Let's just accept what they're offering us.'

But some younger people in their 40s and 50s were saying we could have got more. Some of them were people picked up through the Welfare system, not under Native Affairs. The Stolen Generations group we fought for was picked up under Native Affairs, from the 1900s to 1967. I don't know whether anybody is working on compensation for the people that got picked up under Welfare. My whole focus was on Stolen Generations survivors. I said, 'I'm here for all the kids that were institutionalised. They're the people we're fighting for now.' We discussed that at the board level and with the community, and they said, 'Yeah, we'd love more money, Eileen, but we have to be realistic.' So I said to the younger people, 'We've been fighting for 30 years. You want to keep fighting, you go ahead. But me and the Elders, we're too old now. We've done our fighting. We are just going to accept this. If people feel they have to still fight, there's several lawyers that might take on your case.' We gave them some names and but told them they would no longer have the facilities from the Stolen Generation office itself. I don't think we were cruel. I think we were realistic.

The communication was between me and NIAA, the National Indigenous Australians Agency. They started the payments in March 2022. NIAA was responsible for the money, they were doing all the Territory's Redress. NIAA gave the Stolen Generation office two officers in our Link-Up service, to work with our people in their compensation claims. Andrea, from Alice Springs, was really good. She was the first one to run that office. I knew her mother and I knew her. So we were all right, working with her and her staff.

After Morrison had made that announcement about the compensation, the southern states started to ring up. One day, I was in the office finishing off some of the lists and somebody rang from one of the other states and said, 'Eileen, why didn't you go for all of us?' I said, 'Well, I couldn't because we are under the Commonwealth here. You are under a state government and your state has offered you compensation.' It wasn't very much, mind you. It was about $10,000 or something, I think. I said, 'I feel for you, but my fight has always been for the Northern Territory Stolen Generations group because we have to fight the Commonwealth. The laws that govern us are Commonwealth laws, and that's who we're fighting. So I'm not being selfish.'

We finally, finally got it: acknowledgment and compensation. The Commonwealth government took responsibility for our removal. Then the Stolen Generations people said, 'Eileen, what about our deceased brothers and sisters?' All the time in the back of our minds, Stolen Gen wanted them to address the situation of their deceased people. So we went back to the government, and they said, 'We can't pay for deceased estates!' I said, 'Yeah, but they're Stolen Generations people. They're our brothers and sisters who have passed. Surely you can do something.' We weren't going to let the Commonwealth get away with it. So we went to Shine Lawyers again, and they put a class action in.[71] When Shine Lawyers decided to take that on, I had to do the lists of the deceased people who were in the seven institutions so when the children put in for their parents, they were able to. I got help from all the people who had worked on the lists with me in the first place. Each of them could tell me who was deceased from their groups. Once I had completed the deceased list, I sent the list to the lawyers at Shine.

Remember me talking about Dreyfus, who was our lawyer when we went up against the Commonwealth years earlier? Well, he was the Attorney-General. That's why when they took it to him to get money for the deceased children, he passed it. He gave them 50 million dollars, just like that. That was paid before Christmas 2024 to most of the families of the deceased. When Mr Dreyfus approved the money for our deceased estates, we were happy, but there were still a lot of problems. Because it was a deceased estate, they had trouble with the procedures. Sometimes the executors of a will, who are responsible for the estates, were the children's uncles or aunties, not the children themselves. Shine Lawyers said, 'What are we going to do, Eileen? We can't bypass the law for deceased estates. We have to go through that process.' I said, 'Yeah, but some of the deceased people were married to non-Aboriginal people and we are fighting for the children of the deceased. We're not fighting for the spouses. We want the children to get compensation.' It brought up a lot of problems and took two years, but, in the end, Shine got around it somehow. Finally, before Christmas 2024, they paid most of the children out. Now I believe there's some leftover money because some of people weren't eligible. Instead of them working with nearly 2000 children, they only had a thousand children or so to work with. We heard from Shine Lawyers the other day that they're going back to court for the deceased families because they've got money left over from the 50 million dollars and the children may be entitled to more. Shine had to go back through the courts to the Commonwealth with a proposal to see what they were going to do about the leftover money. I think the Commonwealth wants the money to be distributed among the children. They went back to court, but we haven't heard the outcome.

At around the same time, we did the duty of care class action with Slater and Gordon.[72] Slater and Gordon did duty of care for the institutions. The first ones were the Retta Dixon mob. The Retta Dixon case was done by Bill Piper, another lawyer, separately. He took the case to court for duty of care with the Retta Dixon home. Bill Piper got money for the Retta Dixon people, quite a lot of money apparently. Then Slater and Gordon came to the Stolen Generations people and said they could represent us. The first case they did was Garden Point, with Maxine and a couple of the others. Slater and Gordon won the case for them. That was in 2021, and then Slater and Gordon said, 'We'll do each of the institutions after that.' But we had to talk to the Stolen Generations groups and organise with the lawyers. We told the lawyers to leave the Cooperation[73] out of it, to just deal with the committees from each of the institutions. I did it with Croker Island, me and some of the Croker Island people, and they were also doing St Mary's home in Alice Springs. So the lawyers came to us and said they could help. We had to go to court to do that, but we weren't always sitting in court, the lawyers did it all.

So, duty of care was for not looking after us properly, for not being taken care of properly on the missions. Until Slater and Gordon came to us and started talking about duty of care, we wouldn't have known what that meant. They wanted to know how we were treated on the missions. Many of us said that we'd been beaten. We had to work from a very early age. There was no money. That's why we are getting lost wages now for that. And then any beatings we got, any mistreatment we got, we had to talk to the lawyers and tell them how we felt about it all. Some of the things that happened to us, regardless of how much there was, we didn't talk about it. When the lawyers started to talk to us about these things, we said, 'But we never talked about it.' The lawyers said, 'Well, don't you think it's time you did?' We were ashamed. We didn't want to talk about the things that hurt us. They said, 'People have gone to court because of such things. What about you children?' So we all went on that journey then, with Slater and Gordon, for duty of care. They had to get all our names. We had to register all our names. Garden Point had over a hundred people, I think, and the lawyers came to talk to us about the court case, the class action.

When we put in for duty of care, a lot of the older people said, 'We don't want that, Eileen.' I said, 'Well, if you don't, that's fine, we'll just go with the people that do.' So in the end there were only 12 of us for Croker Island. Some of the older ones didn't want to be part of it because they felt the church was fine. A lot of our older people say, 'But the churches were good.' I look at them and I think to myself, Don't say anything, Eileen, but I know that some of our churches weren't that good. There was abuse from them as well. But the older people are angry with the Commonwealth for putting us in that situation. They're not angry with the churches. But the church is part of that, and the church got money from the government for taking care of us on the missions. If they hadn't got that, they wouldn't have had money to run the missions. Some of our people say, 'Yeah, but they were good to us.' I read about the abuse and I think to myself, Where are these old people coming from? I suppose it's because I understand abuse better than they do because of my work.

A lot of them haven't forgiven the Commonwealth, but they've forgiven the churches. I can't understand that; I wasn't abused by the church, but some people were. I say to them, 'You can't just blame the government. Those people from the churches were our carers. The Commonwealth put us under those carers, and those carers were supposed to do better than they did.' I've got nothing against the church, but that's not the point. I talk to the old people about that boy locked up because the church people couldn't control him. That's terrible when you think about it. Some of the older girls were sexually abused. They don't want to talk about it, but when you say something about one particular missionary, 'Oh, he was no good.' And we'll say, 'Why?' 'Oh, just, he was no good.' I can understand why they don't want to talk about it, so we don't push them.

We also got an apology from the church. After we'd gone through that process with duty of care, we met with them and the lawyers and the Minister Reverend. I forget her name now. Some of our people didn't want to be part of the apology. One of the old girls that was at the meeting with our people, she said, 'I'm not listening, Eileen,' and she walked out of the room and sat out in the foyer, in the waiting area. I brought her back when the Reverend finished. I said, 'Why didn't you want to stay there?' She had a thing against the missionaries. She was in the middle bracket. There were the older people, the middle people, and us little ones. A lot of people don't like apologies because they think, maybe the institution thinks it's all good now and they don't have to do any more. But I thought that apology meeting was good. The lawyers brought the Uniting Church up to meet us and the outcome was really good.

Just the other day, Slater and Gordon, who did our court

case for duty of care, rang and told me that they've got a new building in Brisbane, I think it's their main office. They wanted to name one of the meeting rooms after me, which is quite an honour. I was quite moved because they've been there all the way in our long journey for compensation and acknowledgement. They were successful in getting us compensated for the duty of care on the missions: Garden Point, Croker Island, St Mary's. The lawyers were really supportive; they never gave up.

With Shine Lawyers, they were the first ones to put up a class action for compensation for us survivors. But then the Commonwealth decided to pay us anyway. So they took on the deceased families and Slater and Gordon did duty of care. It was all starting to happen then, but it was an ongoing fight for 30-odd years to get justice for what had happened to us as children. Now Shine Lawyers are doing lost wages because we all worked as children, but we thought it was part of the mission. So it's still going on.

When the government gave us the money, the redress money for the survivors, NIAA asked us if we wanted an apology from the Commonwealth, whether we wanted a personal written apology, or acknowledgement. NIAA asked, 'Do you want a personal apology or a group apology?' You had to fill that in on the application form. I thought about it for a long time. Then Andrea rang me and she said, 'Aunty Eileen, you didn't say on your form whether you wanted an apology or not.'

I said, 'Well, how are you going to do this?'

She said, 'One of my staff, he's a lawyer, he'll talk to you. Tell him how you feel about the apology and what you want in it. We'll draft the apology based on your discussions, send it back to you, and you can okay it. Who would you like to officially present it to you?'

I said, 'You,' because Andrea, she's an Aboriginal girl from

Alice Springs, and it was most appropriate she signed it, not some minister. I talked to the NIAA staff member, David, over the phone about what I wanted in the document. A lot of people didn't want to do that, and then Andrea came to Darwin and presented it to me at Stolen Gen, in a big frame. My acknowledgement is here on my wall now.[74] I helped them write it, because I wanted the apology to also focus on my mother; she didn't understand why they were taking me. I never saw her again until I was 19 years old. I said, 'I want to make sure my mother's acknowledged because this document is for my children, my grandchildren and great-grandchildren.'

Raelene started working with Stolen Gen in 2012 as team leader in Link-Up and she's now the new CEO in charge of the Northern Territory Stolen Generation Aboriginal Corporation. She started as Acting CEO in 2022 when Maisie left. I was the chair of Stolen Gen, I had two or three stints so I was there for a while, but I stepped down because Raelene had become the CEO. I said, 'No, I don't want to be the chair while my daughter's the CEO, may cause conflict of interest.' The board members said, 'No, Eileen, you should still be there, be on the committee.' But by that time, I'd done all the work I wanted to do with the compensation. I worked with the National Redress on Sexual Abuse, I worked in the compensation for NT Stolen Gen survivors, the Territory's Redress. I then worked on the NT Stolen Generations compensation for the deceased, and on the Croker Island duty of care.

Through all those years of fighting for acknowledgement and compensation, we always needed to talk about what happened to us, and that wasn't very easy. A lot of us didn't open up for a long time. We just accepted it and lived our life. We put everything in the back of our minds so we could survive, that is the actual term I'd use. Many of our abused Stolen Generations people lived in shame and silence and put up with abuse from their partners, husbands and wives. The

Commonwealth government removed us from our mothers, Country and culture but never tried to return us or assist us to have the opportunity to reconnect with our families and Country. What a dark history. It still grieves me that the most loving and caring people in my life as a child, my grandparents, passed before I ever returned to Country. When I left as a child, it was like I had nowhere, I had nothing, and that really broke me. If I hadn't had the teachings from my mother, father, grandparents and family as a child, I wouldn't have been as strong as I was. A lot of people still don't believe that Stolen Generations exists, that this happened to children in Australia. That's the reason I wanted to write this book. I want to let the world know what it did to us as children and how we overcame that to be where we are today.

A lot of the Aboriginal organisations in Darwin, they were established by Stolen Generations people. In Stolen Gen, we set up programs dealing with the personal trauma and intergenerational trauma. That's why they wrote that book on my family.[75] From then on, Maisie got the trauma counsellors to come in and speak to the staff and the board. They needed to be trained in dealing with our trauma. What the Stolen Generation office does now is run healing camps so we can address those issues of trauma as a group. We get funds from the Healing Foundation to run these healing camps for the women, the men, and the young people. We sit and talk around the fire, just get together and have a good time and talk about our issues. The meetings or gatherings encourage and support anyone who wants to talk. The staff are there to support us. That's why Raelene's got her staff under training programs so they don't fade out, their wellbeing needs to be checked too. Every now and again the staff might have a get-together themselves, a weekend away somewhere. This is all part of the wellbeing for staff and members of the NT Stolen Generation Aboriginal Corporation.

For a long time I didn't talk to my children about everything that had happened to me. I didn't want to talk about it. Raelene, Shelly and Sheena said, 'Mum, you never told us all this,' and I said, 'No, you are my children. I wanted you to be happy. I didn't want you to know what had happened to me.' Shelly brought it up, she was crying one day. She said, 'Mum, I just watched ***Rabbit-Proof Fence***.'[76] In the movie they took the children away in a car, or a truck. Michelle said, 'You did say something about that once but you didn't really go into detail.' I said, 'Yeah, it's not that I didn't want you to know about it; at that time, I still wasn't comfortable discussing it.' Yet I'd been discussing it all the time with the remote communities, not about me, but about their issues. When it came to talking about my own issues, I never did, and now I understand why some of our people didn't talk about what happened to them. I mightn't have been sexually abused or anything, but there was still a lot of trauma. That's what I said to Shelly, 'At that time I couldn't talk about it.' 'But you were working in the area, Mum, and you never ever said anything.' They knew I was on Croker Island, but I talked about the happy times, not about the effects it had on me.

Then we did talk about what I had experienced as a child. They'd come and say, 'Mum, can you just tell us what happened?' I had to tell them what had happened and how I'd been removed from their grandmother. Their father never talked about going to Garden Point. By that time, we were fighting the Commonwealth, so we were always talking to politicians and media about our experience. From time to time, I sit down with my grandchildren. I seem to open up more to them because they sit and ask questions. The granddaughters – Telena, Ellie, Adaleen, Shania and Grace – if they want to know anything, they ask straight out, the boys too. I have always been honest and open with my grandchildren. As a family we know how important it is to talk about all things.

The number of suicides of our young people really saddens me. That is the reason I want my children, grandchildren and great-grandchildren to have open discussions with their parents and me. If they have problems, I want to be there to help and guide them so they don't feel alone. Young people these days have so much to consider and it's best they have the love, care and support to keep them safe, well and happy.

I really believe if Australia wants to have reconciliation, they have to acknowledge our sad and dark history of the First Nations people of this country, and meet us together. For such a long time, we were the forgotten people. People think Stolen Generations happened so long ago, and yet it wasn't that long ago. They still want to push us in the background. That's what the government has done with Aboriginal people. We're not important. Why should we have a say? Why should we tell our story, be part of government, part of the development of the Territory? Yet we are here, we have been part of our Country and its history for such a long time now. We don't want to be left in the background anymore. We want to be in the forefront again. We want to be able to do things like anybody else, any other Australian. We want to share our Country. We want to share our culture and our history with Australia, whether it's dark or not. It is the history of this Country, whether they like it or not. We, as the First Nations peoples of this country, were affected by colonisation and we want to talk about all of this. We want truth telling, justice and reconciliation. We want people to know and understand the First Nations history and what happened to us, the NT Stolen Generations people.

8

A Life of Advocacy

A lot of my work was with the government or Stolen Gen, but there are many other things I did after I retired – some before, but mostly after I retired. I had a bit to do with archaeology, through Claire Smith from Flinders University. She goes to Barunga every year, where my Raelene and Mally used to live. That's where I met Claire. She had a lot to do with my two uncles: old Peter Manabaru, he was a renowned artist[77] who lived at Barunga and Claire and her husband Gary Jackson used to go and see him all the time, and Uncle Jimmy Wesan from Beswick. They were really senior traditional men.

Claire said to me, 'Eileen, you want to come away with us?' – with her and her archaeology students from Flinders University on a trip to South Africa and other countries.

I said, 'That sounds interesting, who else will be with us?'

'We will meet other people who work in the same area but are at other universities; it's an around-the-world trip. Your two uncles are coming with me and it'd be good if you were there because you can help look after them.' So I went with them, with Uncle Peter and Uncle Jimmy. She had a group of about 10 students from Flinders University, Aboriginal students, doing the archaeological training. They weren't all from South Australia – there was one from Mount Isa, two from Victoria, one, I think, was from Sydney and the rest from South Australia.

So I went with Claire and her students, that was in 1999. We went to England and had a look at all the museums in

London. We flew across to Paris, went to another museum there and the famous museum, the Louvre, and the Eiffel Tower. We then flew to Rome and looked at some great archaeological sites. We saw the Colosseum – what a huge structure! We saw the Trevi Fountain and the St Peter's Basilica. The ancient buildings were beautiful. We travelled to Washington in the US and visited the Smithsonian Museum where I looked at paintings and Aboriginal artefacts from Arnhem Land. I couldn't look at some of the artefacts, because they were men's business and I am forbidden under Aboriginal customs to look at those items. But I was able to look at the pandanus basket weaving done by our women from Arnhem Land in the Northern Territory. We also visited the Jewish Holocaust Museum. It was very interesting but very sad. Some time later I was supposed to travel with Claire and her students to San Francisco and Canada as well, but I couldn't go with her at that time, so I went later on. Because Claire gave me the travelling bug. When I retired, I travelled as much as I could to many countries in the world and places in Australia.

The trip around the world was a really big trip, in 1999, but the highlight was we went to South Africa. We were in Johannesburg and then drove down to Cape Town. We stopped off at Bloemfontein and picked up Sven Ouzman, an anthropology professor, and he took us to sites. One time, we stopped at a vineyard, it was beautiful, and in the morning you'd see the mist on top of the mountains. Another time, we camped at Sven's house. It was a little two-bedroom house and there were 16 of us, so people were sleeping on the floor, on the front porch, back porch, everywhere. It was an enjoyable time for us all. We stayed for one night and then Sven took us up to the caves to look at the archaeological sites. It was so beautiful. We had to get out of the bus to open and close the gates, and this huge ostrich chased us. We were afraid he would stomp on us! The ostriches can really run, you know. So we were all screaming, 'Come on, let's go before he stomps on us!'

We came back down the hill to another little town to get refreshments and something to eat. An old man comes up to me and says, 'How long have you been away from here?'

I said, 'What do you mean?'

'Well, you went away and now you're back.'

'No, I'm not from your country. I'm an Aborigine from Australia.'

'Oh, I thought you was one of our people.' We all had a big laugh about it, but he really thought I was African.

I said, 'No, I'm an Aborigine. Have you ever heard of the Aborigines of Australia?'

'Yeah, they're the same colour like me.'

I said, 'Yes, I am.' All the students cracked up laughing, 'Aunty Eileen, they think that you're from here!' He was so gorgeous, that old man.

In Cape Town, we stayed at the university, did the summer school there and attended a conference.[78] Claire asked me to give a talk at Cape Town University on our Land Rights Act in Australia, because they were interested in what it was for, and whether it was to help us get back to Country. So I gave a talk on that and a little on native title, but not much because native title had only just started then. The next day we went up in the cable car to the top of the mountain, Table Mountain.

I said to my two old uncles, 'You want to come up in the lift with me?'

'No, we don't want to go up there. That's too high. What is that thing for anyway?' says the two uncles.

I said, 'Uncle, you're supposed to be here, protecting me so I don't fall!' They were laughing, but they sat down in that garden and watched it happen. When I came back down, old Uncle Peter said, 'My girl, all these people know we are from Australia, how come?' I said, 'Uncle, you got our flag on your hat.' We started laughing, 'You both got those caps on. Of course they're going to see you from Australia!' But they wouldn't come up in anything, even in Paris, they wouldn't go up in the Eiffel Tower. Mind you, I wouldn't go up in it either. It was too frightening because I have a fear of heights. I do go up when they're not too high, but those places were too high. I went up in the cable car to Table Mountain, and it was beautiful up there.

We had a wonderful time in South Africa. We were participants at all the conferences that Claire organised. We met people there and we attended it daily. This African man, Mandela, he came to the opening and it was lovely to see him. We were in a big tent and one of the students said, 'Eileen, is that Mandela?' and I turned around and looked. I said, 'Yeah, that's him.' Isn't that amazing! He came into the tent. We were there with some African students, and the students from Australia and Cape Town University, but we didn't have a chance to talk to him because they sort of just whisked him in, he said, 'Hi,' to a few people, and then he was whisked off again. I really wanted to sit down and talk to him, but then he was gone, in a flash of an eye he was gone. It was amazing for me because I had read so much about him.

After we went on that big trip, I stayed in touch with Claire and her work, because she is closely aligned with a lot of my family members. That's how I started to have more to do with her, because of her work with the Barunga people and Beswick people. She got working with Rachel Willika and her family from Eva Valley, they're my people too. Claire was working a lot with them and she wrote the book around Barunga.[79] When she comes to Darwin, she comes to see me, and we became closer and closer all the time. Now she's like my little sister. When I went down to Adelaide, I went to her home a few times. I'd be staying with Lorky and then Claire would come and get me and I'd go up to her little hilltop and see her there. It was wonderful to see her work because we've often thought that our sites, archaeological sites, have never been protected. Aboriginal ones have never been protected, really. But as years went on, you could see the work that was happening. I think Claire and her team at Flinders have sort of opened a lot of people's eyes.

Then, a few years ago, she said, 'I want to do your story, Eileen.' It was partly because I started to work for the Stolen Gen and she saw that coverage on the ABC, but she really started after we came back from South Africa. She said, 'Well, Eileen, we should do your story!' I said, 'Oh yeah, and when are you going to have the time?' She and I laughed about it a bit. Then she said, 'Well, every time I come up, we'll do interviews.' It was in our mind for a long time, making this book of mine.

Another thing I did with Claire years ago was to travel around Australia and scream against the Intervention.[80] I retired from working with the Education Department in 2007, the same year as the flipping Intervention[81] came in, remember?

I got really angry because I had retired and I couldn't really talk anymore because I didn't work for the government. That's why I started travelling everywhere with Claire, screaming against the Intervention like a mad woman.[82] We took Rachel Willika with us, and Raelene and her little children, they were with me. We went around Australia to talk on panels of Aboriginal women from the Northern Territory. Talking about the Intervention and how it's affecting our people. We went to Adelaide, Melbourne, Canberra, we went to Sydney, we went to Perth, and Brisbane. We had that big one in Sydney at the Opera House; there were thousands of people there. So we went around talking about the Intervention and why it was so bad for our people. Because I'd stopped work, I was free to do what I wanted to do.

When the Intervention came in, it changed the whole system and took away the control from our people. Brought in town clerks from outside of their communities, white town clerks, all of that. So you wonder why our people went downhill. Because for a time there, they felt they'd lost control, they'd lost face, they'd lost everything. They'd lost their dignity, they lost everything. Because what we had worked on for such a long time in the government before that, was to start giving the responsibility back to our people. To use the structures they have grown up in. Having that respect for their culture and respect for their traditions would help them come back. The traditional structures that were in place almost came to a standstill. All communities before the Intervention were operated and run by the community councils, people of their communities. These were run well and alcohol, drugs and violence were controlled. Because in the old times, the councils were run by the community. The Intervention took away Aboriginal structures in family and community responsibility.

The Intervention blew everything apart. They took away the guidance and the direction of the men within the communities. There were some strong, wonderful men who had been helping me with all that process on the family violence. If I hadn't had those men and those leaders as part of that process, working with my staff and their women, we wouldn't have got as far as we did. When the Intervention came in they were all portrayed as paedophiles, sexual abusers and family violence abusers. A lot of the family violence and abuse is done by men, the perpetrators are men, but that can be prevented with guidance inside the Aboriginal system, with those Elders there, always there, as advisors. I grew up in the Aboriginal system from a child – they were teaching me that when I was a child as well. But the younger people of today don't want to be part of that system. They might learn from when they're little babies, they go and dance and be part of the ceremony, but as they get up to teenage years, they buck the system. All the knowledge they should be getting from the Elders and from the tribal structure is gone. Or it's there, but they don't want to be part of it. They're floating through the community, without guidance. This one old man who worked in the government told me, 'But that kept me grounded, because I grew up through that system. Then as I got older, I was there with the old men all the time and they were the ones, they were my advisors and teachers. They kept me grounded.' But he was raised from little boy right through. When he got to the teenage years where he could have run amuck, he still had the Elders there, they were still his advisors.

The men showed strength and leadership in the communities before the Intervention. Now they felt they had no place in their communities because it looked like the government was blaming men for everything. They felt disempowered. They had no way to go forward because who's going to listen to them if they are being blamed for everything? Of course, some men were doing these things, but there were so many good men working towards making a better, safe and happy community. Watching our strong men and leaders become disillusioned and question their purpose in life was heart breaking. Because in Aboriginal culture, you got the women's business and men's business, and to address issues in the community, you need both. Aboriginal people have those strong laws in place, both women and men's laws and community laws that affect the whole family. It was there and the governments and wider Australia didn't want to see it. The outside world never sees that. They always thought that Aboriginal people had nothing. But we have, we've got rich cultural systems and structures and traditional laws in place that help to guide and direct our clans, and our families. When the white system came in and we became colonised, they took it all away. Of course we hadn't had alcohol. And alcohol is one of the most demeaning and destructive things Aboriginal people have had to deal with. It upsets the family structure. Our people wanted a change from violence, alcohol and abuse.

When the Intervention happened in 2007, I think that's when they started pulling funding from the family violence strategy. It was working, we were getting the men on board and they pulled it out again. We had set up all those men's safe houses as well as the women's safe houses. In some of the communities they still have them, like Ngukurr and Tiwi Islands. This is the Aboriginal system. It's not a white system. I know some of the safe houses are still there because I hear from the women. I ran into one woman when I was out at dinner with Raelene and Gavon. She came up, she was hugging me, crying, and Raelene said, 'Do you know my mother?' That woman said, 'Yeah, your mother was the one that helped us at Tiwi Islands,' – about the family violence. 'She was really good and helped me.' What is so sad is that we still have so many issues facing our people. The Intervention came in and took away the people's responsibilities and broke up the many good ways that helped manage their lives – that was terrible. Our people lost hope: 'We were doing well and now they're going to mess us around.' They didn't have the power to do what they wanted to do in their communities, the government didn't want to listen to the solutions given by the communities. They wanted to make the decisions, then leave, leaving our people out of the decision-making process.

Aboriginal affairs is big business. Aboriginal affairs has always been big business. But our people haven't benefited from it. They give so much money, both the Commonwealth and the States, to Aboriginal affairs. They give a hell of a lot of money, but they still don't know how to use it properly. They've put in so many different things to try and counteract the issues, but it's never really worked. Because, again, the

Commonwealth and the States think that they know better. They'll give the communities a little bit of leeway, but they want to make sure that the money is being used the way they want it, not the way the community wants it. It was different with Marshall Perron. He knew if we could hear from the people, from the women, he'd know the best way the funds could be used. Not many politicians think that way. Governments have denied our way of life and want only their systems in place. A lot of the work I did was to give responsibility back to Aboriginal people, let them work out their system and regain their structures because we've got such a rich and diverse Aboriginal law. We can give so much. But when the Intervention came in, that all got pushed into the background.

When I retired from the government in 2007, I started to work with Charles Darwin University. When Emma and I finished with the government – my colleague Emma Williams from Chief Minister's – we went to CDU because we were setting up the Research and Evaluation Unit. Emma said, 'You want to come back and work with me?' I thought, Oh, here we go again. Emma and I joined Allan Arnold and John Guenther, that was our team, and we were attached to the Northern Institute at Charles Darwin University, doing research and evaluation of government-funded programs for Aboriginal people, both Commonwealth and State. We were going out to communities, working with them, teaching them because they wanted to do their own evaluation on their programs. So Emma and I were still working as a team but now based at CDU. The first programs we evaluated were a suite of projects focused on Aboriginal family violence, from 2007 until 2009. We evaluated the safe houses and family violence programs we had helped set up. I loved that because I was able to go back to the communities and see how it had all developed. Then we went out to look at the safe houses to make sure they were running properly, and getting the proper support and funding required to run them. We also evaluated other family violence programs. We visited different communities, like Canteen Creek and Yuendumu, and ran workshops with the communities, evaluating the progress of the programs to see if it worked within the funding and time frame. Through this process the communities found there were shortfalls that needed to be corrected.

Our evaluation process was quite different from the ordinary evaluation. It was with the people, for the people. Working with them in how they wanted to evaluate that program and to identify the shortfalls, whether they had enough funding, things like that, so they could keep the programs going. Often the programs were funded by the Commonwealth and were short term, and we wanted long-term projects. We didn't want projects finishing after six months. It was an ongoing process. We were evaluating, but we were also looking at ways to ensure the program was going to continue. It had to, otherwise family violence would've become a real mess on the communities. It has in some instances, because the Intervention came in and messed up everything. The women wouldn't give up the safe houses, no matter what, but they didn't get the support they required. After researching and evaluating each project we then, together with the community organisations, wrote a report to the funding agency. Before presenting to the agency we took draft reports back to the organisations to ensure we recorded the true facts. Evaluations were always done in partnership with the organisations. Because our people kept saying, 'We are sick and tired of people coming in and evaluating us and our programs, and we don't have a say in it.' So Emma and I, Allan and John, that's what we did. We were doing it with our people because that was a new way of doing evaluations.

During this time, we also evaluated a traditional healing

program in Alice Springs, because they got funds from the Commonwealth to run it. The Akeyulerre Healing Centre made their own healing medicines, skin products, creams, candles, medicines. They used to go out bush, take the families and children out in the bus, collect the bush ingredients and bring them back to Akeyulerre and boil it up, get it all ready and make everything. They also had a program there where they were working with their people and trying to heal some of them physically and mentally. It's a great program, because it's run by the community people. The program was based in Alice Springs, but the men and women travel out to the remote communities, like Yuendumu, Papunya, all those places in the southern region. At their office in Alice, they had a fireplace we often sat around and just talked. Participating and learning about their products was great and going back to observe the people collecting bush medicines and doing the artwork in their own way. So we had to evaluate the program to see the methods they used, the delivery, and whether there were gaps in the funding. Whether the program needed extra funding to ensure their products were saleable for the public. Whether the funding was used according to the project plans and time frames and whether the communities had improved in their social well-being. We ran community workshops evaluating their programs together with the workers, and the organisation. Then we'd write up a report about the evaluation process and bring that back to the organisation, board and workers, to read and discuss. Once the report was endorsed by the organisation, we could send the report back to the Commonwealth. It was their funding, to the remote communities and to the Aboriginal organisations.

We also had an education stream, teaching our people how to evaluate and research projects and programs. One of the projects we evaluated was at the Tangentyere Council in Alice Springs. We met and worked with staff and trained them in the evaluation process. They were setting up their own evaluation team there. We workshopped everything about the program and it was wonderful to see the staff draw up their own way graphs about how programs should be run. We were training our people so they could do their own evaluations and not have people coming in to do the evaluations for them. They were sick of other people coming in and doing research on them; they wanted to do it themselves, evaluating their own programs. We set up a training module at Charles Darwin so our people could understand what research and evaluation was all about, and we went out to the communities to do the training with them there. Once I went all the way to Canteen Creek; I'd never heard of this community before. John and I flew out there. Emma and I did most of the family violence programs, but where there were other programs, John would come with me, or Allan. I really enjoyed that, going out to the communities and doing the evaluation of their community programs with them. I also gave some lectures and workshops to students at CDU about our work.

After doing that for a while, I tried to retire again but started working with my people at Ngukurr, setting up a committee with the Traditional Owners of Ngukurr, which I'm part of. That lasted a few months. Then Emma called, 'Eileen, can you come back now?' So I went back to work with Emma, Allan and John, who were still there at CDU. We looked at the women's prison programs in Alice Springs and Darwin, that was 2014 to 2017. This was a program where Aboriginal women released from prison were put into their own flats, and were trying to reconnect with their children and family. The program was run through the health services in Alice Springs. We'd visit the women at prison and talk to a few of the prisoners. We started to meet with the women who were released and now trying to live normal lives again. It was amazing to see these women, because some of them had had it really bad. Some of them were in such violent situations that some of them had killed their husbands; that's why they were in prison. They had to try and come back out of that, out of the prison system and get back into their own family lives. We were trying to see whether the program was running according to their way of living and their beliefs. Some of the women did really well, others fell back and returned to the prison system. As long as they weren't anywhere near their violent husbands, they were progressing well. Sometimes the violence was really bad. So Emma and I evaluated that program to make sure that it was actually doing the right thing for the women. We talked to the women, we wanted to see how they felt about the program, whether it was useful for them. We wrote up an evaluation report about the program and sent it to the government.

I'm now sort of retired from CDU, but I am still attached to the university. I still do certain projects from time to time. When Flinders Uni set up their training for the doctors, it's part of the Charles Darwin University. I go in and talk to the trainee doctors about Aboriginal issues, Aboriginal customs, why Stolen Generations people don't often go to doctors, that sort of thing. I started to do this through the training health unit at CDU and I still do it from time to time. I talk to trainee doctors because a lot of them are being sent out to remote areas to work in the clinics, and they want to understand our Aboriginal ways and how to deal with our Aboriginal people in the remote communities. So I do presentations about those issues, and particularly about the Stolen Generations. Because a lot of our Stolen Generations people don't trust health departments or the police, they don't trust anybody. So I go and talk about the way they're feeling and why some of them won't talk about their issues. They might have cancer, but they don't want to talk about it. They don't want to go on dialysis and the reasons why they don't want to go on dialysis.

I'd say, 'Let them tell you how they're feeling. They're the ones that know how they're feeling. Let them explain it to you. You have to build up a rapport with them before they'll open up.' I still do that from time to time. It gets me out and gets me meeting other people and keeps me motivated, I guess.

Charles Darwin University gave me an honorary doctorate, in 2023. The Dean of our Northern Institute, Professor Ruth Wallace, recommended this. She has worked with Emma, John, Allan and me for a very long time and was the head of our unit. Ruth has always known about my work with the government, with CDU and remote communities and my people. Also, she's a young Aboriginal woman, originally from New South Wales, but moved to the Territory and was working at Charles Darwin University. I think Ruth had heard about my presentations with Charles Darwin students and about me giving lectures on Stolen Gen and Aboriginal issues. I suppose she was just watching me doing this all the time.

She said, 'Eileen, we want to recommend you for an honorary doctorate.'

I said, 'And why?'

'Because of the work you've been doing,' – through the uni, the government and the Aboriginal community. Ruth was aware of the work I've done over the years in Aboriginal education, community development, Aboriginal affairs advocacy and human rights. That's why they gave me the doctorate, because of that. At first, I didn't want to accept, but my daughters and grannies reckoned, 'That's an honour. You should take it.'

We had that big function at Charles Darwin University. We were looking at not only me, but a lot of other people, plus the student graduations and everything. I was presented with my honorary doctorate and my family attended my ceremony. My great-grandson Fabian was sitting and listening when Ruth was reading the details about my work and my achievements. He turns around and says to his nana, to my daughter Michelle, 'I didn't know grandma did all those things!' Shelly said, 'Your grandma worked very hard when she was a worker. Now we're trying to slow her down.' This is what Michelle said to Fabian. When his nana told me this afterwards, I just hugged him so tightly. So even though I'd been working all these years, my grandchildren knew very little about my job. Fabian would've been about 12 when that happened. But I've never looked for accolades. I just did my work. We live in this world, do all things. I've never been there for my own benefit. You know what I'm saying? I've always tried to work for my people and for the betterment of them and for their development, not so much my own. I wanted to make sure they had the proper education, and they were able to work in the workforce, things like that.

For a long time, I wouldn't even use the title, then people would ask, 'Aren't you Dr Cummings?' I would say, 'Yes I am.' I've always said it's a wonderful title, but the most important and the most fulfilling title is being a mother, a grandmother, and a great-grandmother, and friend to people, friend to all. The title of being a doctor is fine, and I suppose it's showing respect for what I've achieved over the years and what I've done. To me, it wasn't the most important thing in my life. The most important thing in my life was my people being educated, getting jobs. All the processes that I've put in place, and the development, were helping them get proper jobs. It is wonderful our people have employment in their communities. Working in the safe houses and all of that. So I am Dr Eileen Cummings. It is an honour to have an honorary doctorate, but my most favourite title is being a mother, grandma, friend, and advocate for my people, the First Nations of my country, Australia.

When I slowed down working with CDU – in 2009, 2010 – then I started working on Country, I called it. I worked on my traditional lands of the Ngalakan tribe at Ngukurr. They invited me to come help, so I went out to Country to set up the Traditional Owners' organisation, Millwarparra Aboriginal Corporation. The name 'Millwarparra' is the name of Roper River itself. My uncle, Tex Camfoo,[83] one of the old Traditional Owners (TOs), said, 'We're going to call the new committee Millwarparra Aboriginal Corporation.' We put that in and it went through ORIC[84] to get incorporated. The Ngukurr TO Corporation, that's my Traditional Owners group. I was part of the committee, and I was an executive director of the corporation. I always wanted to do something for my people on Country because even though I'd worked with the Bulman mob – my dad Jukaduk's land – where my mum and everybody ended up living, I was really interested in what happened at Ngukurr. Ngukurr is one of the biggest remote Aboriginal communities, and it has a lot of government services there. Different private businesses are also run at Ngukurr. There is a huge river and people often want to go fishing and touring on our land.

That's what the Corporation is for, liaising and instructing NLC and businesses and managing royalties. Any business that goes there, we meet with the Northern Land Council and the Economic Development Unit, and say whether leases can go ahead or not, things like that. The NLC is a big organisation here, funded by the federal government, and they're supposed to look after all Traditional Owners right across the Northern Territory. There's a lot of us, not just one group. The NLC works with all Traditional Owners right across the top end of the Northern Territory. They are supposed to take instructions from all TOs so they can divvy whatever royalty monies come in for each group. NLC has always been pretty good working with us in relation to our Country. The NLC officer runs it really well; he's a great communicator and we had some wonderful meetings with him. Geoff, the economics officer, puts the leases up on the board: 'This is the lease somebody's just written in, wants to do this on your land, are you happy about it?' He discusses with us, we say yes or no. Last time we agreed with all of them except one, we said we wanted a little more time to think about it. The council wanted to extend their municipal station where they keep their fuel. They wanted to build more on that land. We said, 'No, give us a little more time to think about it and we'll come back to you next year.' Because at that time we were feeling that the Yugal Mangi council was just getting too much control over the land. One of our committee members went out to talk to them to find a solution.

We get royalties from any businesses on our land, for the use of our land. We get paid around $300,000 a year for leases on our Country. We go through a process where the committee and the TOs decide whether we give any of our people the money out of our royalties. We meet with NLC and give instructions on how our royalties are spent. Sometimes it was for medical reasons, to come into hospital, to go to the Royal Adelaide Hospital. Other times it was to do with education for the children. Sometimes it was for sports for their children – they were representing the Territory and travelling and they had no money to do this. So if our people wanted to do those activities and they didn't have the money to do it, well, the Corporation helped them. So committee had to meet and decide and then send the instructions to NLC. That's the process we put in place. Because we felt that NLC didn't meet us often enough. Before that, all that the TOs could do was work through NLC, but they only have meetings once or twice a year with NLC, and so people in the community were left high and dry. We felt we had to address our peoples' social and health wellbeing. They just live on Centrelink and if they want to do other things, we help them with that through our royalties. We also help with funerals.

We set up a system where we had a form they had to fill in, or they come in and say, 'This is what we want and this is how much we require.' The committee would discuss whether that was a feasible amount of money. We had a system where it wasn't just given to everybody but, at Christmas time, each individual would get a bit of money. During the year, when the people had nothing and the royalty money was sitting in a trust in NLC, the committee would write to them with instructions saying, 'So-and-so needs this money for such and such. The committee has endorsed it.' That was the system I had in place.

We had 12 members on the committee, I think, but we always maintained that the chair had to be living at Roper, Ngukurr. If you wanted to be the chair, you'd have to live there and stay there. The chair, Eric, and I established an office at Ngukurr because we wanted to make sure our people had a service there. The community councils are there, but the Traditional Owners are a bit of a separate matter, they do their own thing. So we used some of the money to set up that office, and we bought a car for the chairman and a bus so they could travel to Katherine. After we set up that office, the people on the community could go there and we could talk to the committee from there. We had computers and a phone, and I could talk to them on the phone from town, where I was living. I was the secretary treasurer, so I could do that from town. Being computer literate, I was able to do those letters to the NLC, get the committee to sign them off and endorse it. I drove to Ngukurr sometimes to meet the chair or he would come to Darwin. We'd have meetings for the Traditional Owners, either at Ngukurr, or in Katherine. It was my role as committee secretary to organise meetings of the Corporation every three months, but sometimes if there was a funeral or some urgent medical plan, we would meet to discuss the financial implication. This was a real challenge because we had to get people from Roper River station, Minyerri, Bulman, Katherine and Darwin. But our committee was functional. It gave me great pleasure working with my people and the group. I feel the committee that Eric and I worked was run efficiently and effectively.

For years, I had all this in place and then I had to give up the work on our lands because of my treatment for cancer. This saddened me because I could no longer go out to the community, where I had worked for six years. I just left the committee to their own devices, and that system isn't in place anymore; all the money just sits at the NLC. I said, 'Well, how do people get any help from you?' And they said, 'Oh, they can talk to the committee out at Ngukurr.' But none of them are reachable, really, their phone numbers change every month. When Eric was alive, we had things running well. As soon as he died, poor dear, it all just went downhill. All the younger people got on board and it's not running properly anymore. That's why I tried to go back to see what I could do. I've just started to come back into my group. I'm not on the committee, but I'm back going to meetings now. I just started returning to Country recently, but it's sad because many of our Elders have passed and our history is slowly fading. We had a meeting a few months ago for the Traditional Owners down there and I went to that meeting with my daughter and a couple of my cousins. That's the first one I've been to for the last 10 years, I suppose. But it's not working properly anymore. The committee is failing, everything's ad hoc and not well managed. The younger people don't have the same commitment or skills to run a corporation like Millwarparra. To me, all they look at is monetary gain. They're not looking at what they can do on their communities and how they can help their people. By the time I finished with the committee, I left $800,000 in the bank because the Commonwealth gave Traditional Owners additional money after the Intervention.

Quite a large sum of money, and they just went and spent it on silly things. Soon as I left, they were spending it on cars and giving money here there and everywhere. I said, 'Instead of buying a car, why didn't you buy a bus?' Because a lot of people like to go to Katherine. Apparently, they did purchase a bus, but people were misusing it, and it broke down and couldn't be fixed so they ended up with nothing. I thought, I'm out of it now. I can't do anything about it. When I left they had money in the bank, they had a good relationship with the bank in Katherine, and everything went beautifully. Then they went and blew it. Even the office was damaged and phones and computers misused. But I couldn't do anything about it. I'd left the organisation by that time.

It saddens me because we who all live elsewhere from Ngukurr are being pushed aside by our own clan group because we aren't living on Country. They wanted to only keep the people living in the community as Traditional Owner. They were trying to push out all the Traditional Owners that didn't live at Ngukurr because they wanted to have the say and the money from Ngukurr because we've got a big lot of lease money coming in every year. When I left, they were trying to cut the numbers of Traditional Owners. There were too many children, and they wanted the money to benefit them at Ngukurr, nowhere else. But with Traditional Owners, you can live anywhere. You don't have to live on your land, you're still a Traditional Owner, that's under NLC charter. We come from all over the place to go to the meetings out there. They tried to push us out, the ones not living on Country; they didn't want us there anymore. But you can't do that, because when you have a land claim, all our names are on that land claim list. And you can't just cut off Traditional Owners at a whim. Traditional Owners are there forever. They go through the land claim, they're listed on the land claim. We have found this situation often with our Stolen Generations people, but they forget we didn't leave our lands – we were removed by the Commonwealth government as children. We lost our rights by the removal policy, but not by our Aboriginal laws and customs: we still own and belong to our traditional lands, also according to the NT Land Rights Act.

When this was happening, I was getting treated for cancer. I said, 'No, I can't travel. I'm not coming anymore.' But I sent a letter last year to the anthropologist, 'I'm over my treatment. I seem to be on the road to recovery. I want to still be part of all of this because you all just put us out. Just remember that my grandfather, Yilparrara, was the head of the Ngalakan tribe. I want to be back on the list again.' I said I would be willing to go out to our lands at Ngukurr to work with the committee to get it back on track. That's why I went back to that TO meeting a few months ago. Raelene always attended meetings with me, so she came too. A couple of my cousins also came, we all went back to the meeting to question them. We said, 'None of the Elders there are alive and you young people don't know the stories of this Country, so how can you kick us out?' My grandfather was the eldest of all the of the Ngalakan leaders. Ngukurr – that's on Ngalakan land. That's our Country.

We've also had this difficulty with the land councils, like the Northern Land Council. They're saying, 'You don't live there and you are not part of that Country.' They never took into account that we were forcibly removed from our Country as children under the removal policy. We had no say in the matter so they shouldn't delete us from the Traditional Owners list. They denied all the Stolen Generations people. The land councils have also left us out, we've been denied our own Country. Many of us had a lot of difficulties trying to get back on Country, but because my mother put me on the land claim when she was still alive, I was able to return.

In 2013, I ran for office, but I didn't win. It was a federal election and we had our own Aboriginal party.[85] There was one candidate from Maningrida, me from Darwin and one from Alice Springs, I think. Maurie Ryan, my Croker Island brother, established the Aboriginal party and he said, 'Eileen, you want to run for Darwin?' I said, 'Oh, I don't know. I'm not really a political maniac.' He wanted me to run for the seat of Solomon in Darwin. I thought, Oh, well I might as well. Not doing much. I ran, but I didn't win. I didn't do too badly. What I really wanted to do, was see how our political party would go, because Maurie had put so much work into establishing it. Also, I thought, I might as well do something for our people here in the Northern Territory. That was the first time we put our party in at the federal level, so I was happy with the outcome. Poor Maurie, he was very disappointed, but me and the other candidates weren't – we gave it our best shot.

I haven't run for office since, but I do follow politics. Leading up to the Voice referendum,[86] I had so many people ringing me, asking questions. The phone never stopped. People asked, 'What is the Referendum? Will it help our people? Why should we vote Yes? Will we be able to tell the government our issues and what's important? Will we have a bigger say in our affairs?' Some people said, 'The government has never listened so how will this improve our voice? We've been talking for years and the government never listened, or never heard what we were saying.' I had long discussions with each person and my suggestion was that they think about the Referendum as this could be a way forward. But I never said, 'You should vote for Yes.' I said, 'You think about what you've told me. Will it help us? Will it make life better? Well, consider where our people can run their own programs.' Community-based programs developed in our communities by the people, for the people, because we understand the issues of our people. One good example is the Rangers program. Our people are responsible for looking after Country and protecting Country and sites – what a good program to have.

It was amazing how many of our people wanted the Voice referendum to succeed. The people wanted change and a bigger say in their own affairs. They said, 'We have tried so many things, so let's try this and see if it helps us.' What they saw on the media upset many, but they were willing to vote Yes if it would bring change in Aboriginal affairs. That's why the result was so disappointing. I was really sad about the Voice. You can't have reconciliation in this country because until the people of Australia acknowledge the dark history of its First Nations people, we will never have reconciliation. How can we reconcile if our history isn't shared by all who live in our beautiful country? As First Nations people, we continue to share our land and our culture, but we've been moved aside. The referendum, I thought, would be a way forward, and we've been in a rut for such a long time. I was sad about it. People rang me afterward, like the ABC and others, 'Eileen, what are you going to say?' I said, 'Until Australia acknowledges and understands the sad dark history of First Nations peoples of this land, Australia as a nation will never move forward. It's time for change.'

Shine Lawyers sent out an ad in September 2024 talking about stolen wages, a stolen wages class action. They got $202 million from the Commonwealth for stolen wages in the Northern Territory.[87] They rang me and I told them I didn't think I was eligible. She said, 'Yes, you are, Eileen, what about your mother?'

I said, 'But my mother's gone.'

She said, 'Yes, we're still getting wages for the deceased people, but giving it to their children.' Nobody got paid money back then, the Aboriginal people. My mother worked at the cattle station for 30 years and she didn't get anything, just rations, like flour, sugar, tobacco and tea. The old people who worked for the mission on Croker Island, Mick and Timothy and others, I don't think they were paid. They invited everybody to a meeting, there were nearly a hundred of us, and they had about five or six lawyers there. They were doing a registry, with our current address, any email or telephone numbers, our bank details. I filled in my section on a form and then two old Aboriginal women said, 'Hey, my girl, can you help me?' I helped them fill in their forms. They've got $202 million to distribute between all the people of the Northern Territory. Not much, but it's something. For the money I'll get for Mum, I'm going to go back to Bulman, where Mum now rests in a graveyard, and organise a headstone for her grave. Mum and Dad are both in a graveyard in the community cemetery at Bulman. Mum's sisters and her brothers are also there. I believe that my grandparents, Mum's parents, are there too. If we can find Nana and Grandpas' graves, I will put up headstones for them too.

At that meeting, a lawyer looked at my form and she said, 'That's good, Eileen, but I want you to put yourself down there.' I said, 'What do you mean?' She asked me what it was like growing up on Croker Island. I told her we all did jobs. We had to from when we was about nine or 10, all the way through till we were in our teens.' I said, 'I thought that was part of growing up in a mission. I didn't think of it as work.' She replied, 'Yes, Eileen, it was work. You were nine or 10 and you were working.' I said, 'The only thing I was really scared of was getting washing out of that big hot copper.' I felt I was too little for those big sticks and it was frightening. We used to do gardening and minding the goats, and every second Saturday they'd wake me up and tell me I had to go and cook breakfast for the boys. I was quite happy to do that. The lawyer said, 'Did you ever get any money?' I said, 'I remember one day we're all outside the store and they gave us threepence each. Did you know what I did with my threepence? I went and bought lollies.' She laughed with me and said, 'Well, that's normal, that's what children would do.' I said, 'I had threepence that day. But I don't remember seeing any other money.' It was the Shine Lawyers who told us that we were working when we were children and we shouldn't have been. That's why they're going for the lost wages. But I said, 'No, I'm only putting in for my mother.' I didn't want to go for myself. I've had enough from the Commonwealth. I didn't feel comfortable about that because we already took Croker Island, the mission, to court about duty of care and not looking after us properly. I've done what I had to. I fought them for compensation. Now it's just the lost wages to be finalised. I wanted to get money to put a proper headstone on my mother and grandparents' graves.

Now, I am encouraging the rest of my family to put in for their family members. For Mai, her mother Aunty Kitty actually worked with the buffalo hides. The buffalo catchers used to shoot the buffalos and skin them. The Aboriginal people then had to tend and tan the hides. That was hard work. When Mai found out about the lost wages claim, we were talking about her mum and her people working on buffalo hides. She said, 'No, they never got paid for it.' I said, 'Well, put that in to the lost wages lawyers.' They got tobacco, flour, sugar and tea from the buffalo catcher. I sent her the forms for the stolen wages. And I didn't put in for Dad. I thought, I'd rather let Ronnie's children do it so they can get something out of it. I thought it'd be better coming from them, not me. I've only put in for Mum, because my brother's gone now and only me and Ronnie were her children. My niece Margo and I had a discussion about it and she said, 'All right, aunty, I'm going to put in for Grandfather.' She'll pay for Dad's headstone and I'll pay for Mum's. Of course, all my uncles also worked for the station, so I told their children to put in for them. I told my brother Kenny, 'You got to put in for Dad,' for Uncle

Dick. I said, 'I can't put in for your father. You've got to put in for your father yourself.'

They're all doing it now. I am trying to support them, because they were having difficulty filling in the paperwork. Every day they'd ring and say, 'Eileen, we don't know what they mean here.' So I'd be helping them over the phone to make sure they understood those questions. I said to Ewen, 'You can put your dad's name down there, but if you know your grandparents, put their names down as well.' Those forms are good, it's quite a simple process if you are used to it. And I sure was used to it after all the other compensation stuff. They ask you what your mother's or father's name is and where they worked. You say Bulman or Mainoru. Then you say what sort of work they were doing. They give you a list of all the things that they might be doing, like cattle work. Like, my mother was cooking, she was doing cattle work, cooking, all of that. I had to do instructions with Margo, but she understands computers, whereas Ewen was a little lost. He doesn't understand computers so well. I said to Margo, 'Can you help your daddy Ewen?' And that's now in the courts.

9

The Importance of Family and Community

Ray and I stayed married, and when he got sick, I took care of him for a while until he was able to do it himself. One day I was in Canberra at a conference and the girls rang up and said, 'Dad's moved.' It was a shock to me. They said, 'To Kurringal Flats, he's got a Housing Commission flat.' I said, 'Oh, don't be silly, girls.' What he said was, it was the noise of the children, the grannies, that he couldn't cope with in my household, because the grannies used to often come to my place. Sometimes they'd stay, Shelly would stay with her kids. The children were always around, and he couldn't take that, the noise was too much for him. So he went and saw Housing, and Housing gave him a flat. By that time, he wasn't violent anymore. He was a sick man suffering with cancer. He had big operations in Royal Adelaide Hospital and could no longer talk. I felt it was okay for me to take care of him until he was able to take care of himself. He was still living with us, but he learned to provide for himself because he had to make special foods, he did that himself. When he felt he was confident enough, he moved to his own place. So that would've been about 1986, 87.

We went to visit him; I used to take the grannies to see him every Sunday. That's how we kept the connection going. I didn't want them to lose out on their grandfather, even though he might've been a bastard of a man before his illness. By this time, he was calm. After the cancer buggered him up for good, he became quite a nice man. He wasn't drinking. He was a healthy sick man because he'd still go fishing and riding his bike and all that sort of thing. But he felt more comfortable being in a place on his own. I felt more comfortable too, I think, because I didn't have to worry about it anymore. I knew he'd never be violent again. He used to go to the pub, but not drink. He ran the darts competition and played pool. He'd go fishing on his own, come back with fish for us and for the neighbours around Kurringal Flats. He had always been a nice person, but when he was drunk, he was terrible. The cancer changed him back to the person he was before his drinking.

We used to visit him quite often. I'd take Raelene's children one weekend, Shelly's children the next, Sheena's children the one after, so he saw his grandchildren and they could see him. I didn't think it was fair that the grannies would miss out on their pop. And they'd have a wonderful time with him. He was a good grandfather. The kids just adored him. We were down at football one weekend and one little boy said to my grandson Raymond, 'Your grandpa can't talk!' And he said, 'Of course my grandpa can talk!' They had their own way of talking with Ray, my three eldest grandchildren. He had throat cancer, but he'd write notes all the time, that's how we communicated. He had his own way to communicate with the grannies. He couldn't talk at all, but they thought he could. Gavon was a late talker and I am sure this was attributed to his pop because they had their own way of communicating, talking didn't come into the equation. When Raymond said that to the other little boy, that made me so proud, it brought tears to my eyes. Regardless of his condition, he was their pop and they adored him. He played footy and games with them, they didn't want to leave him when we came to visit. It was a beautiful bonding time for him and his grandchildren.

When Malcolm was born, Ray was dying. He was in the

hospital having chemotherapy. Raelene had just had Malcolm, and Ray kept saying, 'Eileen, I want to see Raelene and the baby. I want to see Raelene and the baby.' When I talked to the doctors, they said, 'No, you can't bring the baby here because he's having chemo.' They were worried about the chemicals, the chemotherapy. I said, 'Oh, can't he just see him?' After a couple of hours, they wheeled Raelene in the wheelchair and I picked up the baby. He was wrapped in his little blanket, and I picked him up and showed him to Ray. And Malcolm smiled at Raymond. He was only a couple of hours old. I lifted him and he looked at his grandpa and smiled. I said, 'Now you happy?' Ray was happy then. We were all crying, even my daughters – they were there, Michelle and Sheena, they were crying. The grannies were crying. Two days later, Ray went into a coma and never came out of it. That was in 2001, when he passed away.

To this day, Malcolm still believes he knows his grandpa. Malcolm's my youngest grandson, the last one. One time, he was only about two or three, kicking the football in the backyard and he kept talking to someone. 'Who are you talking to?' I said. 'To Poppa. Poppa teaching me how to kick the football.' I just looked at him and I said, 'Where Poppa?' 'There! There!' he'd say. You couldn't see anybody, it was his imagination that his poppa was there watching him. Little buggerlugs. And Poppa was a good footballer, both of Mally's granddads were good footballers. So it was amazing, a miracle I've never forgotten, seeing Malcolm do that. The girls, his sisters said, 'You don't even know Poppa.' 'Yes, I do,' he says. We were all flabbergasted because he was only a couple hours old when I held him up for Ray in the hospital and he smiled. What an amazing and wonderful thing. Throughout his life, Malcolm always said he knew his Pop and no one could say he didn't. I get really emotional when I think about this, because they loved their poppa, even though he'd lost his voice. He had all these operations over his face and they still loved him. He was their poppa, his love and theirs were unconditional. The children miss him to this day. They talk about their times with their pop. I am so sad he isn't here to see our grandchildren, great-grandchildren and how much our family has grown. The love and care we share.

I have 10 grandchildren and 15 greatgrandchildren, and I hope there might be more coming. I love them so very much and am so blessed I have them in my life. I rarely speak about my family, but I love being a mother, nana and grandma. Spending happy times with them at family BBQs and Christmas Days and birthdays, watching them grow and develop into beautiful people, a credit to their parents and grandparents. I just feel so blessed to have this wonderful family and so sorry their pop isn't here to see them and our growing clan.

Raelene Rosas is my eldest daughter. After she finished high school, Raelene started work at 16 with NARU,[88] part of the University of Canberra. She worked with Dr Peter Loveday, they used to go bush and do a lot of projects. Raelene would stay with my mother and father out at Bulman, that's why she came back speaking the language quite fluently.

When Sheena left school, she went straight to work and was working in childcare, and Michelle was working in a store; a company that sold stuff for the wharf and boats. My children worked as soon as they left school and then they had partners. Raelene was married to a wonderful man, Mally Rosas,[89] and her children are Grace, Shania and Malcolm. Raelene adopted Grace and grew her up because she was her cousin Patricia's baby. Patricia died of cancer, poor darling, and her husband took care of the two little boys but found it too much to also cope with a new baby. So they talked to Patricia and Patricia just said, 'I want Mally and Raelene to have the baby.' So before Patricia died, Mally and Raelene went to the hospital and signed the necessary papers. Raelene said, 'Oh Mum, I was so nervous,' because she'd never had a child of her own, you know? All of a sudden she had Grace. Aunty Penny, a relation of my mother's, helped her with the baby, because Raelene was living in Barunga at the time. Aunty Penny was married to an old man from Barunga and they helped Raelene with Grace. They looked after Grace while Raelene and Mally were working. Also, Christine and Ronnie went and lived with Raelene and Mally, they moved to Barunga from Bulman and looked after little Grace. Grace used to call Pop Ronnie 'Beeper'. We don't know why, we don't know where that name came from! Raelene also helped out raising the other Ryan kids, Grace's brothers and sister. Grace and her partner Tristan have two daughters. Grace has adopted children, she's taken on her partner's children, Olivia and Ayanna. They move between Darwin and Yarralin, Tristan's community out west. Shania and partner Chance and their son Daikoss live in Darwin. They just had their new baby, Mahleila-Rae. Shania worked for a bank out at Gove for some years but is now living back in Darwin.

Raelene's son Malcolm is an AFL[90] player, originally with the Gold Coast Suns in Queensland before being traded to the Sydney Swans at the end of 2025. I remember him running around as a little boy, he was always football mad, always had a football in his hand from when he was knee high to a grasshopper. He'd say to Grace and Shania, 'Come out here and kick the football to me.' And they'd say, 'No, we don't want to come out there.' When I'd be visiting, I'd say to the girls, 'Go out there and play with your brother.' So they'd go out and kick the football with him. When it was time for him to go to training, Grace drove him. If she couldn't, I drove him. Because Mum and Dad were always working, Mally was working out bush, father Mally. So we all assisted in taking Malcolm to training since junior football. Father Mally was doing all the roads out in the bush on the big graders and then he did truck driving for a while after that. So little Mally, when he got to about seven or eight, he'd jump in the truck with his father and go out on runs on those big semitrailers. I said, 'You going to be a semitrailer driver when you grow up?' 'No, Nana,' he said, 'I'm going to be a footballer.' It was in his head from that high, and now he is. We knew how talented he was when he was a little boy, because he played all sports well. He played soccer, he was talented at that and the soccer community wanted him to stay with it. Then he decided to play rugby and he was good at rugby. He was good at basketball. He's just like Raelene, Raelene's always been sporty. Once he got into football, though, his parents stopped him from playing the other sports. Because the AFL doesn't allow you to play anything else once you become part of a squad. Malcolm has a lot of experience because he's been with the Boomerangs[91] since he was quite young. He went to China and South Africa with them when he was only about 14 or 15. He was in the Australian team, club and Territory football teams, from his junior sports to now. Malcolm got into the elite squad, then the Allies squad, and won the NT Rising Star Award when he was 16. A few years ago, Raelene and I took her grandson Daikoss to visit his Uncle Malcolm in the Gold Coast. We watched a game, which Daikoss loved. We had a great time with all the footballers, families and club officials, they were wonderful and took good care of us. The Club, when playing in Darwin each year, also spend time with our family and we are so welcomed by them. My whole family go to the games to watch and support Malcolm, all wearing the Club shirts.

Our entire family was very sporty. Sport was the thing that held me together. I played a lot of sport, every woman sport you could think of. I encouraged my girls to play sport. Raelene was in Little Athletics at an early age and won in all the sports she participated in. Michelle and Sheena excelled in basketball, soccer, hockey, netball and softball, like Raelene. I played the same sports and our Saturdays and Sundays were very busy. We all represented the State and Territory in our sport at one time or another. I was also a coach, manager and administrator in our sports teams. From 60 years old I participated in the Masters Games in Alice Springs. When we were younger, my husband Ray played Aussie rules, rugby, basketball and he boxed. My grandchildren followed in the same way. Raymond, Gavon and Yowane played Aussie rules, rugby league and rugby union. Gavon played from junior to senior and excelled in rugby league. He was rugby league, through and through rugby, because his father was a rugby man, represented Australia in the under-21 team. Gavon represented the Territory, went everywhere, the other boys too. The girls, my granddaughters, also played sport. I supported and encouraged our grandchildren in whatever sport they chose. Ray missed out on seeing our grannies play sport, but I know he would have been so proud of them all, like when he watched his daughters play sport and showed so much pride in their efforts. Sports also flowed into my great-grandchildren. Jayden and Owen were in athletics and Owen is a rugby league player. I also watched my two-year-old great-grandson Raymond Namambia kick a drop kick in football and his cousins Keelan, Keegan, Jamiah and Jamyson play rugby and football. So sport continues throughout the family.

Raelene was playing A grade softball at the age of 14, she was so good. A woman came across from America – she was going around Australia with a team – and she brought them to Darwin. She said to me, 'Eileen, can I take Raelene to America? Look at her. She's so talented. She can pitch, she can catch, she can hit, she can do anything on the softball field.' But I thought, No way in the world you're going to take my daughter to America.

Above: 9.1 Eileen Cummings with daughters Michelle, Sheena and Raelene, c. 1998

Left: 9.2 Raelene Rosas and her husband Malcolm at the Barunga–Beswick–Bulman turnoff on the Stuart Highway, c. 1987 (Raelene Rosas personal collection)

Below: 9.3 Raelene and Malcolm Rosas with their daughter Shania

Top: 9.4 Michelle Cummings with her sons, Raymond and Gavon

Left: 9.5 Eileen Cummings at Darwin Airport with granddaughters Grace and Shania, c. 1998 (Raelene Rosas personal collection)

Below: 9.6 Eileen Cummings' granddaughters with her brother Ronnie Lindsay, at Bulman during school holidays, c. 2010. L–R: Grace, Eileena, Leanora, Shania. Left foreground: Ronnie's wife Christine Lindsay and their daughter Loretta (Raelene Rosas personal collection)

Above: 9.7 Chris Hemsworth with Eileen Cummings' Bulman family

Below: 9.8 Sheena Cummings with Melissa and John Randall

Left: 9.9 Eileen Cummings with Dorothea and Anita Randall

Below: 9.10 Lorraine Siwes and her children (standing, L–R): Christopher, Phil and Darren, and, at front, Debbie

Above: 9.11 Christine Lindsay with daughter Raelene Rosas (seated), Grace, Malcolm and Shania standing behind

Right: 9.12 Malcolm Rosas with Eileen Cummings' great-grandson Keelan

Below: 9.13 Eileen Cummings with her grandson Malcolm

Above: 9.14 Eileen Cummings with her great-grandson Jamiah

Left: 9.15 Michelle Cummings with her children, Gavon, Raymond and Adaleen

Below: 9.16 Sheena Cummings and her children and grandchildren at Raymond Cummings' gravesite

Above: 9.17 Eileen Cummings with her granddaughters

Below left: 9.18 Eileen Cummings with her grandsons

Below right: 9.19 Malcolm Rosas jnr., Raelene Rosas and Eileen Cummings at Malcolm's induction into the Sydney Swans Football Club (AFL), 2026

She was a friend of Freddy Schmidt's, one of the coaches up here. Fred and his wife, both were American, and he was wonderful, old Freddie. Freddie reckoned, 'Why don't you let her go, Eileen?' I said, 'I'm not sending my child over there. She's only 14.' Raymond said, 'Well, they can go and jump. She's not going to America.' After I had been taken off my mother, no way in the world I was going to let my child go. But we had a good laugh about it, and this coach, she used to come back every now and again. She was a great coach, it was wonderful to watch her and watch the American team, they were something out of this world. Some of our girls were starting to get really good in the Territory. One of the younger girls, later on, did go over there, but she went with her parents. Raelene travelled all around Australia playing softball for the Territory side, her, Shelly and Sheena. That was something I made sure of, that they had other outlets so they couldn't run off and drink and smoke and carry on. That's how it was. Raymond wasn't a drunk until later on in life because he was a sportsman himself. He played football, he played rugby, played basketball and did boxing when he was younger.

Michelle Cummings is my second daughter. She and her partner Marty live in Batchelor. They visit us here in Darwin and we travel to Batchelor some weekends. Michelle separated from the children's father, Thomas, when they were very young. Years ago, Shelly had an accident with her new partner and he was killed. I was in Yuendumu doing a workshop and the police came out there. 'Eileen, you've got to fly back to Darwin. Your daughter was in an horrific accident. We'll run you into Alice and put you on the first available flight.' I just jumped in the police car with the police, got to the airport. Peter Conran was the boss at the time, for the Chief Minister's Department. He rang and said, 'Eileen, we got bad news, Michelle's had a bad accident. She is still alive but she's in a bad way and in hospital. We've got to bring you home.' She was in hospital for three months. They had her in traction and she still has steel plates in her arms and legs. Whenever she flies, she has to take a letter with her, because they never took them out.

Neil, her partner at that time, was testing out a buggy on his family's block; one of these bull buggies you use for buffalo catching on stations. Shelly was there with him, and the children too. Adaleen would've been about two or three, they were very young. The bull buggy turned over, killed Neil instantly as he threw his body over Shelly to try and protect her. He was such a lovely man, he took those children in like his own. It was so sad when it happened, we couldn't tell her straight away. When she came to, she was asking, 'Mum, where's Neil?' The doctor said, 'Eileen, I think you better don't tell her anything just yet. Just say he's in one of the other rooms.' So I had to tell a lie, and I didn't really like to lie. I wanted to tell her the truth. But they said, 'No, she is too unstable, the shock might kill her.' When she started to feel better, I had to tell her. She got out of hospital and started to have these mental issues. Like, it was pointless living. It was pointless having the kids, all of that. Michelle grieved for a long time. I guess that's how she felt. She didn't want to live. Neil was such a lovely man, he used to take Michelle and the children camping and fishing. His family came from Daly River and lived on an outstation, Chuluk. Michelle and her children used to go out to Neil's Country all the time with him. Neil wasn't a drinker, he was a good provider. One of these men that you want one of your daughters to have as a partner. When Neil got killed in the accident, it was so sad. His loss devastated the entire family. It took us all a long time to get over it. But we had to focus on Shelly, trying to nurse Shelly back from that horrible tragedy.

So Raelene, Sheena and I took the children in turns.

Sheena took them for the first three months because I was working. Raelene then took them to Barunga, they lived with Mally and her for six months. At that time Adaleen was very young, she was still going to preschool. I used to go down and visit them with Raelene at Barunga. When Shelly got out of hospital, she went to Raelene, and stayed there and worked at the preschool where Adaleen was. The boys were in school with all the other children at Barunga. The boys, I tell you, loved going to school at Barunga. I used to go down and visit every possible chance I had. I'd just drive the Commodore down and visit them all. One day, I got down there and they had all their little bags packed. Raelene said, 'Well, Mum, they said they're coming back with you.' So I brought the children and Shelly back to Darwin with me, but then Shelly went off, back out bush. She still wasn't well, was still grieving. That's what our people do when they're not well, they go out bush. So from then on, I kept the children with me. I said, 'You go sort your life out, do what you have to do. I'll keep the children.' I was working full time and every time I travelled, they stayed with Sheena. We were living in a flat in Leanyer and the boys were going to Leanyer Primary School; Adaleen was in preschool. We lived just up the road from the school. The flat was a two-bedroom flat, plenty of room for me and the three children. Shelly would come in to see us. She got better after a while, but couldn't settle down for a long time after Neil died. Once she recovered she worked out bush and after a while she set up a business in Gunbalanya, a remote community near Kakadu. She was running a small grocery store with a family friend, Neville. I had the children living with me in Darwin and their business provided a house for us. During the holidays, her children went out bush with her, and sometimes I joined them. Michelle also came into town to see the children on her work breaks. So the kids have been with me from very young, and they're still with me now. I think living out bush helped her, that was her way to deal with her loss. Out bush, she didn't have the stress of living in the city. Adaleen, after she left school, worked in the shop with her mother Michelle. Gavon also found a job, so did Raymond, and they stayed in Darwin.

Gavon still lives with me, because he doesn't like me being on my own. Housing's allowed that, because he is coming and going, he is working out at the mines or at construction sites. He has been a wonderful support to me at all times. Adaleen is Michelle's youngest and her only daughter. I've had her and her son Fabian living with me over the years, and Fabian spent time here after school each day when Adaleen was working, because Fabian's father got shot when he was young in a tragic accident. His father, Fabian senior, was with my grandson Raymond in a car and this fella comes up to the car, off his face on drugs. He turned around and shot Fabian senior. Young Fabian was only three-and-a-half at the time. We've had to have Raymond and little Fabian go through counselling and all that. Fabian still goes to it from time to time. But he and Adaleen have done really well. Adaleen and Fabian lived with me and Gavon for some time after his father's tragic death. We have been part of Fabian's life from a baby to 10 years old. They have their own home now, but I attend his school sports and school gatherings, being a proud great-grandmother. He is attending high school and doing an apprenticeship in engineering. I'm so proud of his efforts.

Shelly's eldest son, Raymond, is my eldest grandson, so his children are the eldest great-grandchildren. Jayden and Owen are 19 and 20. They have grown into wonderful young men. Raymond and Erin split up when the boys were very little, but the kids have always been in our family. Some years ago, Erin met a lovely man and they have two more children that I treat like my great-grannies as well. Because Erin and I have always been really close. I supported her when she went through some tough times. Both the children are well grounded due to the wonderful job Erin has done in raising them. Both boys have grown into fine young men and have good jobs. Jayden is now a fully qualified plumber, after two years apprenticeship. Owen works in construction at Tindal airport at Katherine. So I'm really pleased with how they've turned out. The boys contact me all the time, and often Adaleen, Fabian and I meet them to have breakfast or dinner. They ring up, 'Nana, can you come out to dinner?' So I'll go to dinner or breakfast with them. It's wonderful we still have a great relationship. I love all my grandchildren and great-grandchildren. They are all so precious and I love them all so dearly.

My youngest daughter Sheena is now married to Charlie, who has been a wonderful stepdad to her children. Sheena has four children and separated from the children's father, Eli, when the children were very young. They moved around a bit and lived in Cairns with the children, because their father is a Torres Strait Islander. Telena, the eldest, and her beautiful daughter Ellianna now live in Cairns. Before that, she lived at Gunbalanya working for a while, and here in Darwin. She is a single mum and has raised her daughter beautifully. Yowane is the next child and only son. He and his partner Shari have three children, Jamiah, Jamyson, and sister Jalylah, and are expecting another child in the new year. I remember when Yowane got his first exhibition of his paintings in Cairns. Ewen and I flew over there. When Yowane was a little boy, around 10 years old, he got into trouble all the time and his mother Sheena would send him to Ewen at Bulman. Yowane is still close to Ewen. Ewen said to me, 'Hey, sis, I've never been on a plane, and you want me to travel to Cairns with you for Yowane's exhibition!' I said, 'Well, you're coming with me. You're going to fly to Cairns now.' He's a really good artist, our Yowane, but doesn't do it anymore, which saddens me. Michelle is the next daughter and has a son, Raymond. Having had a terrible time with his father, Michelle is now a single mum raising little Raymond with the support and encouragement from her mother Sheena and stepdad Charlie. Ellie Eileen is Sheena's youngest daughter. She and her partner Jordan have three beautiful children, Keelan, Keegan and their sister Sienna. Ellie, even though the youngest, supports her mum and her brothers and sisters and their children. She is my only gran that has my name, my Ellie Eileen. She and Jordan have a strong and happy life. Jordan is a great man and a loving father, partner and a support to the family.

My children have never really been away from me. We keep the family together; I don't like separation. Family has to be family, regardless of who they are. Even today people say to me, 'Eileen, you've got a wonderful family and you all stay together.' But it took work getting to this place. I remember one day my eldest, Raelene, said to me, 'Mum, whenever we ran to you for a hug, when we were children, you would flinch, but look how you are with your grannies. Maybe you should have been a grandmother before a mum.' This hurt me quite deeply because I always felt I gave my children a lot of love and care. Other Stolen Generations people, they told me they were the same. I guess we were never shown love, growing up in the missions and homes, so how were we to show it to our children? How were we to become wives, mothers, husbands and fathers when we had no role models as children? We had to learn all this on our own. Many marriages failed and relationships were no better.

Raelene often says that this affected the children, our removal and being in missions and institutions. Our children have suffered the intergenerational trauma of us having been removed from our mothers and family, the love and care of our family. Shelly and Sheena have said it too, 'Mum, it has affected us children.' I know it has. Shelly broke off with her first partner when Adaleen was a baby, the father then remarried and Michelle had to raise her children. Later in life, she said, 'I just didn't have an idea on relationships.' A lot of the Stolen Generations people have suffered with relationships. Our children as well. Some of them haven't made good choices in relationships because that was never discussed. But Shelly's good now, has a good partner in Marty, I think for 10 years or more. Sheena and Charlie have been together for 15 years after she broke up with the father of her children when Ellie was a baby. She left him, moved back to the Territory from Cairns with all her children in tow, and then she met Charlie and they've been married for 15 years. They've got a strong marriage. Charlie has been good to her children because Ellie was very young when he started going with Sheena. Charlie practically grew up all the children. The children call Charlie stepdad. He's a good role model to those children, he's stability in their lives.

Raelene's husband Mally was the same. He was a wonderful man, but he's passed now. He helped to keep the family together. Raelene didn't marry Mally straight away. She lived with him for a long time before she married him. Raelene was the only one who knew, as a child, that their father was abusive. The other two would be asleep or she'd protect them. Raelene was aware of it all, and when her husband tried that on her, she just said, 'No, that's it. No way in the world I'm going to live with that kind of life, because I saw my mother.' She said, 'If you don't pull yourself together, I want you out of my life.' So she divorced him and he went away for a few years. Then he came back, and he said, 'But I want to come home.' She reckoned, 'Well, you know what the rules are.' So they lived together for another couple of years and then they remarried. That was her, she just said, 'No, I saw what my mother went through. I'm not going through that too.' They were really happy after that. Mally held the family together because he was always there to support her sister's children and the family. Mally and Raelene were an anchor, I suppose, in everything. Mally, he was a wonderful man. When we lost him, the family was shattered. We really miss him and are still grieving. Mally, their son, was only 16, he was just getting into football. Mally had a heart attack out in the bush and the medical plane couldn't get to him in time. After that I started donating to CareFlight, that's the flight that picks up people out bush. I donated to them for nearly three years. Now I donate to Smith Family, the education one for kids. I worry about all these little kids that haven't got enough. Their parents can't afford to give them the schooling support, like uniforms, books, excursions.

Because the relationships didn't always work out, my girls have learnt to do things on their own. Raelene grew up her children because Mally was working out bush all the time. I had to laugh one day, Raymond – my eldest grandson – he was carrying on about women and his mother said, 'Watch it!' He said, 'Oh, that's right. I forgot I was raised by women, wasn't I? My nana and all my mums,' – Raelene, Michelle and Sheena. We all just cracked up laughing. The grannies know they've been raised by strong Aboriginal women, and they're proud of it. That's how we made it in this life. Because of my family holding together, we were able to deal with the losses. When Raelene lost Mally, we bonded together, also when my mother died. My daughters are very close. And the grandchildren, they are more like sisters and brothers, even though they are cousins. Because that is the Aboriginal custom, they are siblings. And that's what keeps us going, I guess – we got this beautiful family bond that keeps us all together. A big happy, sometimes crazy, but loving family. And I think we've always tried to keep that bond between us. If anybody gets hurt or something, we get together, the girls get together and talk about it. Whatever happens, we stay together. Because

I was removed as a child, and no way in the world would I allow them to get lost.

My children go backwards and forth to Bulman all the time. When the Bulman mob come to town, they stay with Raelene or Sheena up here, or they stay with Shelly at Batchelor. Wherever there's room, they'll stay. We are interconnected, which is good. My brother's children ring me all the time. Whenever we go out to Bulman, we can stay with any of my family. They often argue and say, 'Well, Eileen and the kids are coming to stay here.' But we all end up being happy and together. I don't do it as much as I used to because of the road, because I don't like travelling so far. Now I wait for them to come and visit me, and they do. Sometimes they even have Christmas with us. One of my brother's boys lives out at Tiwi Islands, married to a Tiwi girl. He rings up all the time, comes into Darwin. I'm never without visitors from my family. I feel so lucky because this connection I've got with them will never die. My daughters have got it, my grandchildren have got it. When my eldest great-grandson, Jayden, was doing his apprenticeship with plumbing, he was sent out to Bulman for six weeks. He rings me, 'Grandma, guess what?' I said, 'Guess what what? Where are you?' He said, 'At Bulman.' I said, 'Well, you'll have to meet all grandma's relations.' So I rang Margo and the family and told them about Jayden. They said, 'Yeah, we knew who he was. As soon as we saw him, we knew he was Raymond's boy.' They were excited about that.

I also have my Croker Island family there. Dad Randall was an amazing man, and I am so grateful for his teachings and that I had a family who loved and cared for me. Mum and Dad Randall have passed, but to this day I have a close and wonderful relationship with my Randall brothers and sisters and their families – Alan, Johnny, Dorothy and Anita. John is still close to me today. That's why I helped to grow up his two children. Melissa, John-boy[92] and their mother Neena lived in the street behind me in Millner. John and Neena broke up and he took off, went working elsewhere. So John-boy and Melissa were part of my household. They lived in the street behind us; they'd be at our place all the time and they grew up with my children. I used to laugh because Melissa would come in, chuck her plastic bag with her clothes on Shelly's bed, John-boy chucked his clothes on Sheena's bed and they'd just move in for a while. Melissa and John-boy were always with me. We used to take them to football and everything all the time, Melissa was always with us in sport and her brother was a great footballer, too. I used to laugh when I was at softball and they'd say, 'Eileen, where is your other daughter?'

I would say, 'What other daughter? Oh, that's Melissa. That's my niece.' But she was like my other daughter because she'd follow Sheena and Shelly around everywhere. To this day, Melissa's still part of me and my family. She often helps me and takes me out. We have some great times together, sometimes in laughter and tears. We lost John-boy to suicide, but his two children are part of me still, too. They ring me and send me photos of their children, and so this is the Randall connection to this day. We are still interconnected, regardless of where we are. The Randalls are still part of my life. When Dorothy comes up from Mutitjulu, we go out together, her, Melissa and I, we go and eat somewhere. Because Dorry doesn't have a lot of fish and crabs because she lives in Mutitjulu, near Uluru, one night she bought two big mud crabs and we sat on the jetty overlooking the sea, cracking them and eating them, having a feast of crabs.

All the children that I was closest to on Croker Island mission lived in Adelaide at some time or another. Lorky was working at a children's home and married to a Dutchman, John Siwes. When we all grew up and had children, I started to go down to Adelaide for holidays every year with my children. We'd fly down there, stay a couple of weeks and then come home to Darwin. We'd fly from here to Alice and then got on TAA, they used to call it in those days. It was Trans Australia Airlines to Adelaide, before Qantas started. Then the airline sometimes put us on a milk run, that's what we called it, when they'd fly from here to Katherine, Tennant Creek, and then Alice Springs. Once something happened to the plane in Katherine. The children and I had to wait there. I took photos of me and the children on the tarmac. I said to Ray, 'We're not doing that anymore, no milk run for us. We are going straight from here to Alice to Adelaide.'

When we went for holidays, Lorky was there looking after us, because she was so caring and she loved us. Her and her husband broke up, too. But his family, John's mother and father, always went from Melbourne to see Lorraine and the children in Adelaide. The old man, he was six foot something, big man with a big, deep voice. When I had Raelene, he was there visiting and he says to me, 'Eileen, I think I'm going to take you and Raelene home with me to Melbourne.' I said, 'I'm not going to Melbourne. I'm going home,' to Darwin, and we all cracked up laughing. They were beautiful people, the Siwes. I still have communication with Lorky's children. Debbie rings up every now and then. Darren rings me because he's working with Claire,[93] that's my nephew, from Lorky. When he comes up here, he comes and sees me. He would never miss us, 'I've got to go and see Aunty Eileen first.' Phillip lives here, so I have a lot to do with Phillip still. Phillip, Lorky's eldest boy, lives out at Humpty Doo, not far from Raelene. So he sees Raelene quite a bit and they're close, because Raelene and him are nearly the same age. We have photos of the two, when they were babies.

When the kids were little and we'd go down for holidays and stay with Lorky I'd meet up with Tarni and her brood of boys, and Laura and her children. Laura was my best mate when we were children on Croker. I'd sometimes stay with Laura for a weekend, me and the children, and then go back to Lorraine's. A lot of the Croker people went to Adelaide, but most of them have passed away now. Lorky's passed. Laura's passed, her sister Eva's in a home down there in Adelaide. Tarni's passed also, but her husband Max still lives here in Darwin with their boys. She moved back to Darwin years ago; they drove all the way from Adelaide to Darwin to live. I don't remember when exactly that was, they've been here for such a long time now. The boys were young. But before they moved to Darwin, when I used to go down to Adelaide for holidays, my children were always running wild with the Siwes and the Gaston children. Sometimes I'd be walking down the street with all these children, all different colours, shapes and sizes. People would look at me and maybe think, 'Those kids can't all belong to her!' Uncle Max, Tarni's husband, is very old now but Raelene will still visit Uncle Max and see the boys and talk to the boys. I'll ring up Michael, Tarni's son, every now and again just to check on Max. 'Oh, Aunty Eileen, I haven't heard from you for a while,' so I ring him just to make sure the connection is still there.

The mission sent Shirley Bliss, Betty Graham and Annette White down to work at the Women's Lodge in Brisbane while I was attending the Methodist training college. Shirley was 17 and still under the Native Affairs and when they got old enough, Betty and Shirley moved to Melbourne to live, while Annette returned to Alice Springs. Later in life, Shirley married that renowned artist, Harold Thomas. If you visit the university here, there's a big painting he did, real big one, about Stolen Generations. The painting was bought and owned by one of the Paspalis family, a rich family in the Territory. I think it was young Tony, he bought it off Harold Thomas for quite a large sum. He said, 'Eileen, I'm bringing it to Stolen Gen[94] so you can hang it in the office.' But we had such a small office, we couldn't hang it, so I said to Tony, 'Can you get me a print of it so I can hang that at the office?' He did me a print, but the original is hanging in the library at Charles Darwin University.

My other cousin Rita married and had all her children in Adelaide, then they moved back to the Territory. Most of the Croker Island people who were sent to Adelaide as children have moved back here, except Lorky. Rita's husband Eric and children moved to Darwin. I think one of the children was a baby when they came back, but they're all grown up now. Rita passed away some years ago, but I still have contact with her children and her family. Natasha lives still at Palmerston with her husband Ray and family. She's a darling girl, I still have a lot of contact with her. Tasha is the one that said to me once, 'Aunty, all those years I thought you were just coming to spend the weekend with us.' She didn't know about family violence then, because Rita and I never told them what was happening until they grew up. I still have a lot of talks with Tasha, my niece, she came to my 80th birthday party with her husband Ray. Tommy Olson married a girl out from Daly River, Emu Springs. His children and wife still live there but he's passed away now. I often saw Tommy – when he used to come to Darwin, him and his family. He'd ring up and say, 'I'm in town, Eileen.' For a long time I stayed in contact with his sons and his daughter. But they haven't come back to Darwin since their father died. One of the boys lived here for a while, but they all moved back to Emu Springs where their mother lives.

Most of my Croker Island families have passed, but their children are still here. They might ring or send me messages. When all this compensation stuff came up, I let them know about it and how to put in the applications. It's my Croker Island family, so I want them close to me. I don't want to lose connection with Rita, Tarni and Lorky, and I keep them close through their children.

So I had a very interesting life, didn't I? I've been fortunate, I think, with the life I've had. I had a happy life at the beginning of my marriage, then I had a terrible life in domestic violence. But I overcame that. We were removed as children from our mothers, our people, our Country. We lost all of that. But because of the strength and the love of my people, I'm back there now and I can go to rest in this world knowing that I'm still part of that family and part of the people out bush, that'll never go away. I think I've grown up my children and my grannies to the best of my ability to make sure they live safe, secure and happy lives, and that they don't miss out on things that I missed out on when I was a child. I want my children, grandchildren and great-grandchildren to be part of my family out at Bulman and Ngukurr, and I want them to have the same advantages of our culture and our heritage, because I've always instilled that in my grannies – that it's important they know where they come from and to be proud of their heritage. I'd say to them, 'Nobody can take that away from you. That's yours for life.' It's wonderful that I was able to reconnect and give this to my children, grandchildren and great-grandchildren. They've got a family that'll take care of them forever. I think I'm so privileged to have that because a lot of Stolen Generations people haven't had it and have lost the connection.

I've been working all my life and I just loved working with my people and advocating for them. Getting into the Aboriginal areas, that was good for me. That's what I wanted, to give it all back to my people; work with my people so that they can gain the benefits of what I've been taught. I have learnt so much from these amazing women in the remote communities, their resilience, strength and knowledge, their pride in their heritage and culture. What a great two-way learning. From these amazing women, my mother and my people, I regained my wonderful culture and heritage. Born of this land, I am Rembarrnga/Ngalakan of Central Arnhem Land, Northern Territory, Australia. I am proud to be an Aboriginal woman Elder of the First Nations peoples of Australia. I have always dreamt of a better time for our country, that we can move forward together in true reconciliation, acknowledging and understanding the dark history of our nation. That's it.

Afterword

As I close this book, my heart is filled with deep admiration and gratitude for Eileen's mother. Her life was a tapestry woven with threads of resilience, love and an unyielding spirit. Through the pages of this book, we have journeyed alongside her, witnessing her strength in the face of adversity and her unwavering dedication to her family and community.

Eileen's mother was not just a figure in her daughter's life; she was the bedrock upon which Eileen built her own path. Despite the heart-wrenching separation when Eileen was four-and-a-half, the bond they shared remained unbroken. Eileen Cummings, born in 1943, is a member of the Rembarrnga/Ngalakan ethnic groups and a member of the Stolen Generations. She was removed from her family at Mainoru Station in central Arnhem Land in 1949. Her departure, initially met with excitement, soon gave way to longing for her mother when a red truck came to pick her up without her mother's knowledge. Eileen was taken to the Maranboy Police Station before finding her new home on Croker Island, a Methodist mission 200 kilometres north-east of Darwin. While Eileen has happy memories of the island, they are tinged with sadness.

Over the years, Eileen has grown used to telling her story to students, journalists, politicians, psychologists and lawyers. Despite growing up away from her mother, Eileen's mother's wisdom, kindness, and courage were the guiding lights that shaped Eileen into the remarkable woman she is today. Every story shared, every lesson taught, and every act of love has left an indelible mark on Eileen's heart and soul. Her legacy is one of profound impact, not only on her family but on everyone who had the privilege of knowing her.

Eileen's achievements are many. She was the first Indigenous person in the Northern Territory to qualify as a pre-school teacher and has held various roles, including policy adviser to the Northern Territory Chief Minister in the Office of Women's Policies. She coordinated the consultation in the development of the Aboriginal Family Violence Strategy and has been a tireless advocate for the Stolen Generations, working to bring compensation to those affected. Eileen's work as Chairperson of the Northern Territory Stolen Generations Aboriginal Corporation and her candidacy in the 2013 Federal Election for the Australian First Nations Political Party are just a few examples of her dedication to her community.

A significant milestone in Eileen's advocacy was the historic class action settlement for descendants of the Stolen Generations in the Northern Territory, which received final approval in the NSW Supreme Court. The Commonwealth agreed to pay more than $50 million in compensation to family members, bringing recognition to those still experiencing the impacts of the Stolen Generations. This class action, involving about 1200 people, was launched against the Commonwealth in 2021 and officially deemed successful in August 2024. Eileen, as the lead claimant, played a crucial role in this long, hard battle, which signified something greater than financial settlement – it was about acknowledging the trauma and seeking justice for both living and deceased members of the Stolen Generations.

This is a tribute to Eileen's mother, a woman whose life was a beacon of hope and inspiration. Her story reminds us of the power of love and the importance of standing up for what is right. It is a reminder that even in the darkest times, there is light to be found in the love and support of those who care for us.

Thank you for joining us on this journey. May the legacy of Eileen's mother continue to inspire and guide us all, and may her memory be a blessing to everyone who reads her story and provides a way for us to live and work together to ensure a better world.

Ruth Wallace (she/her)
Pro Vice Chancellor, Charles Darwin University

Appendix A: Eileen's family tree

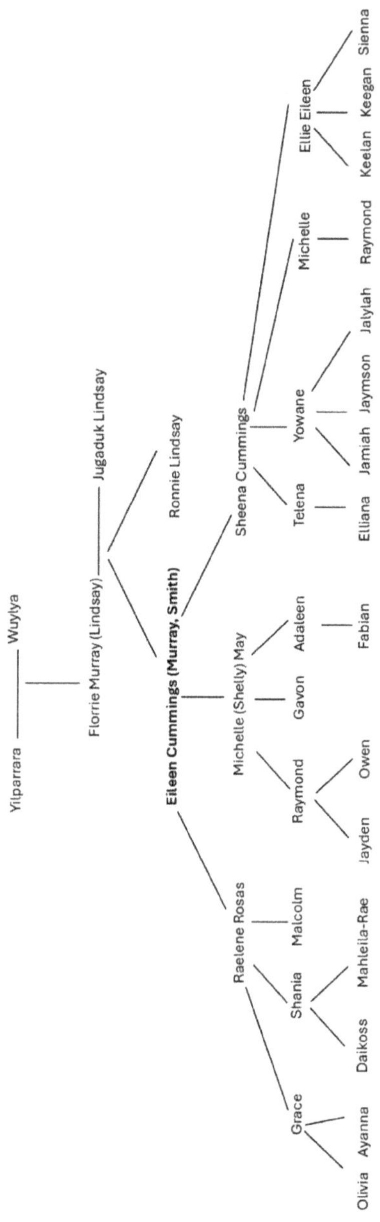

Appendix B: List of major legislation and other important events relevant to this story[95]

1844 Ordinance for the Protection, Maintenance and Upbringing of Orphans and Other Destitute Children and Aborigines Act: statutory basis for the removal of Aboriginal children from their homes
1910 Territory Acceptance Act: Put Aboriginal affairs in NT under Commonwealth control
1911 Aboriginals Ordinance: Chief Protector made legal guardian of all Aboriginal children, even if they had living parents. This became the legal basis for child removal. This was continued in later Aboriginals Ordinances (1918–1947), which replaced the 1911 Ordinance.
1953 Welfare Ordinance 1953: replaced the earlier Aboriginals Ordinance, but kept the same powers
1958 Child Welfare Ordinance 1958: governed the removal of children considered neglected
1994 'Going Home Conference' held at Kormilda College in Darwin
1997 *Bringing Them Home* report, result of the National Inquiry into the Separation of Aboriginal and Torres Strait Islander Children from Their Families (1995–1996)
1998 Northern Territory Stolen Generation Aboriginal Corporation is incorporated
2001 Cubillo and Gunner v The Commonwealth of Australia
2001 Apology to the Northern Territory stolen generation issued by Northern Territory Chief Minister Claire Martin
2007 Northern Territory National Emergency Response Act 2007 ('The Intervention')
2008 National Apology to Aboriginal Australians, especially the Stolen Generations, issued by Prime Minister Kevin Rudd
2018 National Redress Scheme for people who experienced child sexual abuse while in an institution established in response to

the Royal Commission into Institutional Responses to Child Sexual Abuse (2013–2017)

2021 Territories Stolen Generations Redress announced by Prime Minister Scott Morrison

2023 Confirmation by the NSW Supreme Court of the Northern Territory Stolen Generations Class Action, which compensates the families of deceased members of the Stolen Generations

2023 Settlement of a class action lawsuit against the Uniting Church and Commonwealth for the abuse and neglect of children living at the Croker Island Mission

2024 Settlement of the Northern Territory Stolen Wages Class Action to compensate Indigenous people in the Northern Territory who worked between 1933 and 1972 for little or no wages, or their descendants

References

Altman, Jon C. and Melinda Hinkson (eds) 2007 *Coercive Reconciliation: Stabilise, Normalise, Exit Aboriginal Australia*. North Carlton: Arena Publications Association.

Archibald-Binge, Ella 2021 When Eileen Cummings jumped in the back of a truck, she had no idea that her life was about to change forever. *ABC News*, available at https://www.abc.net.au/news/2021–07–07

Austin, Tony 1989 Doomed to whither and disappear: Aboriginal and European relations in 1888. In V. Dixon (ed.) *Looking Back: The Northern Territory in 1888*. Darwin: Historical Society of the Northern Territory.

Austin, Tony 1992 *Simply Survival of the Fittest. Aboriginal Administration in South Australia's Northern Territory 1863–1910*. Darwin: Historical Society of the Northern Territory.

Australian Government 1958 *Assimilation of Our Aborigines*. Canberra: Australian Government Printer.

Australian Government 1961 *One People*. Canberra: Australian Government Printer.

Australian Government 1962 *Our Aborigines*. Canberra: Australian Government Printer.

Aboriginal and Torres Strait Islander Commission 2000 Aboriginal and Torres Strait Islander Peoples and Australia's Obligations under the United Nations International Covenant on Civil and Political Rights. A report submitted by the Aboriginal and Torres Strait Islander Commission to the United Nations Human Rights Committee.

Barta, Tony 2008 Sorry, and not sorry, in Australia: how the apology to the stolen generation buried a history of genocide. *Journal of Genocide Research* 10(2): 201–214.

Buck, Ronnie 1995 *Ronnie Buck. Bulman 1989*. Bulman Oral History Series. Barunga, Northern Territory: Barunga Press.

Camfoo, Nelly 1995 *Nelly Camfoo. Bulman 1989*. Bulman Oral History Series. Barunga, Northern Territory: Barunga Press

Camfoo, Tex 1995 *Tex Camfoo. Bulman 1989*. Bulman Oral History Series. Barunga, Northern Territory: Barunga Press.

Camfoo, Tex and Nelly Camfoo (authors) and Gillian Cowlishaw (ed.) 2000 *Love Against the Law. The Autobiographies of Tex and Nelly Camfoo*. Canberra: Aboriginal Studies Press.

Commonwealth of Australia 1937 Initial conference of Commonwealth and State Aboriginal Authorities. Canberra: Government Printer.

Cowlishaw, Gillian 2009 *Rednecks, Eggheads and Blackfellas. A Study of Racial Power and Intimacy in Australia*. Sydney: Allen and Unwin.

Jaensch, Dean and Robyn Smith 2015 *Turning 40: The Legislative Assembly of the Northern Territory 1974–2014*. Darwin: Historical Society of the Northern Territory.

Fitzgerald, Roxanne 2023 Stolen Generations survivors reach settlement with Commonwealth, church for historic abuse at Croker Island Mission. *ABC News*, available at (accessed 25 May 2025).

George, Minnie 1995 *Minnie George. Bulman 1989*. Bulman Oral History Series. Barunga, Northern Territory: Barunga Press.

Gibbs, Alma 1995 *Alma Gibbs. Bulman 1989*. Bulman Oral History Series. Barunga, Northern Territory: Barunga Press.

Harlow, Sue 1997 *Tin Gods. A Social History of the Men and Women of Maranboy*. Darwin: Historical Society of the Northern Territory.

Human Rights and Equal Opportunities Commission 1997 *Bringing Them Home. The National Inquiry into the Separation of Aboriginal and Torres Strait Islander Children from their Families*. Sydney: Human Rights and Equal Opportunities Commission.

Jangawanga, George 1995 In *Hitler Wood Katcherelli, George Jarudaku and George Jangawanga*. Bulman 1991, pp. 10–12. Bulman Oral History Series. Barunga, Northern Territory: Barunga Press.

Jaurdaku, George 1995 In *Hitler Wood Katcherelli, George Jarudaku and George Jangawanga. Bulman 1991*, pp. 4–9. Bulman Oral History Series. Barunga, Northern Territory: Barunga Press.

Katcherelli, Hitler Wood 1995 In *Hitler Wood Katcherelli, George Jarudaku and George Jangawanga. Bulman 1991*, pp. 1–3.

Bulman Oral History Series. Barunga, Northern Territory: Barunga Press.

Lea, J.P. 1987 *Government and the Community in Katherine, 1937–1978*. Darwin: North Australia Research Unit, Australian National University.

Lee, Peter 1992 *Peter Lee. Bulman 1989*. Bulman Oral History Series. Barunga, Northern Territory: Barunga Press.

Lindsay, Florrie 1995 *Florrie Lindsay and Dorothy Murray. Bulman 1989*. Bulman Oral History Series. Barunga, Northern Territory: Barunga Press.

Lovegrove, T.C. 1978 Legislation and Policies for Northern Territory Aboriginals over 27 years. Unpublished report submitted to the Northern Territory Department of Aboriginal Affairs.

Megarrity, Lyndon 2018 *Northern Dreams. The Politics of Northern Development in Australia*. Melbourne: Australian Scholarly Publishing.

Merlan, Francesca 1978 Making people quiet in the pastoral north: reminiscences of Elsey Station. *Aboriginal History* 1(2):70–106.

Read, Peter 1981 *The Stolen Generations*. Sydney: New South Wales Government Printer.

Read, Peter 1999 *A Rape of the Soul so Profound*. Sydney: Allen and Unwin.

Read, Peter and Jay Read (eds) 1991 *Long Time, Olden Time: Aboriginal accounts of Northern Territory History*. Alice Springs: Institute for Aboriginal Development.

Robinson, Bandicoot 1995 *Bandicoot Robinson. Bulman 1989*. Bulman Oral History Series. Barunga, Northern Territory: Barunga Press.

Rose, Deborah Bird 1991 *Hidden Histories*. Canberra: Aboriginal Studies Press.

Smith, Claire 2008 Communication Barriers Thwart the Intervention. *ABC Opinion* online, 30 March, available at: https://www.abc.net.au/news/2008–03–31 (accessed 25 May 2025).

Smith, Claire 2020 Country, Kin and Culture: Survival of an Australian Aboriginal Community. 2nd edition. Kent Town: Wakefield Press.

Smith, Claire and Gary Jackson 2008 Income Management in the NT: Food for Taxis. *ABC Opinion* online, 6 October, available at https://www.abc.net.au/news/2008–10–06 (accessed 25 May 2025).

Smith, Claire and Gary Jackson 2016 Manabaru. In N. Brown (ed.) *Speak to Me: Conversations with the Flinders University Art Collections*, pp. 98–99. Adelaide: Flinders University.

Smith, Claire, Gary Jackson and Eileen Cummings. Let's Make it Work! Re-thinking the Community Development Employment Program in the Northern Territory. A 36-page submission on CDEP Discussion Paper March 2008 Review of Community Development Employment Program.

Smith, Robyn 2024a *Licence to Kill. Massacre Men of Australia's North*. Darwin: Historical Society of the Northern Territory.

Smith, Robyn 2024b Northern Territory. In Nicholas Barry, Alan Fenna, Zareh Ghazarian, Yvonne Haigh and Diana Perche (eds) *Australian Politics and Policy*. Sydney: Sydney University Press.

Stack, Ella 2013 *Is There Anyone Alive in There? Our Cyclone Tracey, Darwin, Christmas 1974*. Darwin: Historical Society of the Northern Territory.

Stephens, Matthew and the Northern Territory Stolen Generation Aboriginal Corporation 2020 *The Cummings Family; Family, Belonging, and Connections to Country: A Family Case Study of the Intergenerational Impacts of the Stolen Generation*. Darwin: Northern Territory Stolen Generations Aboriginal Corporation.

Welfare Branch, Northern Territory 1961 Beswick Aboriginal Reserve. Unpublished manuscript held at the Northern Land Council, Darwin.

Welfare Branch, Northern Territory 1967 Beswick Aboriginal Reserve. Unpublished manuscript held at the Northern Land Council, Darwin.

Notes

1 A short history of Eileen's mother's life was recorded by Gillian Cowlishaw. *See* Lindsay, Florrie 1995 *Florrie Lindsay and Dorothy Murray. Bulman 1989*. Bulman Oral History Series. Barunga, Northern Territory: Barunga Press.

2 For a history of the interrelationships between Aboriginal people, pastoralists and government policy at Mainoru station see Cowlishaw, Gillian 1999 *Rednecks, Eggheads and Blackfellas. A Study of Racial Power and Intimacy in Australia*. Sydney: Allen and Unwin.

3 For the potency of this threat in the Northern Territory, see Merlan, Francesca 1978 'Making people quiet in the pastoral north: reminiscences of Elsey Station'. *Aboriginal History* 1(2):70–106; Rose, Deborah Bird 1991 *Hidden Histories*. Canberra: Aboriginal Studies Press; Smith, Robyn 2024a *Licence to Kill: Massacre Men of Australia's North*. Darwin: Historical Society of the Northern Territory.

4 This term was coined by Peter Read on this basis of his work with Aboriginal children who were removed from their families in New South Wales. See Read, Peter 1981 *The Stolen Generations*. Sydney: New South Wales Government Printer.

5 Aboriginal word for a non-Aboriginal person, usually a white person.

6 Mataranka Falls.

7 Nelly Camfoo's life is recorded in N. Camfoo (1995), T. Camfoo (1995) and Camfoo, Camfoo and Cowlishaw (2000).

8 More than 200 km.

9 For an example of the practical implementation of assimilation policies in this region: Welfare Branch, Northern Territory 1961 Beswick Aboriginal Reserve. Unpublished manuscript held at the Northern Land Council, Darwin; Welfare Branch, Northern

Territory 1967 Beswick Aboriginal Reserve. Unpublished manuscript held at the Northern Land Council, Darwin.

10 Bamyili was originally named Beswick Creek and later renamed Barunga.

11 The report written by Patrol Officer Ryan of the Native Affairs Branch about his removal of Eileen and the other children.

12 Lorraine Rouster (later Siwes).

13 Rita Fisher (later Tingey).

14 For historical background see Harlow, Sue 1997 *Tin Gods. A Social History of the Men and Women of Maranboy*. Darwin: Historical Society of the Northern Territory.

15 Retta Dixon was a home for Aboriginal children removed from their families, located in Darwin.

16 Tania Ryan (later Gaston) and Shirley Bliss (later Thomas).

17 Claire Smith from Flinders University.

18 For an overview of policies in the Northern Territory for these years see Lovegrove, T.C. 1978 Legislation and Policies for Northern Territory Aboriginals over 27 years. Unpublished report submitted to the Northern Territory Department of Aboriginal Affairs; Lea, J.P. 1987 *Government and the Community in Katherine, 1937–1978*. Darwin: North Australia Research Unit, Australian National University; Austin, Tony 1992 *Simply Survival of the Fittest. Aboriginal Administration in South Australia's Northern Territory 1863–1910*. Darwin: Historical Society of the Northern Territory. For an analysis of the history of Commonwealth control of the Northern Territory see Smith, Robyn 2024b Northern Territory. Chapter 10 in Nicholas Barry, Alan Fenna, Zareh Ghazarian, Yvonne Haigh and Diana Perche (eds) *Australian Politics and Policy*. Sydney: Sydney University Press. For a history of development policy in northern Australia see Megarrity, Lyndon 2018 *Northern Dreams: The Politics of Northern Development in Australia*. Melbourne: Australian Scholarly Publishing.

19 For detailed information on the process in the Northern Territory see Human Rights and Equal Opportunities Commission 1997 *Bringing Them Home. The National Inquiry into the Separation of Aboriginal and Torres Strait Islander Children from their Families*. Sydney: Human Rights and Equal Opportunities Commission, Chapter 8.

20 Commonwealth of Australia 1937 Initial conference of Commonwealth and State Aboriginal Authorities. Canberra: Government Printer. See also Austin, Tony 1989 'Doomed to whither and disappear: Aboriginal and European relations in 1888'. In V. Dixon (ed.) *Looking Back: The Northern Territory in 1888*. Darwin: Historical Society of the Northern Territory.
21 Margaret Anne Somerville was cottage sister on the Croker Island Mission 1941–1964 and led the evacuation of Croker Island children during the Second World War. This evacuation was also called the 'Croker Island Exodus' and is portrayed in a 2012 documentary, directed by Steven McGregor, who is also mentioned in Chapter 6.
22 The Bungalow was a home for Aboriginal children removed from their families, located in Alice Springs.
23 Garden Point Mission was a home for Aboriginal children removed from their families, located on Melville Island.
24 Australian Indigenous Ministries.
25 Pre-eclampsia.
26 Raymond Cummings.
27 For an overview of the impact of Cyclone Tracy on Darwin residents see Stack, Ella 2013 *Is There Anyone Alive in There? Our Cyclone Tracy, Darwin, Christmas 1974*. Darwin: Historical Society of the Northern Territory.
28 Tuberculosis.
29 John Charles Hargrave, surgeon who worked towards eliminating leprosy in the Northern Territory.
30 Weemol is a small outstation community 5 km from Bulman.
31 Bagot is an Aboriginal community in Darwin. Belyuen is an Aboriginal community located on Cox Peninsula, across the bay from Darwin city.
32 For public booklets on government assimilation policies during this period, see Australian Government 1958 *Assimilation of Our Aborigines*. Canberra: Australian Government Printer; Australian Government 1961 *One People*. Canberra: Australian Government Printer; Australian Government 1962 *Our Aborigines*. Canberra: Australian Government Printer.
33 Baghetti is an outstation about 30 km from Bulman.
34 Malcolm Rosas jnr, Eileen's grandson and ex Gold Coast Suns, currently Sydney Swans footballer.

35 Also called waddy, an Aboriginal hardwood club.
36 Councils are Aboriginal organisations running each Aboriginal community.
37 Batchelor Institute of Indigenous Tertiary Education.
38 For a history of development policy in northern Australia see Megarrity, Lyndon 2018 *Northern Dreams. The Politics of Northern Development in Australia*. Melbourne: Australian Scholarly Publishing.
39 See Austin, Tony 1992 *Simply Survival of the Fittest. Aboriginal Administration in South Australia's Northern Territory 1863–1910*. Darwin: Historical Society of the Northern Territory.
40 Marshall Perron.
41 The UN Fourth World Conference on Women, 1995.
42 Rita Tingey, from Croker Island.
43 Claire Martin, Chief Minister of the Northern Territory 2001–2007.
44 *The Northern Territory National Emergency Response Act* (2007–2012).
45 For an overview of the Northern Territory National Emergency Response, see Altman, Jon C. and Melinda Hinkson (eds) 2007 *Coercive Reconciliation: Stabilise, Normalise, Exit Aboriginal Australia*. North Carlton: Arena Publications Association. For an analysis of the immediate impact of the Intervention on the communities of Barunga and Manyallaluk see Smith, Claire 2008 Communication Barriers Thwart the Intervention. *ABC Opinion online*, 30 March (accessed 25 May 2025) and Smith, Claire and Gary Jackson 2008 Income Management in the NT: Food for Taxis. *ABC Opinion online*, 6 October (accessed 25 May 2025).
46 The *Going Home Conference*, held in Darwin at Kormilda College.
47 The National Inquiry into the Separation of Aboriginal and Torres Strait Islander Children from Their Families (1995–1996) resulted in the *Bringing Them Home* report (1997). This report played a pivotal role, many events that happened subsequently and are mentioned here were recommendations of this report, such as official apologies and acknowledgement by governments and churches, compensation, assistance in returning to Country. For more information on this process, see Stephens, Matthew and the Northern Territory Stolen Generation

Aboriginal Corporation 2020 The Cummings Family; Family, Belonging, and Connections to Country: A Family Case Study of the Intergenerational Impacts of the Stolen Generation. Darwin: Northern Territory Stolen Generations Aboriginal Corporation.

48 Mark Dreyfus, attorney-general of Australia 2013 and since 2022.

49 Cubillo and Gunner v The Commonwealth of Australia (2001).

50 The 1994 *Bringing Them Home* report.

51 John Howard, Prime Minister of Australia 1996–2007.

52 Kevin Rudd, Prime Minister of Australia 2007-2010, issued a National Apology to Aboriginal Australians, especially the Stolen Generationss, on 13 February 2008. For analysis within an historical context, see: Barta, Tony 2008 Sorry, and not sorry, in Australia: how the apology to the Stolen Generations buried a history of genocide. *Journal of Genocide Research* 10(2): 201–214.

53 Healing Foundation, a national Aboriginal and Torres Strait Islander organisation established in 2009.

54 Maisie Austin, NT Stolen Generations activist and CEO of NTSGAC until 2022.

55 Michael Gunner, Chief Minister of the Northern Territory 2016–2022.

56 Charles Darwin University.

57 Bernadette Shields, Halpin Hart.

58 Scott Morrison, Prime Minister of Australia 2018–2022.

59 Malarndirri McCarthy, now Australian Minister for Indigenous Australians.

60 Ken Wyatt, Australian Minister for Indigenous Australians 2019–2022.

61 Julia Gillard, Prime Minister of Australia 2010–2013.

62 Jenny Macklin, Minister for Indigenous Affairs 2007–2013.

63 Penny Wong, federal minister 2010–2013, and since 2022.

64 Gary Gray, federal minister 2010–2013.

65 The National Redress Scheme for people who experienced institutional child sexual abuse started in 2018 and was established in response to the Royal Commission into Institutional Responses to Child Sexual Abuse (2013–2017).

66 Dr Matthew Stephens is a freelance history consultant focused on the history of the Northern Territory. He completed two book projects about members of the Stolen Generations with the

Northern Territory Stolen Generation Aboriginal Cooperation: *Lance Stott; 'You gotta tellem right story': A Case Study of the Intergenerational Impacts of the Stolen Generations* (2020) and the book about the Cummings family.

67 Matthew Stephen's extensive research on the intergenerational impact on the Cummings family of Eileen having been stolen as a child, including research on the Croker Island mission, was published as: Stephens, Matthew and the Northern Territory Stolen Generation Aboriginal Corporation 2020 *The Cummings Family; Family, Belonging, and Connections to Country: A Family Case Study of the Intergenerational Impacts of the Stolen Generation*. Darwin: Northern Territory Stolen Generations Aboriginal Corporation.

68 Starting in 2017.

69 For media coverage of Eileen's role see Archibald-Binge, Ella 2021 When Eileen Cummings jumped in the back of a truck, she had no idea that her life was about to change forever. *ABC News*, available at https://www.abc.net.au/news/2021-07-07/stolen-generations-class-action-nt-eileen-cummings/100274420 and Fitzgerald, Roxanne 2023 Stolen Generations survivors reach settlement with Commonwealth, church for historic abuse at Croker Island Mission. ABC News, available at https://www.abc.net.au/news/2021-07-07/stolen-generations-class-action-nt-eileen-cummings/100274420 (accessed 25 May 2025).

70 Prime Minister Scott Morrison announced the Territories Stolen Generations Redress Scheme on 5 August 2021; see also Read, Peter 1999 *A Rape of the Soul so Profound*. Sydney: Allen and Unwin.

71 Northern Territory Stolen Generations Class Action: A class action lawsuit against the Commonwealth to get compensation for the descendants of deceased members of the Stolen Generations, launched in 2021, settled in 2022 and confirmed by the New South Wales Supreme Court in 2023.

72 A class action lawsuit against the Uniting Church and Commonwealth to get compensation for abuse and neglect of children living at the Croker Island Mission, settled in 2023.

73 The NTSGAC.

74 A personal acknowledgement to Eileen, in a letter from May 2023. A personal acknowledgement is one element of redress under the Territories Stolen Generations Redress Scheme.

75 Stephens 2020 The Cummings Family; Family, Belonging, and Connections to Country: A Family Case Study of the Intergenerational Impacts of the Stolen Generation.
76 A 2002 movie about a group of Aboriginal girls removed from their families in 1931.
77 For more information see Smith and Jackson (2016).
78 4th World Archaeological Congress, Cape Town, South Africa, 1999.
79 Claire Smith 2020 (1st edition 2004) *Country, Kin and Culture: Survival of an Australian Aboriginal Community*. Kent Town: Wakefield Press.
80 Claire organised public panels across Australia for women from the Northern Territory to speak about the impact of the Intervention on their communities.
81 The Northern Territory National Emergency Response, commonly referred to as the Intervention, was a set of measures implemented in 2007. The justification given was the Little Children are Sacred report, published in June 2007, which outlined the results of an inquiry into child sexual abuse, commissioned by the Northern Territory Government. As a result, the Commonwealth was granted extensive powers to intervene in Aboriginal communities within the Northern Territory.
82 I also wrote some submissions on policy, see, for example, Smith, Claire, Gary Jackson and Eileen Cummings. Let's Make it Work! Re-thinking the Community Development Employment Program in the Northern Territory. A 36-page submission on CDEP Discussion Paper March 2008 Review of Community Development Employment Program.
83 Tex Camfoo's life is recorded in N. Camfoo (1995), T. Camfoo (1995) and Camfoo, Camfoo and Cowlishaw (2000). The oral histories of other Aboriginal people living in Bulman around 1989, collected by Gillian Cowlishaw, are included in the references.
84 Office of the Registrar of Indigenous Corporations.
85 Australian First Nations Political Party.
86 In the Australian Indigenous Voice referendum, held on 14 October 2023, voters were asked to approve the instalment of a body called the Aboriginal and Torres Strait Islander Voice as a representation in the federal parliament and government.
87 In September 2024, the Commonwealth Government settled

the Northern Territory Stolen Wages Class Action and agreed to pay up to $202 million to Indigenous people in the Northern Territory who worked between 1933 and 1972 for little or no wages, or their descendants.

88 NARU = ANU (Australian National University) North Australian Research Unit.

89 Malcolm Rosas snr.

90 Australian Football League.

91 The Flying Boomerangs, the men's underage Indigenous Australian rules football team.

92 Johnny Randall jnr, son of Johnny Randall snr.

93 Darren Siwes is an artist based in Adelaide. He has done some work with Claire Smith and is enrolled in a PhD programme at Flinders University.

94 The Northern Territory Stolen Generation Aboriginal Cooperation.

95 For a summary of the constitutional history of the Northern Territory see Jaensch, Dean, and Robyn Smith 2015 Turning 40: The Legislative Assembly of the Northern Territory 1974–2014. A Summary of the Constitutional History of the Northern Territory', page xi. Darwin: Historical Society of the Northern Territory.

Acknowledgements

We extend our gratitude to the many people who supported the creation of this book. We thank Senator Malarndirri McCarthy, Minister for Indigenous Australians, and Professor Ruth Wallace, Pro-Vice Chancellor of Charles Darwin University, for finding the time to write the Foreword and Afterword for this volume. Darren Siwes, the son of Lorraine Siwes, who was stolen at the same time as Eileen Cummings, kindly enhanced the quality of photographs included in this volume. Matthew Stephens provided digital copies of Figures 3.5, 3.14 and 7.3. Gary Jackson, the husband of Claire Smith, generously proof-read this book at both copy-editing and proof stages. We are grateful to Shannan Dodson, the CEO of the Healing Foundation, which supported the participation of community people at the prelaunch of this book at the 10th World Archaeological Congress, which was held in Darwin in June 2025.

The idea for this book arose when Eileen Cummings and Claire Smith were travelling in South Africa in 1999. It took a long time before we were able to focus on it. The current text is based on interviews with Eileen Cummings conducted by Claire Smith and Jana Anvari between July 2019 and April 2025. Eileen Cummings thanks her family in Darwin and at Bulman for their unstinting support over many decades. Unless otherwise stated, all photos are from Eileen Cummings' personal collection.

Wakefield Press is an independent publishing and distribution company based in Adelaide, South Australia. We love good stories and publish beautiful books. To see our full range of books, please visit our website at www.wakefieldpress.com.au where all titles are available for purchase. To keep up with our latest releases, news and events, subscribe to our monthly newsletter.

Find us!

Facebook: www.facebook.com/wakefield.press
Twitter: www.twitter.com/wakefieldpress
Instagram: www.instagram.com/wakefieldpress

www.ingramcontent.com/pod-product-compliance
Ingram Content Group Australia Pty Ltd
76 Discovery Rd, Dandenong South VIC 3175, AU
AUHW010905290526
427915AU00004B/6

9 781923 388185